Jewish Roots of American Liberty

The Impact of Hebraic Ideas on the American Story

Edited by Wilfred M. McClay
and Stuart Halpern

New York • London

First American edition published in 2025 by Encounter Books, an activity of Encounter for Culture and Education, Inc., a nonprofit, tax-exempt corporation.
Encounter Books website address: www.encounterbooks.com

Manufactured in the United States and printed on acid-free paper. The paper used in this publication meets the minimum requirements of ANSI/NISO Z39.48-1992 (R 1997) (*Permanence of Paper*).

FIRST AMERICAN EDITION

LIBRARY OF CONGRESS CATALOGING-IN-PUBLICATION DATA IS AVAILABLE

Library of Congress CIP data is available online under the following ISBN 978-1-64177-479-6 and LCCN 2025026138.

CONTENTS

PART FOUR
The Meaning of Jewish History for Americans

PREFACE

The volume before you arose out of a series of conferences and programs under the banner "Restoring the American Story," directed primarily at educators working in both Jewish and non-Jewish school settings and educational nonprofits. "Restoring the American Story" addressed itself to the various ways that the American tradition and the Jewish tradition are intertwined, and speak in strikingly similar and mutually supportive ways to some of the most fundamental human concerns—concerns that are foundational to what we call Western Civilization. Much of the book consists of papers and presentations arising out of these programs, particularly a conference held at Yeshiva University in the spring of 2023, convened by the two editors of this volume, and attended by a lively group of teachers and other educators from around the country. We are grateful for the generous support of Mitch Julis, Elie Gindi, and the Jack Miller Center in these efforts. Other contributions have been added, and in some cases solicited for this volume, as the editors discerned gaps and potential points of interest and illumination.

The net effect of the volume's content, we hope, is a demonstration of the closeness and foundational character of the relationship between the American experience and the Jewish experience, and the nature of the Hebraic impact on the United States. It would be an understatement to say that this closeness has eluded the awareness of both groups for much of American history. On the contrary, there has been a general assumption that the two traditions were intrinsically antagonistic to one another. But the workings of history have clarified that relationship. In recent decades, the rising challenge of a militant secularism in the West, openly hostile to Israel and to many elements of the traditional Judeo-Christian heritage, has made believing Christians and Jews able to see how much they have always had in common. A new awareness of a deep and intrinsic affinity for one another has begun to take hold; and we believe this volume can be of great assistance to dedicated teachers and others who want to further that growing awareness and convey its blessings to a rising generation.

The insight cuts two different ways. Jews owe an immense debt to America, which has been for them an incomparably generous and welcoming land in which they have been permitted to dwell in relative security and have been able to flourish as they have in few other places on the planet in their long and often troubled history. They also know that America has been a stalwart supporter from the very beginning of the modern nation of Israel, in whose existence and thriving so much of Jewish hope is invested. Even in the months after the October 7, 2023, attack on Israel by Hamas terrorists, the support of the American people for Israel has not wavered, even as that of their government has at times been less certain.

But it is equally true that America owes a profound and incalculable debt to the Jews. It is they who provided the deep metaphysical, moral, and anthropological foundation upon which much of the American experiment in democratic self-government was erected, and who have gone on to contribute in ways large and small to the soul of America, and its making and improving.

This collection of essays takes account of both forms of indebtedness, and in so doing, seeks to foster a spirit of mutual understanding and gratitude that reflects a proper perspective on the American-Jewish relationship. We hope this perspective will take root and deepen as the twenty-first century unfolds.

The collection begins with Wilfred McClay's argument for the teaching of American history in faith-based schools, an argument that reverses the usual order of such controversies. The question usually arises in the secular setting of public schools, where the teaching of and about religion is generally regarded as a betrayal of the neutrality to which such institutions should be committed. In religious schools, there is likely to be an equal and opposite predisposition, to concentrate on the inculcation of religious teachings and meta-narratives, which are viewed as superseding the particular history of the nation-state the student inhabits. But both assumptions are flawed in the American instance because, as McClay argues, they fail to take into account the way in which America's secular political order supports free and independent religious faith—and in turn, the way that faith plays a foundational role in forming and upholding American political life. The very possibility of human freedom, that most American of aspirations, depends upon a prior willingness to embrace the Judeo-Christian understanding of man as bearing the image of God. Hence our liberty should be understood as a gift of God rather than a dispensation of man or a construction of the human imagination. For Americans, a proper understanding of liberty cannot exclude God from its formulation.

What follows then is a section of five contributions showing in various ways how profoundly the Hebrew Bible directly and indirectly influenced the formulation of America's political institutions. Dov Lerner's elegant essay demonstrates how John Milton, the great Puritan poet of seventeenth-century England, and the most widely read author in eighteenth-century America, used the Bible to undermine inherited political belief in the necessity of social hierarchy, and open American minds to the notion of man's inalienable rights. Mark David Hall argues that it was the Judeo-Christian tradition, not the Enlightenment, that provided the "main reason" for the embrace of religious liberty in America, and the warm embrace of Jews and Judaism shown by President George Washington in his famous letter to the Hebrew Congregation of Newport, Rhode Island. Daniel Dreisbach's masterly essay shows how the Hebrew Bible's influence permeated the political makeup of early America, and makes the case that those generations saw Biblical religion as indispensable to the American experiment in republican self-government. John R. Vile focuses on a little-known story of the Hebraic origins of America's iconic Liberty Bell, while Shaina Trapedo recounts the history of the first book printed in the American colonies, a copy of the Psalms, which would have an incalculable influence on American life and letters.

The second section is devoted a consideration of the cultural influences on American life wrought by Biblical figures and ideas. Most of the section is devoted to portraits by Stuart Halpern dealing with the American career of great Biblical personalities who came to be adopted into the American imagination as culture heroes: David, Esther, Samson, Elijah, and Daniel. Wilfred McClay argues in his essay that the weighty themes explored by Nathaniel Hawthorne, America's first great novelist, drew upon a Hebraic strain in American letters, a sober counsel of restraint and limitation that served as a counterpoint to the utopian and romantic excesses to which the new nation was prone. Ariel Clark Silver shows how the enigmatic figure of Hagar, the Egyptian mother of Abraham's first son, has served great American writers as an emblematic representative of themes such as dispossession and exile.

The third section combines political and cultural themes, showing how American presidents have understood and sought to influence the American-Jewish relationship. Tevi Troy offers an overview of what American presidents, from Washington to Biden, have thought and said about the Bible: some of it good, some of it forgettable, some of it awkward, but always respectful. Then we are treated to the texts of Washington's famous and justly celebrated correspondence with Hebrew congregations in Savannah and Newport, including the letters to him from each congregation's leadership, to which he was responding. Daniel Dreisbach returns with a penetrating exploration of the Biblical elements in Abraham Lincoln's great Second Inaugural Address of 1865, and the section concludes with 1905 letters to Jacob H. Schiff from Theodore Roosevelt and his Vice President Charles W. Fairbanks regarding the 250th anniversary of Jewish settlement in America, and with a generous accounting by President Calvin Coolidge of Jewish contributions to American democracy.

Finally, we conclude the book's offerings with three reflections on the distinctive meaning of Jewish history, suitable to be read by all

Americans of whatever religious persuasion. Jonathan D. Sarna, the dean of American Jewish historians, offers a short, incisive essay answering the question "Why study American Jewish History?" Rabbi Meir Soloveichik, director of the Zahava and Moshael J. Straus Center for Torah and Western Thought at Yeshiva University and rabbi of Congregation Shearith Israel in New York City, the oldest synagogue in the United States, offers a magnificent and haunting statement of what Jews have meant, and continue to mean, to America. Written in the wake of the October 7, 2023 attacks by Hamas terrorists, and the subsequent upsurge of anti-Israeli sentiment on college campuses, often expressed in the most violent and threatening terms, his essay recounts the long story of Jewish persecution and exclusion through much of the history of Europe—and uses that history to illuminate the dramatic difference in the way Jews have been received in America.

In Soloveichik's view, the present crisis represents a potential turning point for America, because the crisis faced by Israel is also a crisis faced by America. The fate of the Jews and the fate of the United States are now clearly bound together as never before. We are seeing a recrudescence of the old antisemitic hatreds that disfigured Europe for so many centuries, and from which America became such a welcome refuge. If it is to continue to play that role, the US must recover its faith in itself, which is grounded ultimately in a faith in the God of Abraham, Isaac, and Jacob, and in the transcendent moral order that God created and sustains. There is much at stake. But there is also much reason for hope.

Following along similar lines, but raising them to an even higher level, Eric Cohen's concluding essay "The Message from Jerusalem" is a *tour de force* which insists upon the existential necessity, not only for America, but for Christianity and for the West, of a recovery of the strong Hebraic foundation that undergirds it all. "The Christian yearns for Jerusalem," Cohen remarks, "because the Christian world itself is in a moral—indeed a metaphysical—crisis." Jews and Christians now face the same moral challenge. And yet it seems that Western Christians, having learned the wrong lessons from their past, have become passive and guilt-ridden, unwilling or unable to defend themselves and their civilization against the moral, cultural, and political forces that assault it. That condition cannot go on. "For Western civilization to flourish," Cohen insists, "Judeo-Christian moral disarmament, or moral surrender, must come to an end." Enter the Jewish people, once again, in a development that past history could never have predicted. Without God's election of the Jews, the Biblical understanding of human life would never have come into being. The Jews, Cohen says, are the Divine message in the bottle, the hope of the world.

Perhaps as a final reflection, then, it is appropriate to recall the words of the late great Rabbi Jonathan Sacks, the former chief rabbi of the United Kingdom, in a brilliant essay called "How the Jewish People Invented Hope." In that essay, Sacks points out that the heart of Judaism is "a belief so fundamental to Western civilization that we take it for granted... the belief in human freedom." This stands in contrast to the belief in a pitiless and inexorable fate, such as the ancient Greeks believed in, or the modern determinisms of Marxist history, or Freudian psychology, or Darwinian evolution. According to these and similar understandings of the human condition, our belief in our freedom is an illusion.

But it has never been so in the Hebrew Bible, in which God exists apart from nature, and speaks the world into being. He creates all that exists out of nothing, merely by speaking the word *Yehi*, "Let there be," an act of radical freedom expressing His sovereign will. And we are told that God makes man in His image, which means that we share in some measure of his freedom. Indeed, the transgression of Adam and Eve confirms that we were granted just such freedom, even if what they did with it was an abuse of that freedom.

Freedom is the native fuel of hope. It has been that for the Jews, through all of their history. But it also has been so in the history of America, a land of hope whose operating premise has always been that we are not condemned to live out our lives under the conditions into which we are born, but have the freedom to transform those conditions—to "make something of ourselves," as we are wont say; a simple expression that carries with it a profound assumption about who and what we are. "To be a Jew," concludes Sacks, "is to be an agent of hope in a world serially threatened by despair," to struggle "against the world that is," doing so "in the name of the world that could be, should be, but is not yet." The very same things can be said of being an American. There is a deep commonality there. That common mission, clearer to us today than ever before, is the source of the living connection between the two, which this book seeks to celebrate and pass along.

CHAPTER ONE

Why We Teach American History in Faith-Based Schools

Wilfred M. McClay

Why should knowledge of religion be a part of a standard education for all Americans? And why should a faith-based education, particularly a Jewish one, include an acquaintance with American history? These are not the same question. But they have similar answers, because they both involve the way in which America's secular political order supports independent religious faith—and in turn, the way that our faith plays a foundational role in forming and upholding our political life.

This is about more than the First Amendment's guarantees of religious liberty. It is about the nature and status of religion itself in the American legal and political order. That controversy is nothing new, of course. It runs through much of American history, taking on different guises and embracing different antagonists and issues at different times. But it has achieved a unique importance at this historical moment, when our public life seems more intent than ever upon the principle of neutrality in all things and upon understanding that principle in a way that would deprive religion of its independent moral and culture-creating power.

But what is so special about religion that it should receive any such "special privileges"? Why should we treat a church or other religious association differently than we treat any other social club or cultural organization, or treat the rights of a religious adherent any differently than we would treat the expressive liberties of any other individual? These are the questions our fellow citizens increasingly ask.

The drive to ask such questions is perhaps a sign of the growing secularity of so much of our public life. But there is no denying the fact that, in some sense, religion and religious institutions have never been treated according to a principle of strict neutrality. To be sure, the recognition and support of "religion" is something dramatically different from the establishment of a particular religion, a distinction that the First Amendment sought to codify. The fact remains, though, that something like a generic Biblical monotheism has long enjoyed a privileged public status in America.

Examples abound. One still sees the name of God on American currency, in the Pledge of Allegiance, in the oaths we take in court, and in the concluding words of presidential speeches. Chaplains are still employed by the armed services and the Congress, and the latter still duly commences its sessions with the invocation of a prayer. The tax exemption of religious institutions remains intact, at least for the moment. Our most solemn observances, such as the National Day of Prayer and Remembrance in the wake of 9/11, are held in the Washington National Cathedral, and are conducted in a manner that draws heavily on the liturgical and musical heritage of Western Christianity. One could compose a long list of similar examples. We are far from being officially secular, even if we may be tending in that direction. As alarming as the present moment seems at times, it is well to remember that such periods of aggressive secularity have come and gone in our past. There is no reason to assume that the current spasm of secularism will be permanent. It was during the religious revival of the 1950s that the words "under God" were added to the Pledge of Allegiance. But they were drawn from concluding words of Lincoln's Gettysburg Address, delivered almost a century before. Certain themes have had a way of reasserting themselves.

But let's return to the question of privileging religion. Secular critics complain that the public expression of religion flies in the face of the principle of separation and represents an illegitimate coercion of conscience. In addition, there are respectable *religious* arguments against religion's being granted a privileged status. Some of them are reminiscent of the views of Roger Williams, the great American religious dissenter of the seventeenth century, and recall one of the central arguments against any establishment of religion: that installation of a state religion inevitably leads, in the long run, to perfunctoriness, place-seeking, faithlessness, coercion, cooptation, atrophy, and spiritual death. In other words, the establishment of religion is bad for religion.

When one looks at the sad and irrelevant state of the empty established churches of Europe today, one sees the power of the argument. In my tradition, the Christian tradition, the Church is referred to as the bride of Christ. But where there is an established state-supported church, the bride of Christ is likely to turn into a kept woman. By contrast, as Alexis de Tocqueville was able to see as early as the 1830s, the American style of religious freedom kept religion vital and energetic, precisely by making it voluntary. People went where they wished. Indeed, many Christians, particularly those drawing on the Anabaptist tradition, would contend that when churches are cut loose from entanglement in the polity and its civil religion, committed only to being a people set apart, they are freed to be more Christian: more radical, more sacrificial, and more faithful.

But Tocqueville also argued that religion was an essential feature of American democratic life, "the first of [our] political institutions."[1] In other words, he argued that there would always be some degree of entanglement of politics and religion, and that such an entanglement was by and large a good thing. Was he right? Let me offer five arguments in support of this view. These surely do not exhaust all the possibilities, but begin to suggest some of the reasons why it is right and imperative for us to teach our children both about their religion and the history of the nation to which they belong—and why teaching the one is part and parcel of teaching the other.

First, there is what I will call the *foundational* argument, which points back to our historical roots and to the animating spirit of the American Founders and the Constitutional order that they devised and instituted.

The Founders had diverse views about a variety of matters, very much including their own personal religious convictions, but they were in complete and emphatic agreement about one thing: the inescapable importance of religion, and of the active encouragement of religious belief, for the success of the American experiment.

Examples of this view are plentiful. John Adams insisted that "Man is constitutionally, essentially and unchangeably a religious animal. Neither philosophers or politicians can ever govern him any other way."[2] And the universally respected George Washington was a particularly eloquent exponent of the view that religion was essential to the maintenance of public morality, without which a republican government could not survive. The familiar words of his Farewell Address in 1796—"of all the dispositions and habits which lead to political prosperity, Religion and morality are indispensable supports"—can be made to stand in for countless others from John Adams, Benjamin Rush, John Jay, and more.[3]

That this high regard extended to religious institutions as well as individual religious beliefs is made clear by Washington's remark, in 1789, that "If I could have entertained the slightest apprehension that the Constitution framed in the Convention, where I had the honor to preside, might possibly endanger the religious rights of any ecclesiastical Society, certainly I would never have placed my signature to it."[4] If we are looking for a plausible grounding for our deference paid to religion, we can begin with the testimony of the Founders of the American constitutional order itself.

And for Jewish Americans, there is something more. There are the quiet but thrilling words of Washington, now president, in his great letter written in August 1790 to the Hebrew congregation in Newport, Rhode Island: "It is now no more that toleration is spoken of, as if it was by the indulgence of one class of people, that another enjoyed the exercise of their inherent natural rights. For happily the Government of the United States, which gives to bigotry no sanction, to persecution no assistance requires only that they who live under its protection should demean themselves as good citizens, in giving it on all occasions their effectual support."[5] Thus the foundational argument.

Very well, you may respond, but that was then and this is now. Why should we feel bound by the Founders' beliefs or their eighteenth-century mentalities? None of the Founders could possibly have envisioned the cultural and religious diversity of America in the twenty-first century. Their vision assumed a degree of cultural uniformity that would be beyond our power to restore, even if we wanted to. Well, perhaps. But the very fact of that diversity itself leads to a second argument for attention to religion, a *pluralistic* argument which would seek to protect religion all the more zealously as a source of moral order and social cohesion. Let me explain.

There is a reason why accounts of the history of American immigration and of the history of American religion so often end up relating the very same history. From the mid-nineteenth century on, every new wave of immigration to America brought peoples for whom a set of distinctive religious beliefs and practices formed the core of their identity. Some of the worst examples of religious prejudice in our nation's history come out of the cultural clashes and anxieties of these years; but so too did the idea of *pluralism* as a central feature of American life. As Richard John Neuhaus and Peter Berger came to formulate it, "This nation is constituted as an exercise in pluralism, as the *unum* within which myriad *plures* are sustained."[6] The persistence of regional, religious, ethnic, and other differences, so long as they are not invidious in character or dependent upon unjust or illegal discriminations or restriction, is something to be desired, because it means that the moral communities within which consciences are formed—churches, synagogues, mosques, and the like—remain healthy. Hence in America, the national purpose rightly understood ought to seek, not to undermine particular affinities or purposes, but to strengthen them. Hence a faith-based account of the national history will include its ability to embrace pluralism.

I would add that it is essential that religious freedom be understood not only as an individual liberty but also as a *corporate* liberty, a liberty that applies to and inheres in *groups* and defends the integrity and self-governance of such groups. How could it be otherwise, since a religion, like a language, is an inherently social phenomenon, quintessentially an activity of groups rather than the property of isolated individuals? Religious freedom must be understood in this dual aspect, protecting not only the liberty of individuals, but also the liberty of churches, synagogues, and other religious institutions and communities: protecting their freedom to define what they are and what they are not, to control the meaning and terms of their membership, to freely exercise their faith by the way they choose to raise their families and order their community life, seeking to embody their religion's moral self-understanding in lived experience.

There are, of course, limits to this autonomy, as there must be to all liberties and all forms of pluralism. Religious liberty is not a *carte blanche* or an all-purpose, get-out-of-jail-free card and its limits cannot be established once and for all by the invocation of some pristine abstract principle. But its essential place in the healthy life of the *plures* should ensure for it a high degree of respect and set the bar very high for any government action that would have the effect of burdening religion's free exercise. That respect and that high bar have generally been affirmed by the federal courts and the Congress. A faith-based education should recognize and be grateful for this.

A third argument for religion's special place might be called an *anthropological* one. Human beings are theotropic by their nature, inclined toward religion, and driven to relate their understandings of the highest things to their lives as lived in community together, both metaphysically and morally. Whether this characteristic can be attributed to in-built endowment, evolutionary adaptation, or some other source, it would seem to be a good thing for the secular order to affirm our theotropic impulses rather than seek to inhibit their expression.

Indeed, the vote of public confidence implied by such affirmation naturally engenders a sense of general loyalty to the polity and binds religious believers affectionately to the secular political project far more effectively than would an insistence upon a rigorously secularist public square. Indeed, the latter course would present the very real danger of producing alienated subcultures of religious believers whose sectarian disaffection with the mainstream could become so profound as to represent a threat to the very cohesion of the nation. Secularists who worry about religion's taking an outsized role in public life would be better advised to give some strategic ground on that issue, and acknowledge the theotropic dimension in our makeup, even if they believe it to be a weakness or debility.

Such acknowledgement has the added benefit of promoting the development of a healthy civil religion, which is nothing more than an expression of our incorrigible need to relate secular things to ultimate purposes. Civil religion promotes political and social cohesion, while serving as a visible embodiment, of sorts, of the generalized thing we call "religion." But there are better and worse ways of doing this. Civil religion can, of course, be extremely dangerous, a form of playing with fire, and is viewed with understandable suspicion from all quarters. It borrows from the energy of specific faiths but always carries with it the danger of usurping and displacing them and underwriting a pernicious idolatry of the state or the nation. Hence it needs to be kept on a short leash.

Properly understood, the American civil religion also draws upon sources of moral authority that transcend the state and are capable of holding the state accountable to a standard higher than itself. A civil religion can be, as Yale sociologist Philip Gorski recently argued, "a mediating tradition that allows room for both religious and political values."[7] And the more that the activity of specific religions is accorded respect in the public sphere, the less likely it is that a civil religion will be successful in displacing them. A faith-based education will want to take account of this.

A fourth argument might be called the *meliorist* argument, which would acknowledge religion's special place in American life because of the extensive social good that religious institutions have done and continue to do in the world, because the doing of such good works is an essential part of the free exercise of religion. This argument follows in the footsteps of the Founders' emphasis on moral formation of citizens and also embraces the role of religious groups in abolishing slavery, promoting civil rights, running orphanages, caring for the indigent, and the like. But it has also taken on a weight of its own, given the vast scale and scope of charitable, medical, and educational activities still undertaken by religious groups today. Let the Catholic Church stand as a powerful example of this. The Catholic Church is the operator of nearly six thousand primary and secondary schools, enrolling 1.7 million students, and 665 hospitals (comprising nearly 16 percent of American hospitals and 17 percent of hospital beds), and 1,600 continuing care facilities, making it the operator of the largest private educational and health-care systems in the country.[8] In addition, Catholic Charities USA is, as of 2022, the thirteenth largest charity in the nation (the fourth largest being the religiously oriented Salvation Army).[9]

Last but not least, there is an argument that I will call *metaphysical.* It is often said that religious freedom is the first freedom, since it is grounded in the dignity and integrity of the human person, which requires that each of us be permitted to fulfill our right, and duty, to seek and embrace the truth about our existence and live out our lives in accordance with our understanding of that truth. This is, or should be, a universal freedom because the great questions of human existence are not the exclusive province of professors and savants, but belong to us all. Any good society, committed to the flourishing of its members, should recognize and encourage and support that search. To acknowledge that fact in a public way, with an explicit recognition of the valuable place of religion, is an important declaration about the value a society places on the spiritual and moral life of its members.

But there is far more to the metaphysical argument than that. Indeed, there is a growing recognition that, in a postmodern world dominated by immense bureaucratic governments and sprawling transnational business corporations, entities that increasingly seem to operate in tandem, behemoths that are neither responsive to the tools of democratic governance nor accountable to national law, nor answerable to any well-established code of behavior, religion serves as an indispensable counterweight. It is an essential resource for the upholding of human dignity and moral order, for speaking truth to power, for giving support to the concept of human rights, and for insisting that a voice of moral urgency—whether celebrating, exhorting, or rebuking—never becomes banished from the cold logic of instrumental rationality. A faith-based education will be bolstered precisely by the knowledge that it is needed to play this important role in counteracting the negative tendencies of even the most benign secular institutions.

Religion has played this role before in American history and done so heroically. Evangelical religious conviction provided the animating force behind what was arguably the greatest reform movement in American history, the nineteenth-century movement to abolish slavery. The moral leadership of Pope John Paul II played a key role in bringing about the end of Soviet tyranny in Eastern Europe. As the sociologist Jose Casanova eloquently argued in his 1994 book *Public Religions in the Modern World*, the modern world runs the risk of being "devoured by the inflexible, inhuman logic of its own creations," unless it restores a "creative dialogue" with the very religious traditions it has eviscerated or abandoned.[10] And that dialogue will not be fruitful unless we sustain and protect the special public standing that religion has hitherto enjoyed.

There is an even deeper question here—the question of whether our freedom itself, and more generally the liberal individualism we have come to embrace in the modern West, is sustainable without the Judeo-Christian religious assumptions that have hitherto accompanied and upheld it. For example, the Italian writer Marcello Pera has argued that it is a dangerous illusion to believe that ideas such as the dignity of the human person can be sustained for long without some ultimate grounding in the deep normative orientation of the Judeo-Christian tradition. Ironically, the very possibility of a "secular" realm of politics, which we embrace in the West as a good thing (and which is the necessary basis for any robust understanding of religious freedom), may depend upon the presence of certain specifically Biblical distinctives, embodied in culture as much as in doctrine.

Pera's concerns had been precisely anticipated by one of the most religiously heterodox figures of early American history, Thomas Jefferson. On one of the panels decorating the walls of the Jefferson Memorial in Washington appear these searing words: "God who gave us life gave us liberty. Can the liberties of a nation be secure when we have removed a conviction that these liberties are the gift of God? Indeed, I tremble for my country when I reflect that God is just, that His justice cannot sleep forever."[11]

In that passage, Jefferson was speaking of the moral scourge of slavery and asking, rhetorically, whether there could be any moral justification for the failure to extend the blessings of liberty to all men. But there is a larger implicit point. Jefferson was saying that the very possibility of human liberty itself, the liberty of every man and woman, is dependent upon our prior willingness to understand liberty as a gift of God, rather than a dispensation of man. The name of God serves as far more than a mere rhetorical device in this context. Even a world-class skeptic like Jefferson understood that erasing the name of God from the foundations of American public life could lead to fearful consequences—which provides yet another reason why defending the special status of religion in American life is not merely a reasonable and defensible path, but one of fundamental importance, and a reason why a faith-based education will benefit from teaching students how their faith is grounded in and protected by the extant political order.

PART ONE

The Influence of the Hebrew Bible on the American Founding

CHAPTER TWO

John Milton: Breaker of Chains

Dov Lerner

In a vast, dark cave, a colossal warrior lies face down, dazed, in a lake of raging fire. But slowly he stirs, lifts his shield, and stands to see his soldiers writhing all around him in pain. Wracked by the shame of defeat, the soldiers gaze up at their titanic leader for solace or counsel or relief. He then provides a speech that lifts their spirits, heals their wounds, rallies them back to their cause, and pledges to avenge their losses and win the war. The once dazed warrior now seems daring, dauntless, and audacious; he appears intrepid and inspiring and courageous; he embodies valor and gallantry, power and loyalty—and seems to be the very personification of all that is noble and heroic. And his name is Satan.

This is the scene with which the blind English writer John Milton opens his twelve-book-long epic poem *Paradise Lost*, first published in 1667. The question that has perplexed so many since its inception is why.

John Milton was a prolific author who had spent his life trying to guide souls toward heaven, and society toward a Biblical vision of liberty—he was what one historian called "the purity of Puritanism."[1] And yet, in the epic poem that has become his most enduring legacy, he seems to celebrate, even venerate Satan, the seditious angel who fell into hell after rebelling against God.

Though it is true that, by the end of *Paradise Lost*, Satan's persistent insurrection comes at a cost to himself, he seems no less heroic for it; though he falls, he is a figure of almost unflinching conviction whose charisma captures the imagination. Milton gave Satan power, prestige, and appeal with page after page of soaring poetry—giving him lines and scripting him speeches that bring his fellow angels to their feet and centuries of readers to a state of complete awe. So once more we ask: why did an English Puritan pen a poem that hails Satan as a hero?

The answer is that he was sowing, poetically, the seeds of human dignity and inculcating a need for a very specific species of liberty. But first we need some context.

BACKGROUND

Milton lived through a time of unprecedented change in the systems of English government—the only time in its history that the people killed their king and Parliament served as a pure republic. Oliver Cromwell, then the leader of the English commonwealth, turned to John Milton to use his pen in defense of both the King's execution and the Parliamentarian revolution. For years he served as the principal diplomat and propagandist for the republic—promoting religious reforms and defending regicide—holding a post called the *Secretary for Foreign Tongues*. During those eleven years his reputation for erudition grew as he became the most prolific composer of political treatises and a prime architect of modern liberal democracy.

But in 1660, eleven years after the execution of Charles I, the republic fell and England saw the return of the king's son Charles II, who brought about a restoration of the monarchy that remains in place to this day with the reign of Charles III. By this time, Milton had lost his sight and—as a result of the restoration—had gone into hiding. His writings were banned and burned, and survived only as a result of friends in high places. The rest of his life was spent quietly in London where he published books on English grammar and British history. He also produced what many now consider to be a work of unrivaled imaginative genius that shook his world and continues to shape ours.

Milton described the nights of those last decades as filled with insights inspired from on high, which he verbalized in daylight to his daughters, who wrote down the lines that built the epic poem he called *Paradise Lost*. Though he does seem to celebrate Satan, what Milton was *actually* doing, from the very start, was tearing apart an insidious vision of the human condition pioneered in ancient Greece—a vision that he felt had come to infect psyches, defile societies, and suppress liberties all across the West for close to twenty centuries.

Even though, with the return of the king, he ceased publishing explicitly political treatises, the themes that lay beneath his early convictions did not die. Milton brought them to life, exquisitely and lyrically, subtly but unmistakably, in a poem that sought to do three specific things—shatter the Greek idea of narrative epic, reconfigure the arena of Western ethics, and depict a distinct form of liberal politics—all inspired by the Hebrew Bible. This essay will trace these three transformations, first in epics, then in ethics, and finally in politics, knowing that the seeds that Milton sowed in Westminster eventually came to fruition here in the United States.

BIBLICAL EPICS

An epic is a story that speaks of great battles and grand deeds in a high style that draws the eyes and captures the imagination. The Western epic tradition peaked in the ancient world with Homer's *Odyssey* in Greece and Virgil's *Aeneid* in Rome. Though these tales differ in many ways, they share a sense of what makes a hero that remains pervasive to this day.

Perhaps the most well-known version of this vision can be found in the mythic tradition ascribed to Peisander of Rhodes, who is supposed to have composed the tale of Hercules as we know it. In this telling he faces ten so-called labors—with an extra two being set to correct for successes achieved on the back of deception. In each of these labors or ordeals, Hercules is put to a test where he depends on his stamina, strength, tactics, and intellect to overcome a mythic enemy, beginning with the Nemean lion, the Lernaean Hydra, and the Erymanthian Boar.

But on the other side of the Mediterranean, there resided a small nation of tribes inspired by prophets rather than oracles and driven by history rather than myth, which spoke of a similar tradition—but they seem to ground it in an altogether different, far less epic, vision of the hero. The sages of Israel contend in the Mishna—among the earliest strata of rabbinic literature—that their principal patriarch, Abraham, underwent *asarah nisyonot*, ten tests.[2] They do not enumerate the content of the Abrahamic labors, a detail left to the medieval commentators, but an assessment of the Biblical text of Genesis offers a fairly limited inventory of possibilities. Among other things, Abraham cuts his flesh and leaves his father, expels one son and binds the other, meets a Pharaoh, saves a nephew, and seals a treaty. As Rabbi Jonathan Sacks notes: "[he was] not [a] heroic figure of the kind we find in Greek legends…, For the most part, he…lived quietly, far from the arenas of power and fame."[3]

It is hard to overstate the rift between the imaginative worlds of myth and Scripture as exhibited in these two tales of ten respective tests. Hercules occupies a world of beasts and competes with mythic creatures—his heroism is found in the capacity to ground fiends, bind hounds, and seize hinds. All his enemies and nemeses are external, while his inner world remains apparently static and entirely unseen. In contrast, the drama of the Abrahamic labors unfolds not on the world stage but in the theatre of his soul. All the monsters and obstacles that he faces are found within. His antagonists are not the creatures of myth but the beasts that live in the human heart—doubt, apathy, greed, fear, impatience, and ego.

Where the heroism of Greek myth honors the physical skill and corporal strength to defeat titanic creatures, Biblical heroism hails the power to battle inner demons. It extols the resolve to conquer all impediments to reflection and patience, friendship and self-effacement, penitence and allegiance and care. It is this Biblical alternative to the epic that the rabbinic sages turned into a tenet when, in a comment on Proverbs, they said:

> Who is a hero? One who masters their desire.

Or as another sage put it, in the interpersonal context:

> Who is a hero? One who turns an enemy into a friend.

The topography of Hebraic heroism is the human heart, where words not swords do the hard work—where the mind not the hamstring is the most important muscle. This is precisely what Milton sought to inject into an epic tradition that, as far as he could tell, stressed weapons and war and failed to address our flaws or even attempt to perfect our inner condition. In his words: "Wars, hitherto the only argument / Heroic deemed… / the better fortitude / Of patience and heroic martyrdom / Unsung."[4]

Milton could see that the epics of the ancient world had cast a long shadow. Homer and Virgil had inspired national poets for centuries to tell tales of great battles and fabled knights. But no one, he says, had yet penned a great epic that elevated patience or dramatized the unseen world of ego and restraint, instinct and moderation, impulse and spiritual determination. This aspiration to transform the epic genre suffuses *Paradise Lost* from the first lines to the last.

The poem elaborates on the short story found at the beginning of Genesis in which Adam and Eve are ejected from Eden after they eat fruit from the only forbidden tree. In Milton's retelling, the reason that Eve ate was due to a temptation from Satan in the guise of a snake, who sought to retaliate against God in the wake of his defeat at the hands of Heaven. Along the way, Milton treats us to a series of encounters and conversations between the first human couple and a range of angels, and offers us their respective memories of the war in Heaven and the origins of life on Earth. But Milton does more than simply replace the inhabitants of myth with a cast of Biblical figures or shift the scene from the Aegean Sea to the garden of Eden.

Just like the poets of ancient Rome, he opens his poem with an invocation—a call for inspiration from on high to achieve a feat that, in his words, had been "unattempted yet in prose or rhyme".[5] Milton's aim was to fundamentally revolutionize and reconfigure the epic tradition by deploying a Greek means for Hebrew ends—to tell a great tale of a heroic battle, but to locate that battle within the human heart.

William Poole, in his recent work *Milton and the Making of Paradise Lost*, describes what he calls Milton's "techniques of disruption" and characterizes the poem, writ large, as an act of "creative violence" against the classical epic. He writes:

> [E]pic imitation in Milton carries with it a subtle incrimination of what it imitates. Milton's gods are God; his heroes . . . garden rather than duel; his battles, conducted by angels, are surreal morphs of classical warfare, fought by deathless shape-shifters . . . and the conflicts of loyalty and love are uniquely domestic in focus.[6]

Fundamentally, however, the rift between the world of Homer and the Hebrew Bible, which Milton tries to bridge by injecting the body of myth with the spirit of Scripture, goes so deep as to make the mixture almost impossible which is why staging the poem as a successful play has proved almost insurmountable. At the core of each culture lies a central premise about how to weigh moral worth and thus how we ought to operate in this world, and they are radically different if not completely incompatible. And to further flesh out this incompatibility we turn to the ethical imagination that lay at the foundation of Milton's transformation of the epic.

BIBLICAL ETHICS

Imagine a mature person confronting the diversity of the material cosmos for the very first time. Then imagine they trying to assign relative value to the various elements of the vista before their eyes—trying to determine what in this world is more or less important. They see birds in the trees, diamonds in the dirt, stars in the sky, and fish in the sea, and are awash with a sense that there must be an innate hierarchy in nature. And as they search for the most valuable or vital element of existence, their eyes are drawn to that enormous orb which radiates warmth, is blindingly bright, and at each dawn brings an end to the night—that ball of fire and blazing light that we call the sun.

This response to the material cosmos—what's called an ontology—can be summed up in a single if superficial sentence: what you sense is what you get. For such an ontology, bigger is better; sturdier or stronger is superior; glossier or more gilded is greater; and all *essential* worth—all *moral* value—comes to be ascribed on the basis of *physical*, most often *visual*, traits. And this ontology grew into a creed that defined the Greek ethos and, over time, developed into a concept called the "Great Chain of Being."

This Great Chain, as described by Arthur Lovejoy in a series of lectures on the subject, is comprised of a painstakingly meticulous ladder of created matter that reaches all the way from heaven down to hell, with the level of perfection lessening as one descends the chain—all the way from angels down to inanimate objects.[7] And on each rung of the existential ladder, or within each link of the great chain, lies an internal hierarchy as well. Stones are ranked from diamonds down to dirt, trees from oak down to weeds, and animals from eagles down to beetles. Of course, the hierarchy does not end there; and the cosmic canvas bespeaks a sweeping and intrinsic hierarchy always accessible to the eyes and visual *image*-ination.

From the very first chapter however, the Hebrew Bible contests this perspective, and repudiates any chain that attributess essential value purely on the basis of the sense of sight. Leon Kass, in his reflections on the opening of Genesis, presents the relegation of the sun to a relatively late stage of creation as part of a larger argument for what he calls the "moral irrelevance of the entire visible cosmos."[8] Kass suggests that Scripture assumes that human beings would "follow their eyes" in the absence of an intervention. And that is precisely why God's revelation seeks to suppress any inclination toward a great chain and goes to great lengths to place moral value on agency, choice, and behavior rather than unchangeable traits of a static nature.

Speaking to this divide, Lovejoy notes that Judaism developed "an appreciation of the inner springs of conduct ... that the Greek mind scarcely ever attained."[9] And in the same vein, Hans Kohn, the celebrated political scientist, characterized the ancient Greeks as "the people of sight" and cited Jacob Burckhardt calling them "the eye of the world."[10] But Ancient Israel was what Rabbi Sacks, following Kohn and Kass, calls "a culture of the ear"[11]—a product of a people pushed to overlook their sense of sight and attend to the inner eye.

It is no accident that at least twice a day, traditional Jews cover their eyes and recite the phrase: "*Shema Yisrael,*" "Hear O' Israel." The revolution launched by revelation sought to attune ancient Israel to the world of the mind rather than the eyes, to see glory in peace rather than violence, and to see value in each human being—no matter how tall or strong or shrewd—freely pursuing the awe of Heaven.

So radical, and apparently unnatural, was this revolution in antiquity, that it took centuries of incremental intellectual dents for it to break through to the masses and displace the weight of the great chain. The man who made one of the most enduring dents, in a determined effort to break that chain and show that assigning value on the basis of sight perverts the dignity of human life, was John Milton—who paints Eve's failure in Eden as the result of relying on her eyes.

In Book 9, when Satan finally decides to work his designs on Eve, he possesses a snake and slithers wildly to catch her eye. Then, with her attention fixed, he coaxes her to "see the truth" and eat from the forbidden tree, which—allured by its look—she does. After eating its fruit, she convinces her husband to follow suit, which, after some deliberation, he does—and then they turn to sensual and carnal joy.

But in the wake of their illicit feast and conjugal sleep, the thrill of the taste recedes and the feeling of ecstasy fades and, in Milton's words, they "Soon found their eyes how opened, and their minds /

How darkened..."[12] He then describes how their reliance on their eyes not only obscured their minds and made them cry, but unleashed a wildness within.

The failure of our first parents, for Milton, was the decision to let their instincts subjugate their will; they permitted the scene before their eyes to seize their minds and enflame their appetites, with chaos waiting in the wings. The task to which Milton attunes his reader is the achievement of peace in the mind rather than the possession of that which breeds desire through the eye. And we see this as the poem closes, when Adam is prepared for his expulsion from Eden with a vision for an angel, and then says:

> Greatly instructed I shall hence depart,
> greatly in peace of thought...
> Henceforth I learn, that to obey is best...
> and by small
> Accomplishing great things, by things deemed weak
> Subverting worldly strong, and worldly wise
> By simply meek; that suffering for truth's sake
> Is fortitude to highest victory.[13]

Adam has learnt what Milton understood the Hebrew Bible to be teaching us about the human task in the face of visual creeds like the great chain of being. He now knows that true greatness lies in small acts of goodness; that true strength lies not in the skill to slay another but in the ability to hold sway over the self. The angel responds and confirms Adam's learning with words of comfort that give him and Eve reason to feel that, despite their expulsion from Eden, paradise may still be a possibility.

Appetite shattered human innocence and made an Edenic life impossible. But our mission remains. Given our condition, cultivating the paradise *within* is now the key. In fact, a decade before publishing *Paradise Lost*, when the English republic first fell, a critic of Milton printed a sermon entitled "No Blind Guides," in which he derided Milton's blindness as a sign of Divine displeasure. In response, Milton made the case that true happiness and human flourishing are found not through *sight* but *insight*. In his words, physical blindness "merely deprives things of color and superficial appearance...," but "what is true and essential... is not lost to my intellectual vision."[14]

It is for the same reason that a number of rabbinic commentators insist that someone who is blind should still recite the daily blessing thanking God for "liberating the blind," "*poke'ach ivrim*"—for what makes us truly free is not the utility of physical sight, but the gift of mental insight.[15]

It was with this commitment not only to a scriptural mode of epic but a Biblical notion of ethics that Milton aimed to break the great chain and advocate for a new kind of politics, to which we now turn.

BIBLICAL POLITICS

In 1649, when Charles I stood on the precipice of his execution, he is said to have appealed to the people with a sentence that may strike us as profoundly odd. He said: "A subject and a sovereign are clean different things." But if this sentence seems to us like the rambling of an unrepentant tyrant, that is only because we are all heir to an outlook bequeathed to us by Milton and his peers, who were inspired by their reading of the Hebrew Bible.

For centuries the idea of the Divine right of kings reigned supreme. But it was always more than a simple claim made by princes to have God's private favor—it was a central tenet that gave societies their shape and structure and stability which emerged self-evidently from a belief in the great chain of being. Just as diamonds were essentially superior to dirt, as oak was to weeds, and lions were to lambs—kings were superior to commoners according to the law of nature. To put it simply: "A subject and a sovereign are clean different things."

At the core of the creed that arose from the great chain of being was the belief that the cosmic equilibrium depended on preserving the hierarchies within nature. To complain about the chain, or rebel against it, was a form of heresy that threatened material harmony and courted existential catastrophe. Seen this way, monarchy was understood as constitutive of social order, and killing the king was doing more than protesting a particular political figure—it was to deny the very idea of innate and ordained hierarchy. It was to both invite and incite pandemonium.

Seen this way, to kill the king is to decapitate the body politic and we all know how bodies fare without their heads. There is a reason that royal coats of arms tend to be emblazoned with lions and that crowns have been encrusted with diamonds. There is a reason that the parliamentarians were depicted as cutting down the royal oak and that John Milton was condemned by an enemy as a "blind Beetle that durst affront the Royal Eagle."[16] Kings had their place atop the great chain of humanity and to topple them was to defy nature and play with fire.

When Cromwell and the republic asked Milton to defend their regicide, he cited both Scripture and the rabbinic sages,[17] noting most centrally that: "No man who knows aught, can be so stupid to deny that all Men naturally were born free, being the image and resemblance of God himself."[18] For Milton, what determines any person's status as royal is not their birth but their behavior. In his words:

> They in whomsoever... virtues dwell eminently, need not Kings to make them happy, but are the architects of their own happiness; and whether to themselves or others are not less than Kings.[19]

Seeing people as independent architects, rather than rungs on a ladder involves a stunning revolution in the moral imagination—and an equally stunning shift in understanding how political institutions ought to be built to best serve human flourishing. If we are all part of a great chain that relies on hierarchy for prosperity, the central aims of political institutions ought to be suppressing any ideas of social change, promoting the agency of those born to rule, and depriving those who weren't of power. If, however, it is not cosmic equilibrium that leads to human happiness but inner peace, then the central ambition of political institutions ought to be simply this: promoting the conditions of individual liberty, giving each person the ability to cultivate the paradise within.

Seen this way, we can appreciate how much time, toil, and tempering it took to direct the West away from a deep belief in the great chain of being and to embrace the creed on Benjamin's Franklin's proposal for a Great Seal that reads, "Rebellion to tyrants is obedience to God." At the center of that transformation was our author who, once more, not only wrote revolutionary treatises, but composed an epic poem inspired by the Bible to incline his readers' minds aways from the prospect of a cosmic chain and toward the cause of human freedom.

If we return to the vision that Adam is given by the angel preparing him for eviction from Eden, we read of him foreseeing Noah and his family surviving the flood and going on to live in fraternal peace as intended by Heaven. That peace, however, was to be short-lived, as the angel predicts that one day:

> One shall rise
> Of proud ambitious heart, who not content
> With fair equality, fraternal state,
> Will arrogate dominion undeserved
> Over his brethren, and quite dispossess
> Concord and law of nature from the earth ...[20]

Speaking of Nimrod and feeding off the exegesis—which ties Nimrod's name to the Hebrew verb for rebellion ("*mered*")—Milton has the angel teach Adam and humanity a timeless lesson. There will always be those who follow their eyes and close their minds, those who seek to rise on the back of appetite and glorify violence along the way. Though they will censure others for resisting their rule, it is they—says the angel—who violate the laws of nature.

In response, the appalled Adam calls this son of his a "wretched man" and a "usurper" who steals authority "from God not given"—and then he articulates God's law for all time: "man over men / He made not lord" but "human left from human free."[21]

For Milton, human beings were born to live in liberty and cultivate bliss, first in Eden and then within. It is not by muscle but with the mind that we find our happiness. It is not through sight but with insight that we mine the moral truth. No one has a Divine right to exercise power over others, and politics is comprised of a single, limited enterprise: the promotion of individual liberty for every citizen.

Rabbi Sacks, distinguishing this Biblical vision from the kind of political life implied by Greek myth, concedes that:

> It is not dramatic, heroic, the stuff of Homer or Virgil. But it does stop us killing one another in the name of faith... and helps us, in Robert Kennedy's fine phrase, 'to tame the savageness of man and make gentle the life of this world.'[22]

Milton's Biblical vision is not visually spectacular, as it renders all political power, at best, a necessary evil—and seeks to suppress every exercise of public authority, unless a case can be made that it furthers the liberty of the citizenry. Seen this way, governmental power ought to be used for only two purposes—to keep citizens safe from harm and free to choose—both with the express goal of promoting as much individual happiness as humanly possible.

If this sounds like the right to life, liberty, and the pursuit of happiness, that is no accident. To say that Milton's thought had an impact on America would be like saying a seed has an impact on a tree: his poetry and his prose lie at the root of the US Constitution and beyond.

Reams of research have already shown how he was likely the most widely read author in eighteenth-century America, and how the Founding Fathers, from Jefferson to Madison and Adams to Paine, all cited and relied on his writing. And the pervasive omnipresence of his influence did not end in the generation of Paine's *Common Sense* and Jefferson's *Declaration of Independence*. His line defining God's posture toward humankind—that "man over men / He made not lord"—struck a chord with freedom fighters and abolitionists and feminists, and civil rights activists across the board, well into the twentieth century.

One early American anthologist declared that "Milton is more emphatically American than any author who has lived in the United States."[23] Commenting on that declaration, critic Margaret Fuller explained, "He is so because in him is expressed so much of the primitive vitality of that thought from which America was born." She continued: "He is one of the fathers of this age, of that new idea which agitates the sleep of Europe, and which America, if awake to the design of heaven and her own duty, would become the principal exponent."[24]

We could itemize all the evidence and catalog every reference ever made to Milton in American letters to exhibit how his thought—inspired by the Bible—lies beneath almost every element of constitutional liberty and the American moral imagination. But it can all be encapsulated in a two-line rhyme inscribed on a window at the back of a chapel next to Westminster Abbey, in the center of London. At the bottom of a frame dedicated in 1888 by the Philadelphian George Childs, lies a couplet composed by one of America's so-called fireside-poets—the Quaker and abolitionist, John Greenleaf Whittier. And it reads:

> The new world honors him whose lofty plea for England's freedom made her own more sure,
> Whose song, immortal as its theme, shall be their common freehold while both worlds endure.[25]

Though his work—including *Paradise Lost*—is regretfully now rarely read, the pen of this blind poet led a revolution that broke the great chain and continues to shape our age. On the shoulders of giants and inspired by the Bible, he revolutionized the epic, reconfigured Western ethics, and reimagined modern politics—seeing every life as a Divine gift in which liberty and inner bliss go hand in hand. And this brings us back to our encounter with Satan at the start.

CODA

Looming large over a dark lake of raging fire, Satan may well strike us as heroic at first glance. He has muscle, conviction, stature and charisma, and wields weapons and words in the service of war. But he only remains a hero to those encumbered by the measures of Greek myth—to those who attribute moral value solely on the basis of the sense of sight. Because, despite Satan's size and his skill at inspiring an armed insurrection, a battle rages beneath his skin in which he fails to fight and does not win—deep within, his appetite triumphs over his will and dominates his mind.

In a crucial passage of the poem, having forged a plan to attack man, Satan sails out of hell and makes his way across the cosmos to Earth. Landing near Eden, he stands in the sun but the light becomes too bright for him to bear, reminding him of life in Heaven before the war. The gleaming beams lead him to contemplate the error of his ways and the pain of his loss and to then admit to himself that wherever he goes, agony follows. In his words: "Which way I fly is hell; myself am hell."[26] And it is here, in the middle of a sincere soliloquy, that Satan appears to entertain repentance and apology, but cannot imagine it lasting very long. He says:

> But say I could repent and could obtain
> By act of grace my former state; how soon
> Would height recall high thoughts, how soon unsay
> What feigned submission swore.[27]

He does not doubt that he could be forgiven, for God's grace knows no bounds. What he does doubt, however, is his capacity to sustain his sincerity once the pain of falling fades away. He sees himself as powerless before the forces of pride and passion and resigns himself to eternal, irredeemable defeat—uttering perhaps the most tragic lines in all of English literature:

> So farewell hope, and with hope farewell fear,
> Farewell remorse: all good to me is lost.[28]

It is here, where Satan forsakes hope and caves to his craving that he truly falls, never to rise again. He may go on to deceive angels, tempt humanity, and get our first parents expelled from Eden, but his inability to wrestle within himself leaves him weak and feeble and anything but free. The epic hero thus becomes, in Milton's hand, an epic villain. Incapable of patience and held captive by passions—resident of what one critic calls an "inward prison"—Satan ends up hollow, shallow, and tragic. He stands as an emblem of what leads human beings to hell.

Only in an age still chained by a creed that preaches a need for hierarchy do human beings assign value with their eyes and define heroism through the prism of physical power. It was the ethics of the Bible revealed at Sinai that stirred a moral transformation that sought to break that chain—and in seventeenth-century England, it was John Milton's prose and epic poem that led the way.

Inspired by Abraham's inner triumphs, and—though blind—defined by insight and defiance, Milton defended a revolution that sowed the seeds of the American constitution. With a detailed retelling of Genesis, he has us see that human beings can fail—but he also has us see that they can thrive, if they defend each other's unalienable rights to life, liberty, and the pursuit of the "Paradise within."[29]

CHAPTER THREE

The Judeo-Christian Tradition and the Rise of American Religious Liberty

Mark David Hall

"Inspired by Enlightenment ideas of free inquiry, Jefferson used his reason to argue that government ought to have nothing to do with religious matters other than to guarantee religious liberty."
—Frank Lambert, *Separation of Church and State*

"Religious toleration generally arose from the Enlightenment."
—David L. Holmes, *The Faith of the Founding Fathers*

"In its conception and language, the [Virginia] Statute and the First Amendment were Enlightenment creations."
—Jon Butler, "Coercion, Miracle, Reason"[1]

Scholars routinely assert that the Enlightenment inspired civic leaders in the West to adopt religious liberty. They came to value reason over revelation, the argument goes, and so concluded that it is irrational to kill or persecute in the name of God. While Enlightenment ideas did have some positive influence (especially in Europe), the main reason Americans embraced religious liberty was the influence of the Judeo-Christian tradition. Biblical and theological arguments played key roles in defining and supporting what many Founders called "the sacred right of conscience."[2] In addition to supporting freedom of worship, many Founders believed that citizens should be free to act according to their religious convictions unless the government has a compelling reason to prevent them from doing so. Moreover, most of America's Founders understood that the religious liberty of all men and women should be protected—including citizens who do not share the majority's faith.

Americans of European descent were an overwhelmingly Christian people in the seventeenth and eighteenth centuries. Indeed, as late as 1776, 98 percent were Protestant, 2 percent were Roman Catholic, and there were around two thousand Jews in a handful of cities.[3] Even so, it is necessary to consider the influence of the *Judeo-Christian* tradition because many of the Protestants who settled British North America had a high regard for the Hebrew Scriptures. Religious and civic leaders regularly looked to these Scriptures for guidance, and many were members of traditions that were heavily influenced by rabbinical commentaries on them.[4]

WHY RELIGIOUS LIBERTY?

According to some, a faith commitment necessitates that one be intolerant of other religions or sects. From 325, when Emperor Constantine called the Council of Nicaea to resolve a theological debate, to the founding of the American colonies, it was common for civic authorities to promote what they considered to be true religion. This often included discriminating against or even persecuting those who deviated from the rulers' understanding of Christian orthodoxy. America's earliest colonial leaders, from north to south, were not immune to this temptation, but there was more freedom than is often assumed. Even in Puritan New England, civic authorities did not try to compel belief. Orderly dissenters were tolerated; however, disorderly dissenters like Anne Hutchinson and Roger Williams were not, and upon rare occasion a *very* disorderly dissenter, such as the Quaker Mary Dyer, was executed.[5]

Fortunately, the way Americans approached religious liberty changed in important ways between the establishment of the early colonies and the founding era. They did so for several reasons. At a practical level, despite a desire for homogeneity, almost from the start America attracted diverse groups of immigrants from England and continental Europe.

Even in Congregational New England and the Anglican South there were dissenters from an early date, and the middle colonies were always a muddle. A great illustration of this is a 1771 woodcut of the skyline of New York City. Of the twenty-one buildings identified, most are houses of worship, including those belonging to Presbyterians, Anglicans, Dutch Calvinists, Moravians, Jews, Quakers, Anabaptists, Catholics, Methodists, and others. Admittedly, New York was a particularly diverse city, but there was significant pluralism in each colony. This diversity forced civic authorities to negotiate laws and policies encouraging different groups to get along (sometimes with more success than others).

"Prospect of the City of New York." Woodcut from Hugh Gaine, *New York Almanac*, 1771.

The lot of religious minorities in America improved markedly in the eighteenth century. These advances were aided by Parliamentary legislation, pragmatic attempts to deal with religious diversity, and Biblical, practical, and theoretical arguments for the liberty of conscience made by indisputably pious men such as Roger Williams, William Penn, Elisha Williams, Samuel Davies, Isaac Backus, and John Leland. These religious leaders advocated religious liberty for a variety of reasons, including the conviction that persecution does not work, that liberty of conscience causes true religion to flourish, and that the Bible and Christian theology require liberty of conscience.[6]

Arguments for religious liberty are replete with references to the Hebrew and Christian Scriptures. For instance, in his famous *The Bloudy Tenet of Persecution* (1644), Roger Williams drew from the Hebrew Bible to help describe his ideal of a Christian society:

> According to these blessed *Commandements,* the holy *Prophets* foretold, that when the *Law of Moses* (concerning *Worship*) should cease, and *Christs Kingdome* be established, *Esa.* 2. 4. *Mic.* 4. 3, 4. They shall breake their *Swords* into *Mathookes,* and their *Speares* into *Sithes.* And *Esa.* 11. 9. Then shall none hurt or destroy in all the *Mountaine* of my Holinesse, &c. And when he came, the same he *taught* and *practised,* as before: so did his *Disciples* after him, for the *Weapons* of his *Warfare* are not *carnall* (saith the Apostle) 2 *Cor.* 10. 4.[7]

In such a society, he argued, there would be no coercion in matters of faith, even with respect to religious traditions that he considered to be woefully in error (a list that included numerous Protestant traditions!).[8]

A very common argument was that persecution simply does not work. Far from being a merely prudential argument, the chief concern of critics was that persecution hindered the flourishing of true religion. William Penn, for instance, contended in 1675 that "force makes hypocrites,' tis persuasion only that makes converts."[9] He reiterated this conviction a dozen years later, noting that persecution "converts no body; it may breed *hypocrisy*, that that is quite another thing than *salvation*."[10] Good social and legal policies should produce faithful Christians, not hypocrites.

When religious minorities gain political power, they sometimes forget their commitment to religious liberty. Fortunately, when Penn had the opportunity to craft laws for Pennsylvania, he included a provision in the colony's statutes that protected:

> all persons living in this province, who confess and acknowledge the one Almighty and eternal God, to be the Creator, Upholder and Ruler of the world; and that hold themselves obliged in conscience to live

> peaceably and justly in civil society, shall, in no ways, be molested or prejudiced for their religious persuasion, or practice, in matters of faith and worship, nor shall they be compelled, at any time, to frequent or maintain any religious worship, place or ministry whatever.[11]

Penn may be criticized for guaranteeing religious liberty only for monotheists but, in his defense, there is no record of any citizen of Pennsylvania being anything other than a monotheist until well after he died. Although some Native Americans in the region might be characterized as polytheists, no colony dealt more fairly with, and used less force against, indigenous peoples than did Pennsylvania.[12] The provision clearly protects adherents to Judaism, which might be why Jews settled in Philadelphia as early as 1701.[13]

Arguments similar to Penn's were adopted and reiterated by influential Americans in the eighteenth century. For instance, the Baptist minister Isaac Backus contended in 1773 that

> where each person, and each society, are equally protected from being injured by others, all enjoying equal liberty, to attend and support the worship which they believe is right, having no more striving for mastery or superiority than little children (which we must all come to, or not *enter into the kingdom of* heaven [Matthew 18:3]) how happy are its effects in civil society?[14]

Backus favored religious liberty for its own sake, but he also understood that it had a positive impact on civil society.

In Massachusetts, the pseudonymous author Worcestrienis opposed compulsion in matters of faith because, "instead of making men religious, [it] generally has a contrary tendency, it works not to conviction, but most naturally leads them to hypocrisy."[15] The author had no doubt that religion was beneficial to civil society, and he did not even oppose state "encouragement of the GENERAL PRINCIPLES of religion and morality"; but he rejected compulsion primarily because it did not work.[16]

In 1776, the Presbyterians of Hanover County, Virginia, sent a memorial to the General Assembly where they argued that

> if mankind were left in the quiet possession of their unalienable religious privileges, Christianity, as in the days of the Apostles, would continue to prevail and flourish in the greatest purity, by its own native excellence, and under the all-disposing providence of God.[17]

These believers made a variety of arguments in favor of religious liberty and against religious establishments, but like virtually everyone advocating for these positions a key contention was that religious liberty causes religion to flourish *and* to be purer. In like manner, the future Supreme Court Justice James Iredell remarked in North Carolina's Ratifying Convention that it

> would be happy for mankind if religion was permitted to take its own course, and maintain itself by the excellence of its own doctrines. The divine Author of our religion never wished for its support by world authority. Has he not said that the gates of hell shall not prevail against it [Matthew 16:18]? It made much greater progress for itself, than when supported by the greatest authority upon earth.[18]

During the height of the First Great Awakening Elisha Williams, a Congregationalist minister, Yale rector, member of the General Assembly, and judge on the Connecticut Superior Court, wrote an impassioned plea for religious liberty entitled "The Essential Rights and Liberties of Protestants" (1744). A central contention in this work is:

> That the sacred scriptures are the alone rule of faith and practice to a Christian, all Protestants are agreed in; and must therefore inviolably maintain, that every Christian has a *right of judging for himself* what he is to believe and practice in religion according to that rule.[19]

Williams's argument encapsulates some of the key commitments of the Protestant Reformation—notably *sola scriptura* and the priesthood of all believers. If one truly believes these doctrines, he averred, one must embrace freedom of conscience. To be sure, this is a very Protestant argument and might not have been as effective in Catholic countries. But in a colony that was 99.99 percent Protestant, it worked well.

Williams made other arguments, including what has become a famous appeal (at least among academic students of the founding) to John Locke's social compact.[20] But after citing Locke he returned to his Protestant arguments, noting that everyone "is under an indispensable obligation to search the scriptures for himself (which contains the whole of it) and to make the best use of it he can for his own information in the will of GOD, the nature and duties of Christianity." He moved quickly from this restatement of the argument to the conclusion that "the rights of conscience are sacred and equal in all, and strictly speaking unalienable."[21]

Freedom of conscience was so important that it was common for it to be referred to as a "sacred right." For example, when the Continental Congress wrote instruction to commissioners appointed to Canada in 1776, they included the following charge: "You are further to declare, that we hold sacred the rights of conscience, and may promise to the whole people, solemnly in our name, the free and undisturbed exercise of their religion."[22] Likewise, President James Madison's July 23, 1813, call for prayer connects the "sacred rights of conscience" to our "present happiness" and "future hopes."[23]

One of the most important founding era arguments in favor of religious liberty was based on the theological principle that humans have a duty to worship God as their consciences dictate. A fine example of this is George Mason's 1776 draft of Article XVI of Virginia's Declaration of Rights, which reads:

> That as religion, or the duty which we owe to our divine and omnipotent Creator, and the manner of discharging it, can be governed only

> by reason and conviction, not by force or violence; and therefore that all men should enjoy the fullest toleration in the exercise of religion, according to the dictates of conscience, unpunished and unrestrained by the magistrate...[24]

Mason's draft of Article XVI was reprinted throughout the states and had an important impact on subsequent state constitutions and the national Bill of Rights. But it was not the draft that became law. James Madison, in his first significant public act, didn't deny that all humans have a duty to worship God, but he objected to the use of "toleration" in the article, perhaps because he thought that it implied that religious liberty was a grant from the state that could be revoked. The Virginia Convention agreed, and Article XVI was amended to make it clear that "the free exercise of religion" is a right, not a privilege granted by the state.[25]

In Massachusetts, the Baptist minister Isaac Backus appealed to Matthew 22:21 when he argued that Christians "must render unto Caesar the things that are his, but that it is of as much importance not to render unto him anything that belongs to God."[26] Worship belongs to God alone, so Christians must be free to worship Him according to the dictates of their consciences, not as directed by the state.[27] Several years later, a Baptist elder named Noah Alden asked him how a "bill of rights ought to be drawn?" Among Backus's suggestions was a religious liberty provision that reads:

> As God is the only worthy object of all religious worship, and nothing can be true religion but a voluntary obedience unto his revealed will, of which each rational soul has an equal right to judge for itself, every person has an unalienable right to act in all religious affairs according to the full persuasion of his own mind, where others are not injured thereby.[28]

His fellow Baptist John Leland made a similar argument in his important pamphlet "The Rights of Conscience Inalienable" (1791).[29]

For a final example, consider the Massachusetts Constitution of 1780, drafted in part by John Adams and ratified by an overwhelmingly Congregationalist electorate. Article II of the constitution proclaims that:

> It is the right as well as the duty of all men in society, publicly and at stated seasons, to worship the Supreme Being, the great Creator and Preserver of the universe. And no subject shall be hurt, molested, or restrained, in his person, liberty, or estate, for worshipping God in the manner and season most agreeable to the dictates of his own conscience, or for his religious profession or sentiments, provided he doth not disturb the public peace or obstruct others in their religious worship.[30]

America's Founders routinely made arguments grounded on religious premises to support a robust understanding of religious liberty.

By the end of the Revolutionary era, every state offered significant protection of religious liberty.[31] The federal Constitution of 1787 did not contain a religious liberty provision, but only because its supporters believed the national government did not have the delegated power to pass laws interfering with religious belief or practice.[32] In the face of popular outcry, the first Congress proposed and the states ratified a constitutional amendment stating that "Congress shall make no law respecting an establishment of religion, or prohibiting the free exercise thereof...."[33]

RELIGIOUS LIBERTY FOR ALL

In many early American civic leaders' minds, religious liberty did not necessarily entail religious equality. When delegates to the Constitutional Convention met in Philadelphia to draft a new constitution, Georgia, New Hampshire, Massachusetts, New Jersey, North Carolina, South Carolina, Vermont, and even Rhode Island required civic officials to be Protestants, whereas Delaware, Maryland, and Pennsylvania insisted that they must "merely" be Christians. Only New York, Virginia, and

Connecticut did not have religious tests, but in 1788 New York passed a law requiring office holders to "renounce and abjure all allegiance and subjection to all and every foreign king, prince, potentate and State, in all matters ecclesiastical as well as civil. . . ."[34] The reference to ecclesiastical authorities was widely understood to prohibit Roman Catholics from holding office. Ironically, the new oath permitted Jewish citizens, but not Catholic citizens, to hold civic offices.[35]

Even tolerant, Quaker Pennsylvania had a religious test for civic offices. Its 1776 constitution required office holders to "acknowledge the Scriptures of the Old and New Testament to be given by Divine inspiration," a provision that prevented Philadelphia's Jewish citizens from holding office.[36] The Pennsylvania Constitution of 1776 stipulated that a "Council of Censors" meet every seven years to determine if the constitution needed to be amended. When this body met in 1783, leaders of Philadelphia's Jewish synagogue submitted a petition requesting that the religious test be revised so that Jews as well as Christians could hold public office. The Council considered the petition, tabled it, and took no further action.

When the federal convention met in Philadelphia in 1787, a Jewish merchant from Philadelphia named Jonas Phillips mistakenly thought the body could amend the state's constitution and so petitioned the body to amend its religious test. Of course, the Convention had no power to do this, but it might be telling that a Fourth of July parade in Philadelphia the following year included seventeen clergy, among whom was "the Rabbi of the Jews" who marched arm in arm with two Christian ministers. A feast following the parade included a "separate table with special foods that the Jewish citizens of Philadelphia could eat without violating their dietary laws."[38] When Pennsylvania rewrote its constitution in 1789-90, it amended its religious test to permit any "person, who acknowledges the being of a God and a future state of rewards and punishments" to hold public office.[39] This was obviously still a religious test, but it was one that permitted Jews as well as Christians to hold civic office.

The Federal Convention had no power to amend state constitutions, but it had the ability to draft one for the nation. Understanding that religious liberty should entail civic equality, the delegates included a provision in Article VI that prohibited religious tests for federal offices. Anti-Federalists objected that this would permit "a Papist or Infidel" or "pagans, deists, and Mahometans" to be elected.[40] Many Founders undoubtedly thought that these outcomes would not be ideal, but fortunately they insisted on a constitution that did not favor one religious tradition over others.

By the end of the founding era, many civic leaders had come to embrace the view that the religious liberty of all citizens must be robustly protected. This is perhaps best evident in George Washington's inspirational letter to the Hebrew Congregation in Newport, Rhode Island. His letter to this tiny religious minority promised that:

> All possess alike liberty and conscience and immunities of citizenship. It is now no more that toleration is spoken of, as if it was by the indulgence of one class of people, that another enjoyed the exercise of their inherent natural rights. For happily the Government of the United States, which gives to bigotry no sanction, to persecution no assistance requires only that they who live under its protection should demean themselves as good citizens, in giving it on all occasions their effectual support....
>
> May the Children of the Stock of Abraham, who dwell in this land, continue to merit and enjoy the good will of the other Inhabitants; while every one shall sit in safety under his own vine and figtree, and there shall be none to make him afraid. May the father of all mercies scatter light and not darkness in our paths, and make us all in our several vocations useful here, and in his own due time and way everlastingly happy.[41]

This letter, from the era's one indispensable man, reflects well the Founders' understanding that the religious convictions of all citizens must be respected. Yet it also illustrates the reality that America's Founders did not think that religion must be driven from the public square. There are nine references to Biblical texts in the last paragraph alone, including one to Micah 4:4: "while everyone shall sit in safety under his own vine and fig tree, and there shall be none to make him afraid."[42] This was one of George Washington's favorite verses; we have records of him quoting or paraphrasing it at least fifty times.[43] Like other Founders, Washington's faith influenced his political beliefs and actions, and all Americans—from Jewish citizens in the eighteenth century to Muslim, Hindu, and Sikh citizens today—have benefited from this fact.

Washington's letter is inspirational, but of course the founders did not perfectly protect the religious liberty of all citizens. Neither did civic leaders and jurists in the nineteenth, twentieth, or twenty-first centuries. Nevertheless, we should continue to strive towards the Founders' ideal: that freedom of conscience must, except in the most extreme circumstances, be robustly protected.[44] All Americans have a right to live according to their religious convictions, even if they are members of minority faiths. The moment we start picking and choosing between which convictions we protect and which we don't is the moment we abandon the Founders' commitment to respecting "the sacred rights of conscience."

CHAPTER FOUR

The Hebrew Bible and the Political Culture of the American Founding

Daniel L. Dreisbach

Since the Pilgrims came ashore at Plymouth Rock in 1620, and continuing through the American founding era and beyond, the Bible—especially the Hebrew Bible—has informed how Americans see themselves and their place in the world.[1] The Bible has shaped diverse aspects of American culture, including the arts, education, law, and civil government. Indeed, given its pervasive influence on public culture in general, it would be surprising if the Bible did not leave its mark on the nation's political and legal traditions. The Bible's influence on American political culture and constitutional tradition is so profound that some commentators describe the Bible as America's "founding document."[2]

The Hebrew Bible was a rich source of values, principles, and aspirations for the founding generation in framing their political thoughts and institutions. The "founding era," in the last third or so of the eighteenth century, was a time when the American people began to agitate for their rights as Englishmen. They wanted to fight for and secure political independence from Great Britain and to establish constitutional republics in their respective states and the nation. The Founders were drawn to the Hebrew Bible and, it must be emphasized, interpreted it through the lens of Christian—specifically Protestant—theology, tradition, and practice, not necessarily as it was expounded in Jewish theology or rabbinic commentary. Hebraic texts and themes, in short, were selected and adapted to serve Christian theological and cultural interests. Christian interpretations of the Hebrew Scriptures (the Tanakh or the Old Testament, as it is commonly called by Christians) do not always align with Jewish interpretations of the same text. Adam's sin in the garden as recounted in Genesis 3, for example, was the basis for the Christian doctrine of "original sin" and the attendant Protestant Reformed notion of humankind's radical depravity; the Decalogue's prohibition on taking "the name of the Lord thy God in vain" (Exodus 20:7) was extended in Christian practice (including public laws throughout Christendom) to encompass all three persons of the Trinity; and the following commandment's requirement to keep holy the sabbath (seventh day) (Exodus 20:8) was transmuted in much of Christendom to the first day of the week in commemoration of Jesus's resurrection.

Many in the founding generation looked to the Bible for insights into human nature, civic virtue, social order, political authority, the rights and responsibilities of citizens, and other concepts essential to framing a new political society. There was, in particular, broad agreement that the Bible was useful for nurturing the civic virtue that gives citizens a capacity for self-government. In various representative assemblies of the era, as well as in pamphlets, political sermons, and private papers, founding figures appealed to the Bible for principles, precedents, and normative standards to order their political communities and design their institutions of governance. Some Founders saw in the Hebrew Scriptures political and legal models—such as republicanism and due process of law—that they believed were favored by God and, thus, worthy of emulation in their polities. Starting with the New England Puritans and continuing through the founding era, for example, notions of Hebraic republicanism, as interpreted through the lens of Protestant Reformed theology, found expression in American political thought. (To the Founders, "republican" meant, at least, government by consent of the governed as exercised through representatives of the people.) Other aspects of the Sacred Text, especially Mosaic law, as filtered through canon law, civil law, and English customary and common law, influenced American political and legal cultures, too.

Unfortunately, many people often miss or dismiss these Biblical influences. Indeed, the claim is often made that the American founding was a strictly secular project, achieved in an age when the Enlightenment was in the ascendency and traditional religion, if not rejected outright, was relegated to the sidelines.[3] Drawing on Lockean liberalism and/or civic republicanism, the Founders, it is said, deliberately created a secular republic founded on what some have called a "godless" constitution.[4] I argue that the Bible—both the Old and New Testaments—informed the Founders' political and constitutional thought in significant ways. I contend that there was a consensus in the founding generation that religion (for all but a few, the religion they had in mind was a Biblical religion) was indispensable to their experiment in republican self-government. Perhaps most interesting, it was a view expressed by the Founders most influenced by the Enlightenment, as well as by adherents of orthodox Christianity.

Along with the Bible, the Founders were also influenced by diverse intellectual traditions, including English common law and constitutionalism, Enlightenment liberalism (in manifold forms), and classical and civic republicanism. Drawing attention to the Bible's contributions to the founding is not meant to diminish or dismiss these other intellectual influences on the Founders. Rather, acknowledging the Bible's often ignored role in the founding enriches our understanding of the broad range of ideas that inspired and informed the Founders' political thoughts and shaped their civic projects.

The Bible's presence in the political culture of the founding reflected the religious demographics and culture of the age. Religious historians and sociologists estimate that, at the time of independence, 98 percent or more of Americans of European descent identified with the Protestant tradition.[5] In their study of religion in American society, Barry A. Kosmin and Seymour P. Lachman reported, "At the time of the American Revolution, there were approximately 3.75 million people living in the thirteen colonies. Except for approximately 25,000 Catholics (15,000 of whom lived in Maryland) and 2,500 Jews (500 of whom lived in South Carolina), the inhabitants were all of different and various Protestant denominations. These included not only the British Protestant element, which made up 75 percent of the Colonies' three million whites, but also approximately 750,000 blacks, the vast majority of whom were slaves."[6]

Most Protestants of European descent living in America at the time of independence, either by heritage or conviction, identified with the Reformed theological tradition. The Reformed tradition refers to the vein of the Protestant Reformation associated with the teachings of John Calvin and his followers. Adherents included the New England Congregationalists (descendants of the Puritans), Scottish and Irish Presbyterians, French Huguenots, Dutch and German Reformed congregations, and most Baptists. In his magisterial study of American religious history, Sydney Ahlstrom wrote that the Reformed theological tradition was "the religious heritage of three-fourths of the American people in 1776."[7] Harvard religious historian William R. Hutchison claimed that "At least 90 percent of the colonists... had come out of the Calvinist rather than the Lutheran side of the Protestant Reformation.... [T]he colonists had been at least 85 percent English-speaking Calvinist Protestants."[8] Furthermore, many influential Founders were raised in or affiliated with Reformed congregations.[9] It should be noted, however, that prominent Founders, such as Thomas Jefferson, opposed core tenets of Reformed theology.

Protestant theology emphasized that the Bible was God's revealed word for humankind and authority in *all* matters of faith and practice. Given Protestant representation in society, it is not surprising that the Bible was the most accessible, authoritative, and venerated book in seventeenth- and eighteenth-century America, and that Americans were a biblically literate people. Furthermore, the significant presence of Reformed (Calvinist) Protestants in America is worth noting in this discussion of the Hebrew Bible's influence. Reformed theology, more than any other Protestant tradition, relied on a covenant theology that Reformed Protestants believed was expounded in the Hebrew Scriptures as its essential conceptual and interpretive framework. They believed, in short, that a sequence of covenants recounted in the Old Testament provided the theological framework for understanding God's dealings with humankind. This explains, in part, the Reformed Protestants' extraordinary attraction to and familiarity with the Hebrew Bible.

The Bible figured prominently in the political discourse of the American founding. The Founders read the Bible, as evidenced by their many quotations from and allusions to both familiar and obscure scriptural passages. Biblical language and themes liberally seasoned their rhetoric. Its ideas shaped their habits of mind and informed their political thought. Moreover, many Founders were devoted students of the Bible and a few even wrote Bible commentaries and learned discourses on theology and Christian doctrine and practice.

Following an extensive survey of American political literature from 1760 to 1805, political scientist Donald S. Lutz reported that the Bible was cited more frequently than any European writer or even any European school of thought, including Enlightenment thought.[10] The Bible accounted for about a third of all citations in the literature he surveyed.[11] According to Lutz, "Deuteronomy is the most frequently cited book, followed by Montesquieu's *The Spirit of the Laws*."[12] Biblical sources figured prominently in this study even though Lutz significantly under-surveyed religious sources, excluding from his sample most political sermons that made no mention of secular sources.[13] The Bible still "accounted for roughly one-third of the citations in the sample.... Saint Paul is cited about as frequently as Montesquieu and Blackstone, the two most-cited secular authors, and [the Book of] Deuteronomy is cited almost twice as often as all of Locke's writings put together." About three-fourths of all references to the Bible in Lutz's survey came from political sermons; however, had he surveyed only secular works, the Bible would still have accounted for 9 percent of all citations—"about equal to the percentage for classical writers."[14]

What explains Deuteronomy's prominence in this literature? It is a convenient digest of the Mosaic law and the providential history of the nation Israel. The Old Testament in general provides a narrative of a covenant people who, like the New England Puritan settlers, set out to be governed according to God's word and saw themselves as instruments of God's redemptive plan for humankind. Adherents of Protestant Reformed theology, such as the New England Puritans, believed the covenants so prominent in the history recounted by Moses in the Pentateuch described God's special, covenantal relationship not only with the Children of Israel but also with them. The books of Moses seemed particularly pertinent to many Americans—from the Pilgrim Fathers to the Founding Fathers—because they not only recorded God's dealings with a "chosen nation" but also recounted the establishment of specific political and legal institutions and the processes necessary to govern that nation. When Moses led the Children of Israel out of Egypt, they were, apart from his leadership, without a government. He was directed by God to create a political and legal regime to govern them. This exercise in nation-building is recorded in the books of Moses. Many Americans, especially in Puritan New England, found in these narratives a model for establishing their commonwealths in conformity with Divine standards. Americans believed, in short, that the Book of Deuteronomy described principles, offices, and processes of governance useful in establishing a new political society.

Americans, including the Pilgrims and Founding Fathers, have seen themselves as a chosen people—God's new Israel. The chronicles of the Children of Israel, many Americans thought, offered a sacred guide and example for their own political experiments. They were reliving the Exodus story. The precise contours of the analogy differed depending on who made it and when, but they were often elaborate, and sometimes tortured, comparisons. Significantly, even the Americans most influenced by the Enlightenment and skeptical of the miraculous aspects of the Exodus account embraced this theme. The political repression and religious persecution they had endured in England and from which they fled was their Egyptian bondage. The Stuart monarchs (and, later in the revolutionary era, King George III) were their intransigent Pharaoh. And the treacherous waters of the Atlantic Ocean, which they traversed in search of the promised land, was their Red Sea (in some versions, the Atlantic represented the Jordan River). In a new Canaan, the American settlers, like the ancient Israelites, had to contend with forbidding terrain and hostile inhabitants. The native Americans they encountered were their Moabites and Philistines. Americans even observed that the population of the United States at the time of independence—three million people—was approximately the same as the number of Israelites with Moses in the wilderness.[15] Many Americans of the founding era came to regard George Washington as their Moses who led them out of Egyptian bondage and to a "Promised Land."[16] The providential history of the Hebrew commonwealth and Moses's instructions for creating the legal and political institutions to govern that commonwealth had special meaning for these Americans.

This theme of America as God's chosen nation was embraced by both pious and skeptical citizens, woven into the national mythology, and manifested in diverse national expressions and symbols. The Reverend Israel Evans, one of General Washington's favorite military chaplains, was appointed by the commander-in-chief to deliver a Thanksgiving sermon to the victorious troops near Yorktown, Virginia, on the occasion of General Cornwallis's surrender in October 1781. In a poem purportedly addressed to the assembled soldiers and appended to a published text of the discourse, Evans struck this familiar theme:

> To him who led in ancient days
> The Hebrew tribes, your anthems raise;
> The God who spoke from Sinai's hill
> Protects his chosen people still.[17]

The president of Yale College, Ezra Stiles, delivered a 1783 election sermon before Connecticut's highest officials. His text was Deuteronomy

26:19, a passage describing God's promise to exalt the nation Israel if her people remain a "holy people," which Stiles declared was "allusively prophetic of the future prosperity and splendor of the United States"—"God's American Israel."[18] In 1788, Samuel Langdon, a Congregationalist clergyman (and the former president of Harvard College), declared in an election sermon entitled, "The Republic of the Israelites an Example to the American States," that "instead of the twelve tribes of Israel, we may substitute the thirteen states of the American union."[19] Another New England clergyman observed at the end of the eighteenth century: "It has been often remarked that the people of the United States come nearer to a parallel with Ancient Israel, than any other nation upon the globe. Hence, 'OUR AMERICAN ISRAEL,' is a term frequently used; and common consent allows it apt and proper."[20] Even Thomas Jefferson drew on the comparison between Americans and the Children of Israel, closing his Second Inaugural Address in March 1805 by encouraging all Americans to join him in seeking "the favor of that Being in whose hands we are, who led our forefathers, as Israel of old, from their native land, and planted them in a country flowing with all the necessaries and comforts of life...."[21] A chosen people Divinely delivered from oppression and directed to a promised land of hope and liberty were recurring themes in the political discourse of the age.

The story of Israel's deliverance from Egyptian bondage chronicled in the Book of Exodus, perhaps more than any other story, has resonated with Americans and shaped how they have recounted their own experiences.[22] This is a story about liberation and liberty, hope, and providential deliverance. It tells of God's people enslaved in a foreign land by a tyrannical ruler who defied God's command, delivered by His messenger, to "Let my people go" (Exodus 5:1). When God's people fled from the land of their servitude, the ruler sent his army in hot pursuit. It seemed the people, hemmed in on the banks of a great sea, would be re-enslaved, but God miraculously parted the waters, allowing His people to escape on dry ground and embark on a journey to a promised land.

Americans have recurred to this story at decisive moments in their history, beginning with the seventeenth-century Pilgrim and Puritan settlers in New England who believed they had escaped religious oppression in the Old World in pursuit of religious liberty in a new promised land, and continuing with the eighteenth-century patriots who fought the "tyranny" of "Pharaoh" King George III, nineteenth-century abolitionists who sought the emancipation of African slaves and an end to slavery, and twentieth-century activists who struggled to secure the civil rights of African Americans and other minorities. The Exodus narrative represents poignant themes of liberation and liberty that have resonated through the centuries in the experiences of diverse peoples and communities.

On July 4, 1776, the Continental Congress appointed Benjamin Franklin, John Adams, and Thomas Jefferson to a committee charged with designing "a seal for the United States of America."[23] Franklin proposed an image of Moses standing on the shore and extending his hand over the Red Sea in anticipation of God's supernatural parting and then closing of the waters, allowing the Divinely directed Israelites to escape Pharaoh and his army (Exodus 14). According to Adams's recollection, Jefferson initially recommended a portrayal of the "Children of Israel in the Wilderness, led by a Cloud by Day, and a Pillar of Fire by night" (Exodus 13:21-22).[24] Remarkably, both men, sons of the Enlightenment, drew on familiar Old Testament images of the Children of Israel, who were miraculously released from Pharaoh's bondage just as they hoped Americans would be providentially delivered from King George III's tyranny, as fitting allegorical portrayals of the new nation's plight. The committee eventually recommended a design drawn from Franklin's proposal, which the Congress tabled, and no further action was taken on it.[25]

Enslaved Africans in the New World experienced and heard the same narrative in reverse order: they were transported from their homelands in chains across a great sea to the land of "Egypt" where they were held captive by another Pharaoh. European Americans who compared themselves to enslaved Hebrews in Egypt during their conflict with Great Britain became, ironically, enslaving Pharaohs in African American accounts. In time, African Americans came to identify with the Children of Israel, and in spirituals, sermons, stories, symbols, and manifestos they expressed a yearning for liberation from their Egyptian bondage.

In the nineteenth century, both black and white abolitionists appealed to the Exodus story. In the summer of 1822, Denmark Vesey, a former slave who had purchased his own freedom, was accused of and swiftly convicted and executed for plotting a slave insurrection in Charleston, South Carolina. An informant testified that, at a meeting of the conspirators in Vesey's house, Vesey "was the first to rise up and speak, and he read to us from the Bible, how the children of Israel were delivered out of Egypt from bondage."[26] William Lloyd Garrison, one of the most prominent anti-slavery activists of the nineteenth century, speaking in the voice of Moses in an 1829 Fourth of July oration, thundered: "I call upon the ambassadors of Christ everywhere to make known this proclamation: 'Thus saith the Lord God of the Africans, Let this people go, that they may serve me.'"[27]

The major themes and motifs of the Exodus narrative (an oppressed people yearning for freedom, a tyrannical regime, a leader-liberator of the people, God's deliverance from oppression, and the hope of a promised land) continued to feature in the political rhetoric of subsequent liberation movements, including the early women's rights movements of the nineteenth century and the civil rights struggles of the mid-twentieth century.[28]

The Old Testament concept of jubilee, which directed a periodic release from debt and servitude, also nourished American conceptions of liberty. A celebration of jubilee in Leviticus 25:10 is inscribed on the nation's most cherished symbol of liberty—the Liberty Bell. In 1751, the Pennsylvania Assembly commissioned the great bell with the Biblical inscription "Proclaim Liberty thro' all the Land to all the Inhabitants thereof." The bell was to hang in the soon to be completed State House (Independence Hall) in Philadelphia to commemorate the fiftieth anniversary (Jubilee year) of Pennsylvania's "constitution," the "Charter of Privileges" (1701). Signed by William Penn, the document was a colonial charter of freedom, protecting "Liberty of Conscience," religious profession and worship, and civil liberties. It also expanded self-government for the colonists and affirmed basic principles of the rule of law and property rights.

The bell's profile in the public's imagination was raised to new heights by nineteenth-century abolitionists who adopted it as a symbol for their movement and, in fact, gave what had been known as the State House bell its now famous name, the "Liberty Bell." Images of the bell, often accompanied by the words of Leviticus 25:10, were emblazoned on abolitionist printed material, banners, medals, and the like, becoming a part of the movement's iconography. Liberation movements that followed, including those advocating for women's suffrage and African American civil rights, similarly embraced the bell and the themes encapsulated in its Biblical inscription. Like the Exodus narrative, the theme of jubilee along with the Liberty Bell inspired enslaved and oppressed peoples yearning to be free—a theme sounded in spirituals, abolitionist tracts, and civil rights speeches.

From the establishment of England's North American colonies to the founding era, there were influential Americans who believed the model of political leadership and civil government established by God through Moses and practically developed under Joshua and his successors for the Hebrew nation was worthy of emulation in their own polities.[29] They thought the Hebrew commonwealth, from the Exodus to the selection of Saul as king, was a perfect model of and Divine precedent for a form of civil government most conducive to political prosperity and civil and religious liberty.

The theme that America was analogous to the Hebrew nation and that the newly independent states should emulate the Hebrew commonwealth's "republican" form of government was developed in political tracts and sermons, and even in various deliberative bodies. "A volume," one scholar observed, "would not contain all the politico-theological discourses delivered during the decade prior to the restoration of peace, wherein the Hebrew commonwealth was held up as a model, and its history as a guide for the American people."[30] Most of what the founding generation knew about the Hebrew republic they learned from the Bible. In an influential 1775 election sermon preached to Massachusetts's highest public officials, the president of Harvard College, Samuel Langdon, opined: "The Jewish government, according to the original constitution which was Divinely established, if considered merely in a civil view, was a perfect Republic.... Every nation, when able and agreed," Langdon continued, "has a right to set up over themselves any form of government which to them may appear most conducive to their common welfare. The civil Polity of Israel is doubtless an excellent general model, allowing for some peculiarities; at least some principal laws and orders of it may be copied, to great advantage, in more modern establishments."[31]

In Thomas Paine's popular 1776 revolutionary pamphlet *Common Sense*, he drew on the history of the Hebrew republic to repudiate monarchy and to promote republicanism. Monarchy, he asserted, was "first introduced into the World by the Heathens," and it cannot "be defended on the authority of scripture; for the will of the Almighty[,] as declared by Gideon [Judges 8:22-23] and the prophet Samuel [1 Samuel 8], expressly disapproves of Government by Kings." For nearly "three thousand years," he wrote, the Jewish form of civil government "was a kind of Republic administered by a judge and the elders of the Tribes. Kings they had none, and it was held sinful to acknowledge any Being under that title but the Lord of Hosts." But in their folly, the Jews rejected God's designs for them and insisted on a king to reign over them. Accordingly, Paine reported, "Monarchy is ranked in scripture as one of the sins of the Jews, for which a curse in reserve is denounced against them."[32] On this point, Paine relied on the same Biblical text as Algernon Sidney, the English republican political theorist. Sidney, who was much admired and read by the founding generation, had more than 175 years earlier cited 1 Samuel 8 in reaching a similar conclusion: "I may safely say, the *Hebrew* Kings were not instituted by God, but given as a punishment of their Sin, who despised the Government that he had instituted [amongst the Hebrews]..."[33]

In the heated debate of the mid-1780s on the need for constitutional reform, the influential Founder Roger Sherman of Connecticut responded to an ardent critic of the Articles of Confederation, proposing that "the civil polity of the Hebrews" was a commendable exemplar of civil government:

> And in truth and reality, the framing a perfect and complete system of government for a rising empire, is a most arduous and very important subject; and as he seems desirous of Divine Aid, I would recommend it to him once more to consult his bible, and duly weigh and consider the civil polity of the Hebrews, which was planned by Divine Wisdom, for the government of that people although their territory was small; ... their laws were few and simple—their judges and elders of their cities, well acquainted with the credibility of the parties and their evidences—they held their courts in the places of greater concourse, the gates of the city, and their processes were neither lengthy nor expensive.[34]

Against remarkable odds, Americans had secured independence. They then turned their attention to the difficult task of framing a plan of civil government. Once again, they looked to the Hebrew commonwealth as a guide and model for establishing their own polities. In a speech in the New York convention, delegate John Smith quoted at length Samuel's admonition to the "nation of Israel" when the latter "rejected their divine Ruler" and the "form of civil government" they had received from Heaven in favor of a king to rule over them.[35] The countless "references, parallels, and analogies to the [C]hildren of Israel in their struggle for political liberty would not have been made again and again" in the political rhetoric of the era had they not resonated with the American audience to whom they were addressed.[36] The notion that the United States was "God's American Israel"[37] was deeply embedded in the public's imagination and continued to inform the way many late-eighteenth-century Americans thought of themselves and their place and mission in the human experience.

Among other Biblical texts, Exodus 18:13–27, Deuteronomy 1:9–18, and Deuteronomy 16:18–20 offered Americans guidance on republican government and political leadership. In a 1788 New Hampshire election sermon by the Reverend Samuel Langdon, the Congregationalist minister (former president of Harvard College, 1774–80) and delegate to the New Hampshire convention that ratified the US Constitution, specifically cited Deuteronomy 16:18–19 in arguing that the Hebrew Republic was a laudable model of republican government, an example of the phenomenon mentioned above.[38] Among the civic lessons Americans of this age thought that this and similar Old Testament passages taught, at least implicitly, were that civil government was ordained by God and under His authority.

Moreover, God ordained the office of civil magistrate and instructed His people to select their civil magistrates.[39] The voice (or consent) of those to be ruled in selecting civil magistrates was the first action in the formation of the civil government. The claim was thus made that a polity so organized was a "government of the people." Insofar as the civil magistrates the people selected to represent them were not restricted to a titled or privileged class, but from "out of all the people" (Exodus 18:21, 25), this process embraced a republican principle of civil equality. God, they believed, had identified specific qualifications for civil magistrates. Those qualifications were expressed most concisely in Exodus 18:21: "able men, such as fear God, men of truth, hating covetousness."[40] Civil magistrates were accountable to the people to exercise good judgment in the performance of their official duties, and they must rule justly and wisely in conformity with God's standards.[41] Civil magistrates must also respect the rule of law and due process of law.[42] They must always pursue justice.[43] Early Americans also believed that the Bible proposed a model of civil government that was republican and decentralized. The people's representatives in the Hebrew republic served in various bodies from the local to the national levels.[44] There is a rudimentary form of federalism in the separation of powers between magistrates in "thy gates" and "throughout thy tribes" (Deuteronomy 16:18).[45]

In addition to the model of republican government provided by the Hebrew commonwealth, many Founders thought that Biblical law and morality were essential to their political experiment in republican self-government and liberty under law. Indeed, this was a virtually unchallenged assumption of the age. The Founders knew they had embarked on a bold and novel experiment in self-government. They believed that if this experiment was to succeed, the people must be both educated and virtuous. The political literature of the founding era is replete with the assertion that education and religion are the indispensable twin pillars on which their system of republican self-government rested. First, the populace must be sufficiently educated for citizens to make well-informed decisions about how best to govern themselves. Second, the people must be sufficiently virtuous to maintain the personal responsibility and social discipline necessary for a regime of self-government to succeed. In erecting and maintaining this second pillar—civic virtue—the Founders believed that religion played a vital role, either for genuinely spiritual or utilitarian reasons.

Even those Founders who rejected the Bible as God's revealed word valued the Scriptures as a tool for moral instruction. The challenge the Founders confronted was how to nurture personal discipline and social order in a political system committed to self-government. Authoritarian rulers and tyrants used the whip and rod to compel subjects to behave as they desired, but this approach was unacceptable for a free, self-governing people. In contrast, the Founders looked to religion—specifically the moral instruction found in Scripture—to provide internal monitors that would prompt citizens to behave in a disciplined, responsible fashion and, thereby, promote the social order and stability necessary to facilitate self-government. A self-governing people had to be a virtuous people who were controlled from within by an internal moral compass, which would replace external control by the whip and rod.

Historian James H. Hutson has referred to this notion as "the founding generation's syllogism": "virtue and morality are necessary for free, republican government; religion is necessary for virtue and morality;

religion is, therefore, necessary for republican government."[46] Some Founders took this one step further, arguing that religious liberty was a desirable precondition for effective republican government insofar as it unleashed religion and religious expression and their beneficent influence in society.[47] The Founders knew from history that religion could survive in the face of state persecution; however, they also believed that freedom—freedom of religious belief and expression—could facilitate a vibrant religious culture that, in turn, would nurture civic virtue.

The political literature of the founding era is filled with expressions of religion's vital role in a regime of republican self-government. The idea was espoused by Americans from diverse religious, intellectual, and political traditions, walks of life, and regions of the country.[48] No one expressed this idea more famously or succinctly than George Washington in the Farewell Address (1796): "Of all the dispositions and habits which lead to political prosperity, Religion and morality are indispensable supports." He then proceeded to cast doubt on the supposition that morality could be maintained in the absence of religion.[49] David Ramsay, a delegate to the Continental Congress and the first major historian of the American Revolution, also expressed this idea succinctly, writing in 1789: "Remember that there can be no political happiness without liberty; that there can be no liberty without morality; and that there can be no morality without religion."[50] Benjamin Rush, a venerated signer of the Declaration of Independence, opined in 1786: "[T]he only foundation for a useful education in a republic is to be laid in RELIGION. Without [religion], there can be no virtue, and without virtue there can be no liberty, and liberty is the object and life of all republican governments."[51]

Religion, in short, was thought to be the well-spring of the civic virtue essential for republican self-government. A moral people respected social order, legitimate authority, oaths and contracts, private property, and the like; and such civic virtue, it was believed, was nurtured by the Bible and the Christian religion. Thus, many Founders regarded the Bible as indispensable to their republican project. With this idea in mind, John

Adams called the Bible "the most republican book in the world." This is a remarkable statement. How is the Bible "republican"? "[W]ithout national morality a republican government cannot be maintained," Adams explained, and "[t]he Bible contains... the most perfect morality... that ever was conceived upon earth." Therefore, he said, the Bible is "the most republican book in the world."[52] The Bible is a republican book, in other words, because it nurtures the civic virtues in citizens that are essential for a system of republican self-government to succeed.

Adams was not alone among his contemporaries in expressing this idea. John Dickinson, the acclaimed "penman of the Revolution," similarly remarked that "The Bible is the most republican Book that ever was written."[53] Arguments connecting religion, civic virtue, and self-government, as well as descriptions of the Bible as a "republican book," were commonplace in late eighteenth-century political discourse.

The United States Constitution hammered out in Philadelphia in 1787 gives evidence of a political vision informed in part by the Bible, despite the rise of secular influences in the eighteenth century. Although it is difficult to definitively establish that constitutional provisions were derived from specific Biblical texts, the lineage of selected constitutional principles can be traced to Biblical concepts that had previously found expression in Western legal tradition, especially in English common law, as well as in colonial laws and customs.

Those who reject that there were Biblical influences on the Constitution note that records from the Constitutional Convention reveal few mentions of the Bible during the delegates' deliberations on substantive provisions. It is a mistake, however, to draw conclusions regarding the Bible's influence or lack of influence on the US Constitution based solely on the number of references to God and the Bible in the text of the Constitution or records of Convention debates. The surviving records of Convention deliberations, including James Madison's famous notes, are abbreviated and arguably unreliable in some respects. There is no verbatim record of the Convention proceedings. Again, some commentators dismiss claims of Biblical influence on the Constitution because the delegates, according to extant records, only occasionally referenced the Bible explicitly during substantive debates. This analysis, however, misses the multiple channels through which the Bible exerted its influence on the political, legal, and constitutional traditions that informed the Constitution.

Convention delegates occasionally invoked the Bible in surprising and interesting ways. For example, during debate on the qualifications for public office, Benjamin Franklin spoke in opposition to any proposal that, in his words, "tended to debase the spirit of the common people.... We should remember the character which the Scripture requires in Rulers," Dr. Franklin said, invoking Jethro's advice to Moses regarding qualifications for prospective Israelite rulers, "that they should be men hating covetousness."[54] Significantly, in his speech on August 10, 1787, when he appealed to a Biblical standard in this debate on a substantive constitutional provision, Franklin informed his fellow delegates in unambiguous language that his source was "Scripture," and then he appropriated specific Biblical language (he was alluding to Exodus 18:21). Beyond a few explicit references to the Bible in the sparse surviving records of Convention proceedings, the Bible's influence on the Constitution was manifested in various ways.

First, general theological or doctrinal propositions regarding human nature, civil authority, political society, and the like informed conceptions and institutions of law and civil government that influenced the Constitution. The Constitution's basic design, defined by the separation of powers and checks and balances, reflected an awareness of the Christian doctrine of "original sin" and the necessity to guard against the concentration and abuse of government powers vested in fallen human actors. This view of a sinful human nature, emphasized in Reformed (Calvinist) theology, was expressed in the Constitutional Convention.[55] In remarks made on July 11, 1787, James Madison acknowledged a fellow delegate's strong view regarding "the political depravity of men, and the necessity of checking one vice and interest by opposing to them another vice & interest.... The truth was," Madison concurred, "that all men having power ought to be distrusted to a certain degree."[56] One cannot appreciate the most fundamental features of American constitutional design—limited government, federalism, separation of powers among the three branches of the national government, checks and balances, representative government, and rule of law—without understanding this Reformed theological doctrine of radical depravity and the attendant necessity to check humankind's fallen nature.[57]

Another constitutional feature with theological implications concerns oath taking, at least as oaths were understood in the late eighteenth century. The Constitution's four oath provisions found in Article 1, § 3, cl. 6; Article II, § 1, cl. 8; Article VI, cl. 3; and Amendment IV arguably mandated a profoundly religious act, reflecting explicitly theological propositions. Moral philosophers and constitutional framers in the founding era and well into the nineteenth century typically defined an oath as a solemn appeal to God for the truth of what is said by a person who believes in the existence of a supreme being and in a future state of rewards and punishments.[58]

Second, the founding generation saw in the Bible political and legal models that they thought worthy of their consideration and, perhaps, incorporation into their political and legal systems. In Article IV, § 4, cl. 1, the Constitution requires every state to maintain "a Republican Form of Government." As previously mentioned in the section on Hebraic republicanism, the political discourse of the founding era is replete with appeals to the Hebrew "republic" described in the Hebrew Bible as a Divinely inspired model for republican government worthy of emulation in their own political experiments. From various Biblical passages chronicling the Hebrew polity, some Americans derived support for specific republican principles, such as government by consent of the governed, as exercised through representatives chosen by the people. These appeals emphasized that republicanism apparently enjoyed Divine favor, but they typically glossed over the nuts and bolts of the Hebrew government. The Bible, it seems, was more useful for revealing God's appreciation for republicanism in general than for detailing the specific design and structures of the Jewish polity. Reassuring a Bible-reading public that republicanism was a Divinely approved form of government was important in affirming the legitimacy of the political regime the Founders envisioned.

Most of what the founding generation knew about the Hebrew Republic they learned from the Hebrew Bible. They were well aware that ideas like republicanism found expression in traditions apart from the Hebrew experience, and, indeed, they studied these traditions both ancient and modern. Although the Founders did not seek to replicate the Hebrew model in its details, its Biblical precedent reassured many pious Americans that republicanism was a political system that enjoyed a Divine imprimatur.

Third, the US Constitution includes specific provisions that were almost certainly derived from or informed by the Hebrew Bible. For example, Article I, § 8, cl. 5, grants the Congress the authority to "fix the Standard of Weights and Measures." This provision, wrote Sir Edward Coke in his *Institutes of the Laws of England* (published in the mid-seventeenth century and widely recognized as an authoritative commentary on common law), was "grounded upon the Law of God." Coke, the most eminent English jurist of the age, cited Deuteronomy 25:13–14 in support of this claim of Divine provenance ("Thou shalt not have in thy bag divers weights, a great and a small. Thou shalt not have in thine house divers measures, a great and a small."),[59] although he, like subsequent commentators, could have cited numerous other supporting Biblical texts (see, e.g., Leviticus 19:35–36; Proverbs 11:1, 16:11, 20:10, 23).

The Article III, § 3, cl. 1 provision that convictions for treason be supported by "the testimony of two witnesses" conforms to a familiar Biblical mandate, asserted in both the Old and New Testaments, requiring multiple witnesses of malfeasance for conviction and punishment (see Deuteronomy 17:6, 19:15; Numbers 35:30; Matthew 18:16; John 8:17; 2 Corinthians 13:1; 1 Timothy 5:19; Hebrew 10:28). For centuries, leading English legal authorities have acknowledged that requiring multiple witnesses in selected legal contexts was, if not derived from the sacred text, affirmed by the authority of Scripture. "And it seemeth that by the ancient Common law," Sir Edward Coke wrote in his *Institutes of the Laws of England* (The Third Part, 1644), "one accuser, or witnesse was not sufficient to convict any person of High Treason.... And that two witnesses be required, appeareth by our books, and I remember no authority in our books to the contrary: and the Common law herein is grounded upon the law of God expressed both in the old and new Testament."[60] In support of this proposition, Coke cited Deuteronomy 17:6, 19:15; Matthew 18:16; 2 Corinthians 13:1; and Hebrews 10:28, in addition to earlier commentators on the English law. These authorities confirm that a multiple witness rule, buttressed by the weight of Biblical authority, was grafted into selected common law procedural practices and, eventually, found expression in English statutory law.[61]

The principle was written into early colonial laws, such as article 47 of the Massachusetts "Body of Liberties" (1641).[62] Other colonies followed suit, as did states in crafting their laws following independence.[63] (Significantly, in *Cramer v. United States*, 325 U.S. 1 [1945], the US Supreme Court noted that "the two witness requirement... was a familiar precept of the New Testament, and of Mosaic law.")[64]

The interpretation and application of the Eighth Amendment's prohibition on "cruel and unusual punishments" have provoked much controversy and debate. From early in the colonial experience, Biblical law, even more than common law, informed American notions of what constituted cruel and unusual punishment. The Massachusetts "Body of Liberties" (1641), for example, included a prohibition on "inhumane Barbarous or cruell" punishments (art. 46), and it limited corporal correction to "forty stripes" (art. 43), as directed by Mosaic law (see Deuteronomy 25:3: "Forty stripes he may give him, and not exceed: lest, if he should exceed, and beat him above these with many stripes, then thy brother should seem vile unto thee.").[65] These provisions were reaffirmed in the Massachusetts "Laws and Liberties" (1648), as well as in subsequent laws of the Commonwealth and other colonies. Significantly, the limitation on corporal punishment was rooted in Biblical law and a departure from common law.[66]

The Mosaic injunction placing specific limitations on acceptable physical punishment also found expression in the regulations and laws of the new nation. Among the punishments for misconduct authorized by Congress in June 1775, a soldier in the Continental Army could receive a "whipping not exceeding *thirty-nine* lashes."[67] The first Congress under the US Constitution similarly reflected Mosaic law when it authorized the punishment of flogging "not exceeding thirty-nine stripes."[68] Why thirty-nine stripes when the Hebrew Scriptures allowed for a maximum of forty? The most likely explanation is found in Judaic traditions regarding corporal punishments that eventually found expression in rabbinic literature reducing the maximum number of lashes to forty less one (i.e., thirty-nine) to avoid exceeding the Biblical provision due to a miscount.[69]

The Bible's influence on the American constitutional tradition arguably extends far beyond the examples presented here. Scholars have identified additional constitutional provisions that reflect Biblical influences, including measures addressing due process of law, presidential pardon power, and corruption of blood. In the context of Western legal culture, these and other provisions, it is argued, were almost certainly informed or affirmed by a Biblical tradition. In other examples, the Bible played a supporting role, buttressing or supplementing the rationales for a constitutional measure and reassuring a Bible-reading people that the provision bore a Divine imprimatur.

Tracing intellectual influences is not always easy or certain. Simply counting the number of references to God or the Bible in the surviving records of the Constitutional Convention is not the only way to establish Biblical influence on the Constitution, or the lack thereof. Evidence indicating influence is sometimes found in unusual and unexpected places. In the search for intellectual influences on the American constitutional tradition, one must look wide and dig deep for evidence of Biblical influences that may have subsequently found expression in American law.

In an increasingly secular age, the claim that religion contributed to the nation's founding is often contested. However, it is indisputable that Biblical themes and principles have long informed how Americans see themselves, their place in the world, and their experiments in civil government and law. These Biblical influences were derived as much, if not more, from the Hebrew Scriptures, as interpreted through the lens of Christian theology, than from the New Testament. Americans have looked to the Hebrew Scriptures for insights into social order, political authority, civic virtue, man's relationship to God and with his fellow man, and the like, which they believed would assist them in organizing their own polities. Their political experiments in republican self-government and ordered liberty cannot be adequately understood without acknowledging the Bible's contributions. Other traditions and perspectives, to be sure, informed the founding and merit careful study alongside the Biblical influences. Yet, if we miss or dismiss the Bible's contributions to the American political order and constitutional tradition, we will fail to appreciate the broad range of ideas that contributed to the creation of the American civil order.

CHAPTER FIVE

The Hebraically Inspired Liberty Bell and Its Role in the American Story

John R. Vile

At a time when it is common to hear sirens blaring, automobile horns honking, the sounds of industrial machines at work, and words and music from our phones, iPads, radios and televisions, it may be difficult to appreciate the role that bells played before the modern age. Their ringing announced the time of day; called legislators into session; pealed sounds of joy, sorrow, or of impending threats; called laborers to dinner; invited worshippers to church; and jingled as sleds traversed the snow. Bells were often visible in the steeples of houses of worship and were objects of community pride.

One such bell—the Liberty Bell—has taken its place as an iconic symbol of the United States along with the US flag, the Statue of Liberty, Uncle Sam, and the American Bald Eagle. The words inscribed on the bell speak much like such documents as the Declaration of Independence, the US Constitution, the Bill of Rights, and other amendments to the US Constitution.

Today, the Liberty Bell is displayed in a separate pavilion outside the Pennsylvania State House (where the Declaration of Independence and US Constitution were signed), now known as Independence Hall, along with accompanying panels about its history. Although the bell has been largely silent since it cracked in the 1830s or 1840s (dispute still exists about the actual cause and date), sounds of liberty continue to resonate throughout the land.

The Pennsylvania Assembly ordered the bell from England in 1751, likely in an effort to commemorate the fiftieth anniversary of William Penn's Charter of Privileges, which among other liberal provisions recognized religious liberty. The bell was inscribed with a passage from Leviticus 25:10. The inscription on the bell, from the King James Version of the Bible first published in England in 1611, says "Proclaim Liberty throughout all the land unto all the inhabitants thereof." That verse is from a passage that elaborates on the Fourth Commandment, which required Jews "To remember the Sabbath day and make it holy" (Exodus 20:8). In addition to Leviticus 25:10, the Liberty Bell also recorded that it had been created "By order of the Assembly of the Province of Pensylvania [sic] for the State House in Philada."

The scripture from the law of Moses inscribed on the bell referred to the Biblical Year of Jubilee: during every fiftieth year the land had to lie fallow, all debts were to be forgiven, and all slaves were to be freed. Although it is not clear whether ancient Israelites actually ever implemented a Jubilee year, the aspiration to do so reflected the experience of the Hebrews in escaping from bondage in Egypt on their way to the Promised Land. Christians believe that Jesus referred to this passage when, in announcing his ministry in Luke 7:16-21, he proclaimed among his callings that of proclaiming "liberty to the captives."

The bronze bell, which is largely a combination of copper and tin, was originally cast by Thomas Lister of the Whitechapel Foundry in London, England, and weighed about 2,080 pounds. Unfortunately, the bell cracked, probably when first tested, after reaching Philadelphia by ship. It was subsequently re-melted and recast by John Pass and John Stow of Philadelphia, not once but twice (it did not produce a sweet sound after the first recasting) before being hung in the steeple of the State House, where it announced the start of legislative sessions. Accordingly, it also contains the words "Pass and Stow/MDCCLII," which note the date of its last recasting. A twin bell that arrived later from England was in turn connected to a clock whose face was on the outside wall of the building.

Americans pride themselves on the desire of many of their European settler predecessors for religious liberty. Those who get the most credit—the Puritans, who wanted to purify the Church of England from what they believed to be its Roman Catholic excesses, and settled in Massachusetts—were unwilling to extend the religious liberty that they came to enjoy to those of other faiths, some of whom subsequently founded the colonies of Connecticut and Rhode Island. In contrast to their colonial contemporaries, the Puritans based many of their laws on those of Moses, often citing the chapters and verses corresponding to definitions and penalties for crimes. By contrast, William Penn, a Quaker who had faced persecution in England for his beliefs, interpreted Scripture as a mandate to guarantee broad freedoms of religion to colonists in Pennsylvania and Delaware, even though members of his religious tradition dominated the Pennsylvania legislature for many years.

Quakers were not particularly popular among Patriots during the Revolutionary War, largely because most of them were pacifists; some interpreted such pacifism as either cowardice or lack of patriotism. Nonetheless, the city of Philadelphia, the most populous in the colonies, became the gathering point for the First and Second Continental Congresses, in which the colonists expressed their growing opposition to the taxes that the British Parliament was attempting to impose on them. Believing that they had brought their rights as Englishmen with them, the colonists did not believe that a body in which they were not physically represented had the right to tax them. The Magna Carta (1215) and other English documents had articulated this principle of "no taxation without representation." Delegates who gathered in Philadelphia for the first Congress at Carpenters' Hall and in the second Congress at the Pennsylvania State House eventually decided that continuing subjection to Britain was a form of slavery, akin to that of the Israelites in Egypt, which they had to repudiate.

In the Declaration of Independence, which the Congress adopted on July 4, 1776, Thomas Jefferson articulated the principle that all men are created equal and are equally endowed by their Creator with the rights of "life, liberty, and the pursuit of happiness." Jefferson's rationalistic view of liberty and his personal view of a deistic God differed in many ways from that of Moses. But he understood that, like the ancient Israelites, Americans desired to govern themselves free of foreign domination. Moreover, the view that God had created all human beings accords with the creation accounts in the Book of Genesis, and the Declaration's opposition to the king reflects elements of thought articulated by Israel's priestly prophet in I Samuel 8.

The proclamation of American independence was celebrated throughout Philadelphia and the rest of the colonies with the ringing of bells and other signs of joy, but it is uncertain whether this included the Liberty Bell or not. The steeple on the State House where it was housed was in a state of disrepair, and citizens might have feared excessive ringing. This did not prevent novelist George Lippard (1822-54) from printing a fanciful story in 1847 in which a white-haired elderly man waits for news that the Congress had voted for independence and that he should therefore ring the bell. Lippard's widely-reprinted story ends with the evocation: "Let us search for the origin of the great truth, which that bell proclaimed, let us behold the great Apostle [William Penn] who first proclaimed on our shores, ALL MEN ARE ALIKE THE CHILDREN OF GOD."[1]

The Revolutionary War succeeded in overturning British rule in 1783. Just as many Puritans had likened their journey from Europe to America to that of the Israelites crossing the Red Sea, so also many interpreted the victory over the British as an example of God's providence and his concern for the oppressed.

America's first experiment with self-government under the Articles of Confederation, similar to the time period in Hebraic history prior to the installation of King Saul that corresponded to the rule of the judges, was not particularly successful. This confederal system vested primary sovereignty in the thirteen states, which resembled the twelve tribes of Israel. The unicameral congress, in which states were equally represented, had limited powers and needed to requisition taxes and troops from states—and they often failed to comply. Many key matters required the consent of nine of the states and constitutional amendments required unanimous state approval.

In time, delegates from twelve of the thirteen states (all but Rhode Island) gathered once again in Philadelphia to revise this constitution. But rather than amending it, the fifty-five delegates developed a new plan, the main outlines of which remain in effect today. Although it strengthened the national government, the document—formulated from an understanding of a flawed human nature that was grounded in both Hebrew and Christian Scriptures—divided power among three branches of the national government (separation of powers), and continued to share authority between the national government and the states (federalism). Although the new government created a president who served as commander-in-chief of the armed forces, it limited his powers and subjected him to four-year renewable terms and even the possibility of impeachment and removal.

The new Constitution was the product of many compromises on a variety of subjects. In a compromise between states with large and small populations, representation in the new bicameral Congress was awarded according to population in the House of Representatives and equally in the Senate, where each state had two votes. The president was indirectly selected by the people (rather than by Congress) through an electoral college mechanism that remains the subject of criticism to this day.

The most problematic compromises involved the issue of slavery, which was more prominent in southern than in northern states, dating back to the importation of slaves to Virginia in 1619. In part because many of the delegates believed that the institution would die out on its own, a majority was willing to leave the issue of slavery largely to state discretion. Without mentioning the word slavery—an institution that contradicted the principles of equality and self-determination in the

Declaration of Independence—delegates allowed the slave trade to continue for another years, provided for the return of fugitive slaves, and even granted slave states additional representation in the House of Representatives (and the Electoral College) by counting slaves as three-fifths of a person.

Although William Penn had not outlawed slavery, Quakers developed into its strongest opponents, and the percentage of slaves in Pennsylvania never rose to the level of states to the south. In 1780, Pennsylvania passed a law providing for gradual emancipation, although some remnants of slavery lasted through the 1840s. Four of the first five US presidents owned slaves. Most northern states followed Pennsylvania's example in gradually abolishing the institution. Over time, southern leaders who had once defended slavery as a necessary evil began to argue that it was a positive good even for the slaves. In turn, northern politicians who had once turned a blind eye to the institution became increasingly convinced that the nation could never achieve the goals of the Declaration of Independence if slavery continued; William Lloyd Garrison called for immediate emancipation regardless of consequences. Much controversy centered on whether slavery would expand into US territories. This led to crises in 1820 (the Missouri Compromise) and 1850 (the Compromise of 1850) and ultimately the Civil War (1861-65).

Previously known simply as the Old Bell, the bell gained its new name from abolitionists who frequently symbolized their cause with the Liberty Bell, including the publication of a series of Liberty Bell gift books that included the bell along with its Hebraic inscription on their covers. This occurred as African Americans within the United States increasingly identified their own situation to that of the Israelites in Egypt in songs such as "Go Down Moses."

On the way to his presidential inauguration, Abraham Lincoln visited Independence Hall, where he would have seen the Liberty Bell. He raised a US flag with stars representing all thirty-four existing states, stating that he would rather be assassinated than abandon the principles of the Declaration of Independence. Following his assassination, his body would lie in state in view of the Liberty Bell on April 22 and 23, 1865.

After the Civil War, the nation adopted the Thirteenth Amendment, abolishing slavery in 1865; the Fourteenth Amendment, recognizing the citizenship rights of African Americans in 1868; and the Fifteenth Amendment, prohibiting discrimination in voting on the basis of race in 1870. The Liberty Bell was then used to rekindle national unity. As the nation celebrated its centennial in 1876, John Shoemaker, who chaired the Philadelphia Centennial Committee, observed that "Cracked and shattered as the bell may be[,] the base upon which that motto is cast remains firm and solid, and shaken as has our country been with the din of battle and bloody strife, that principle remains pure and perfect for all time to come and the whole text, Liberty Jubilee, will be literally carried out in 1876. 'Liberty can now be proclaimed through all the land to all inhabitants thereof.'"[2]

Beginning in 1885 and continuing through 1915, the Liberty Bell took a series of seven tours that heightened its importance in the popular mind. Unlike the Liberty Bell, famous documents could be reprinted, countless US flags could be made and flown, and the National Anthem could be sung almost anywhere. Trains carried the bell to the World's Industrial and Cotton Exposition in New Orleans (1884), the World's Columbian Exposition in Chicago (1893), the commemoration of the Battle of Bunker Hill in Boston (1903), the Atlanta Cotton States and International Exposition (1904), the Interstate and East Indian Exposition in Charleston, South Carolina (1902), the Louisiana Purchase Exposition in St. Louis, Missouri (1904), and the San Francisco Panama-Pacific International Exposition and the Panama-California Exposition in San Diego (1915). People gathered along tracks and in train stations throughout the land, often lifting their children when the train stopped to touch or even kiss the bell.

In time, concerns about the bell's safety prevailed and the tours ended. By that time, an increasing number of tourists could travel to Philadelphia to see the bell for themselves. Although it was now stationary, the Liberty Bell was increasingly used as an advertising symbol and the bell was reproduced in miniature as a symbol of the nation's highest values. In 1926, the Union of Jewish Orthodox Congregations had erected a replica of the Liberty Bell in New York City, spelling out the words from Leviticus in transliterated Hebrew as "*u'kratem deror ba'aretz le-khol yoshvehah*."[3]

The bell was an especially useful symbol in raising money for war bonds and in emphasizing America's commitment to liberty during the Cold War period. In time, each of the states was presented with a replica of the Liberty Bell to display.

In his 1963 "I Have a Dream" speech, which he delivered on the steps of the Lincoln Memorial in Washington, DC, Dr. Martin Luther King he quoted "My Country 'Tis Of Thee," with its declaration, "let freedom ring." Looking forward to the day when freedom would ring throughout the land, he included whites and blacks, Jews and gentiles, Protestants and Catholics, all of whom had supported the civil rights movement, in his vision.

In 1976, in anticipation of crowds for the celebration of the bicentennial, the bell was moved outside Independence Hall to its own pavilion (which was replaced by another in 2003). During the bicentennial celebrations, President Gerald Ford observed that, although the Liberty Bell was not a church bell, it contained a Bible verse that "refers to the ancient Jewish year of Jubilee," during which "the land and the equality of persons that prevailed when the Children of Israel entered the land of promise" were restored.

The Liberty Bell Pavilion has served as a site for demonstrations on a variety of issues. Concerns raised when it became known that the new pavilion for the Liberty Bell would be only yards away from the location of the house where George Washington kept slaves while he served as president, prompted the National Park Service, which now administers the site, to create an outline of the house and to provide visitors with information about the slaves who had served there. It remains common to view the bell as a symbol of the distance that has sometimes existed between national rhetoric and actual achievement.

The last goal articulated in the Preamble to the US Constitution is the securing of "the Blessings of Liberty to ourselves and our Posterity." Like the Year of Jubilee to which the verse engraved on the Liberty Bell refers, the bell serves as both a marker of past achievements—especially in extending liberties to those who were originally excluded from full participation in the US political system—and an aspirational symbol of still wider liberty under law for future generations.

American Jews, many of whom have viewed the United States as the modern land of promise, continue to express pride that the Liberty Bell displays a passage from their Scriptures and that they are able to exercise their religious freedom in America at a time when Jews have been persecuted in many other nations. Although the United States has hardly been free of religious bigotry, the First Amendment (adopted in 1791) guarantees the free exercise of religion—Christianity or any other—to all.

CHAPTER SIX

Psalms and the American Founding

Shaina Trapedo

In July 2021, one of the great wonders of the literary world—Shakespeare's First Folio—was up for sale at Sotheby's in New York as part of its "Fine Books and Manuscripts, Including Americana" block.[1] While owning one of the 235 remaining copies in the world was out of the question, I just had to be in the room where it happened. Although the room's population was sparse, the auctioneer opened the bidding at $800,000 and two minutes and $2 million later, the Folio had a new private owner.

The next item up for auction was a copy of the first edition of the Geneva Bible, translated from Hebrew and Greek into English and printed in 1560, and bound together with "The Whole Book of Psalmes: Collected into English Meeter, by Thomas Sternhold, John Hopkins, and others, Conferred with the Hebrew, with Apt Notes to Sing Them Withall."[2] For half a century, the Geneva Bible was the dominant version in Protestant England, and eventually, King James had to ban printing new editions so his 1611 authorized translation could compete. Bidding started at $100,000 but the bids that came in were under the seller's reserve price and the Bible wasn't bought.

Just after that, in rapid succession, a previously unrecorded copy of the official Massachusetts printing of the Declaration of Independence that had been "folded in eights for dispatch"[3] and the US Constitution and the Bill of Rights from the Virginia Convention in 1788, "intended to be sent to the governor or legislature of one of the other twelve states," were promptly purchased.[4] Apparently, when in the course of human events a piece of American history is up for sale, people are willing to spend between two and three million dollars (respectively). If material culture can offer some insight into how society views different types of wisdom—from Shakespeare's exploration of the human condition to the Founding Father's ratification of rights and freedoms—that morning, I couldn't help feeling sorry for Scripture. And this wasn't the first time.

In 2016, a first edition of the King James Bible sold for close to $400,000.[5] Four years later, a copy of Shakespeare's Folio went for almost $10 million. Even adjusting for availability and inflation, that is a significant discrepancy. While auction houses aren't necessarily domestic economies, they do reflect the edges of what markets might bear. Rare editions of the Bible have rarely fetched more than six figures in the last few decades, whereas Shakespeare's Folios have not gone for less. These gaping numbers suggest that the perceived monetary (and perhaps moral) value of the bard has eclipsed that of the Bible in the twenty-first century. That is, until we turn our attention to a very specific section of Scripture—the Psalms.

In 2013, the world record price for a printed book sold at auction was set by the Bay Psalm Book, the first book printed in British North America in 1640, which Sotheby's sold for $14.2 million.[6] While the story of that Psalter—one of only eleven remaining of the 1,700 originally produced—is fascinating, the Psalms of the Hebrew Bible are not only of inestimable value to Western literature and culture, but to America's founding in particular.

In Jewish tradition, King David—the "sweet singer of Israel" (2 Samuel 23:1)—composed a significant portion of *Sefer Tehillim* (the Book of Psalms), with numerous chapters attributed to other named authors, including Asaf, Heman, and the sons of Korah, as well as others including Moses and Solomon identified in rabbinical literature. The Hebrew introductory terms of *mizmor, maskil, shir, michtam, shigayyon,* and others indicate the Psalms were intended for musical performance with a variety of instruments to accompany the Levite choir on the steps of the Temple. Within the Hebrew Bible, as Yael Ziegler and other scholars have argued, the Psalms are unique. While several poetic sections record God's greatness and prophetically convey Divine messages, the Psalms capture the religious experience from the perspective of human beings.

> Let all those who seek thee rejoice and be glad in thee; let such as love thy salvation say continually, the Lord be magnified (40:16).[7]

Whereas the Hebrew Bible predominately conveys God's desire for a relationship with creation, the Psalms give us insight into the earth-bound efforts of seeking a relationship with God. It "contains words of human search and concern," writes Rabbi Abraham Joshua Heschel, most notably in the collected compositions of *Tehillim* in which "the spontaneity of the Biblical man found its expression."[8] The Midrash declares, "Everything that David said in his book, he said corresponding to himself, to all of Israel, and to all times." As such, its 150 chapters have been recited for centuries by Jews seeking protection, healing, prosperity, penance, consolation, companionship, direction, favor, fortitude, an expansion of wisdom, and an ending of exile.[9]

Yet the particularism of Israel's experience encapsulated in the Psalms has found universal appeal in various communities and contexts, especially in Early Modern England, when new translations and adaptations flourished. In addition to the Psalters formally commissioned by monarchs as Head of the Church of England during the sixteenth century, the Psalms were translated and printed more than any other book and thoroughly embedded in the lives of English citizens, from personal diary entries to the public theater.[10]

> The Reformation did nothing to dampen enthusiasm for the Old Testament poetry of David the poet-king (as it was generally believed that he was the author of all the psalms), including specifically the seven

> Penitentials, on the contrary.... Behind the impetus of Luther, whose commentary on the seven was published in 1517, and of Calvin's, then Clément Marot's and Théodore de Bèze's translations in the immensely influential Geneva Psalter, the psalms became even more widely read, translated, paraphrased, memorized, said and sung than ever before.[11]

As poet and Anglican cleric John Donne averred, the Psalms were "the manna of the Church. As manna tasted to every man like that he liked best, so do the Psalms minister instruction, and satisfaction, to every man, in every emergency and occasion."

Sternhold and Hopkins's metrical Psalms, first published in 1549, retained popularity into the seventeenth century and beyond. Yet as Heather Dubrow has shown, the fluctuating use of the Psalms within the established church reveals "complex tensions accompanying the shift of authority to the laity."[12] Dubrow traces the impact of the Psalms on conceptions of poetic audience in Protestant England by repositioning David as author, auditor, and ambassador in his discourse with the Divine. Through her readings, Dubrow imagines the early modern Protestant congregation singing psalms as performers and audience—singers and listeners—at once. With the Psalms' consistent position that God never abandons the oppressed, it is little wonder that they appealed to persecuted Christian reformers and writers like Luther, Milton, and the Puritans, who compared themselves to Israelites embarking through the wilderness toward a new promised land.

Following the Pilgrims, the Puritans arrived in Massachusetts in the late 1620s. Not long after, they "realized in the New World they didn't have one of the great objects of education and learning—a printing press," which was essential in making the Bible available for study and "key to their mission ... of living a Godly life and setting an example for other people."[13] The first step to solving their intertwined religious and pedagogical problem was to send for a press and printer from England. Although printer and minister Jose Glover died en route to Cambridge, Massachusetts, his widow Elizabeth, and his assistant Stephen Daye, managed to set up America's first printing press in 1639.[14]

The next question, of course, was *what* to print first. The colony's committee of thirty elders, including John Cotton and Richard Mather, knew they needed a book that was both utilitarian and theologically significant. It didn't take long for a work of singular import to emerge. As a sacred text, the Psalms were central to religious practice. Every family in Massachusetts Bay Colony would have taken a Psalter to church for singing as part of the liturgy and used it at home for Bible study. While a practical choice, printing a new Book of Psalms also offered a political opportunity.

As the literary scholar Robert Alter has demonstrated, mostly recently in his own English translation of the Psalms, every act of translation is an act of interpretation. It was the received translation/interpretation of the Hebrew Psalms (such as those produced by Sternhold and Hopkins) that the Puritans disapproved of and sought to correct. In the preface to *The vvhole booke of Psalmes faithfully translated into English metre* (quickly adopted by every congregation in the colony and colloquially known as the Bay Psalm Book), the compilers address the corrective path of their project in the text's preface:

> For although we have cause to bless God in many respects for the religious endeavours of the translators of the psalms into metre usually annexed to our Bibles, yet it is not unknown to the godly learned that they have rather presented a paraphrase than the words of David translated . . . and that their addition to the words, detractions from the words are not seldom and rare, but very frequent . . . and that their variations of the sense, and alterations to the sacred text too frequently, may justly minister matter of offense . . . [whereupon] we might enjoy this ordinance also in its native purity: we have therefore done our endeavour to make a plain and familiar translation of the psalms and words of David into English metre, and have not so much as presumed to paraphrase to give the sense of his meaning in other words; we have therefore attended herein as our chief guide the original, shunning all additions . . . avoiding all material detractions from words or sense.[15]

Although the Puritan translators strived to replicate the "native purity" of the original Hebrew content and cadence, many scholars have found their lyricism lacking. Take, for instance, their rendering of Psalm 23. In the King James Version, which closely follows the Hebrew, Chapter 23 begins: "(A Psalm of David.) The Lord is my shepherd; I shall not want. He maketh me to lie down in green pastures: he leadeth me beside still waters." The "paraphrase" and "variations of the sense" shunned by Puritans are easily observable in Sternhold and Hopkins's approach to Psalm 23, which bypasses the Hebrew *ro-ei* (my shepherd) and swaps lying down for standing, all while maintaining a rhyming stanza of alternating eight and six-beat lines:

> The Lord is only my support,
> and he that doth me feed;
> How can I then lack any thing,
> whereof I stand in need?

To restore the literal meaning of Scripture, but also preserve a meter for singing in services, the Bay Psalm Book renders these verses as follows:

> The Lord to me a shepherd is,
> Want therefore I shall not,
> He in the folds of tender grass
> Doth cause me down to lie.

Although Robert Frost likely had something else in mind when he defined poetry as what gets lost in translation, his quip befits the clunkiness of the Bay Psalm Book, which was designed to be functional rather than beautiful. For twentieth-century American musicologist Irving Lowens, the Bay Psalm Book was the predictable result of "a committee of thirty New England divines, more distinguished for their piety and learning than for their poetic gifts."[16] As if applying the *talem qualem* rule to its translation of *Tehillim*, Henry Wilder Foote asserts the Puritans' Bay

Psalm Book "key to understanding of their religious life; and it was the fountain-head of that great stream American hymnody of which it is the direct spiritual."[17]

Beyond its religious significance, reprinting the Psalms was a material act of nonconformity. "From the point of view of our world here in America," David Redden suggests, the Bay Psalm Book marks "the beginning of our Western Civilization."[18] No doubt, the text's spiritual and intellectual influence surpassed Puritan pulpits. It was the leading Psalter for the next century as it was read and sung by the country's Founders, though, of course, its Biblical source stretches back millennia. The copy that Sotheby's auctioned in 2013 had belonged to Boston's storied Old South Church, established in 1669, and was one of many originally used by the church's prayer-goers and patrons over time, including Samuel Adams, the young Benjamin Franklin, and William Dawes, who, like Paul Revere, was dispatched from Boston to warn the patriots the British were coming. It was from the Bay Psalm Book that some of the country's earliest thinkers first encountered the ideas that would inspire a nation.

By the time delegates gathered in Philadelphia for the First Continental Congress in 1774 to discuss a coordinated response to the British, they represented a variety of Christian communities—Episcopalians, Quakers, Presbyterians, Anabaptists, and Congregationalists—yet they were far from a monolithic whole.[19] When it was proposed that the meeting commence with a prayer, there was much debate about whether it was appropriate, and, if so, which denomination's minister would lead. Samuel Adams, who declared he was "no Bigot, and could hear a Prayer from a Gentleman of Piety and Virtue, who was at the same Time a Friend to his Country," recommended episcopal clergyman Jacob Duché, who was promptly summoned.[20] The next day, September 7, 1774, Duché invoked the words of King David to convene the assembly in Carpenter's Hall.[21]

After reciting a psalm that summons Divine force against foes and concludes with the assurance that one day all will rejoice in God favoring a "righteous cause" (Psalms 35:27), Duché offered a spontaneous personal prayer for the success of their collective mission. In recounting the event in a letter to his wife, John Adams marvels, "It seemed as if Heaven had ordained that Psalm to be read on that Morning," having had "an excellent Effect upon every Body here," and then adds, "I must beg you to read that Psalm… it would be thought providential."[22] In this case, providence proves stranger than fiction. Like Ahithophel—King David's sagacious advisor turned betrayer—Duché used "the power of covenantal thinking to unite disparate groups" but ultimately deserted Congress, sided with the British, and died in disgrace.[23]

While the American founding is full of complexity, with numerous theological and ideological crosscurrents as represented in the country's early relationship with the Psalms, the Hebrew Bible's "influence exists alongside Cato's Letters, the philosophy of John Locke, and Plutarch's exemplars of civic leadership and moral purpose."[24] Yet the impactful spirit of the Psalms extends far beyond the nation's nascence. If, as Percy Bysshe Shelley asserted, "poets are the unacknowledged legislators of the world,"[25] then America's authors have both charted and challenged the country's sense of civic and moral virtue through their verses, often using *Tehillim* as a touchstone.

Born in 1807, Henry Wadsworth Longfellow came of age in a young nation and achieved great renown at home and abroad as the predominant American poet of his day. With an eye for antiquity and an ear for hymnody, Longfellow wrote for a country that felt the strongest stirrings of aspirational promise but would come to know the deepest levels of personal and political tragedy. For a time, Longfellow was drawn toward Jewish literature and history, even penning an eloquent elegy upon visiting "Hebrews in their graves" at the Newport cemetery. In his poem, "A Psalm of Life," Longfellow adapts the ancient Israelite mode to represent the American spirit regarding "strife" as a key component of progress. "Dust thou art, to dust returnest, was not spoken of the soul," he reminds readers, and urges them to "act in the living Present! Heart within, and God o'verhead." For half a century, Longfellow served as the voice of a people hyperattentive to history-making and their own "footprints on the sands of time."[26]

Keenly aware of the spiritual and political dimensions of poetry, Ralph Waldo Emerson sounded the call for a voice that would rise to the occasion of a new nation in his 1844 essay "The Poet." Walt Whitman's response still resounds today. While Whitman pioneered an essentially American free verse in *Leaves of Grass* (1855-61)—which took America as both its Muse and exploratory subject—as Matt Miller finds in his study of the poet's creative process, "[t]hat Whitman was aware that his line seemed biblical is undeniable, and he was surely influenced, even if only unconsciously, by English translations of the Bible's Hebraic rhythms."[27]

Even when intoning the discords of battle and the strains of death he witnessed during the Civil War, Whitman, like David, notes "in the midst God's beautiful eternal right hand," being ever-present in "the stricture-knot call'd life."[28] Whitman offers us a complicated but unflappable faith in God and country that is at once expansive, inclusive, and life-affirming. American wordsmiths from Robert Frost to Amanda Gorman have been stretched by the structural and spiritual elements of the Psalms, and continue to engage with Scripture even in an age when fewer Americans claim association with a religious group.[29] Though the common reader (and even uninitiated artists themselves) might miss the Biblical valences of their verses, the imprint of the Hebrew Bible is found on the strands of rhyme across American shores.

When the Psalmist wrote that God's words are "more to be desired than gold, even much fine gold" (19:10), he was not anticipating the modern auction market, but the sentiment holds just the same. In May 2023, a decade after their record-breaking sale of the Bay Psalm Book, Sotheby's held another historical auction in New York City. This time, it was standing room only, and the item up for auction was the Codex Sassoon Bible, "the earliest, most complete Hebrew Bible extant dating to the late ninth to early tenth century, [which] has long been a foundational cornerstone to civilizations and communities around the globe and is arguably the most influential book in human history."[30] At $38.1 million, its purchase price far exceeded any sale of Shakespeare's Folio, and I think even the bard himself would have capitulated. Rather than going into the hands of a private collector, the Codex Sassoon was purchased to become a permanent exhibition of the ANU Museum of the Jewish People.

Even though the Codex Sassoon Bible will reside behind tempered glass in Israel, its priceless ancient wisdom is freely available to all, as it has been for millennia. From Revolutionary rhetoric to American abolition to modern-day international diplomacy, the evocative imagery and moral inspiration of the Psalms have moved history forward. More than four hundred years ago, Shakespeare wondered, "Is it not strange that sheep's guts should hale souls out of men's bodies?"[31] Perhaps, but it is my hope that the strings of David's harp continue to compel us toward the fullest expression of national peace, prosperity, and purpose.

PART TWO

Influences of the Hebrew Bible on American Culture

CHAPTER SEVEN

The Shepherd of American Courage

Stuart Halpern

Viewers of King Charles III's May 2023 coronation and consumers of Netflix's *The Crown* notwithstanding, Americans have a history of hating on kings. As burgers are grilled and beers raised at barbecues every year on July 4, liberty-loving Americans, of course, celebrate the Revolutionaries who declared independence from England's King George III. As the Founding Fathers put it, "The history of the present King of Great Britain is a history of repeated injuries and usurpations, all having in direct object the establishment of an absolute Tyranny over these States."[1] Yet few of these full-bellied fans of freedom are aware that an ancient Biblical king actually helped inspire the colonists in their fight for independence from England.

Seeking reassurance that their rebellion against the British was in line with God's wishes, colonial ministers sought a model of military might and spiritual standing. They found it in the figure 1 Samuel 13:14 calls "a man after God's own heart": David.

As James P. Byrd notes in his *Sacred Scripture, Sacred War*, Congress issued a May 26, 1779, statement to inspire its weary citizens amid the harshness of ongoing battles. It invoked the young shepherd boy David's slingshot-powered defeat of the sword-wielding Philistine giant Goliath.

> America, without arms, ammunition, discipline, revenue, government, or ally; almost totally striped of commerce; and in the weakness of

> youth, as it were with a "staff and sling" only, dared in the name of the Lord of Hosts' to engage a gigantic adversary, prepared at all points, boasting of his strength, and of whom even mighty warriors "were greatly afraid."

Hoping that providence would guide their hand against the mighty and arrogant British troops as it had David's makeshift weapon against an overpowering foe, Congress saw in the American cause a similarly righteous struggle that, they prayed, might merit a miraculous victory.

This wasn't the first time David had been cited in support of the colonists. John Witherspoon, who taught James Madison and served as president of the College of New Jersey (later Princeton), had wondered, in a 1776 sermon: "Has not the boasted discipline of regular and veteran soldiers been turned into confusion and dismay before the new and maiden courage of freemen in defense of their property and right?"[2]

The Book of Psalms, traditionally attributed to David, had an "overwhelming" popularity in Revolutionary America, Byrd notes. Wartime preachers cited this book from the Hebrew Bible five times more often than the New Testament's Book of Revelation, with no message more timely than David's poetic proclamation in Psalm 144 that God taught his "fingers to fight."

Ironically, a couple of decades prior to the Revolution, David's speech against Goliath as they readied for battle had been used to inspire Native Americans fighting *alongside* the British against French troops. Hyping up for the heat of battle like Rocky heading to the ring to the chords of "Eye of the Tiger," Jonathan Edwards—whose famous father of the same name had sermonized about "Sinners in the Hands of an Angry God"—spoke of a slingshot in the hands of a simple shepherd. Speaking in 1755 from his frontier post in Stockbridge, Massachusetts, he addressed a primarily Native American congregation by recalling David's verbal shot across the bow: "Thou comest to me with a sword, and with a spear, and with a javelin; but I come to thee in the name of the Lord of Hosts, the God of the armies of Israel, whom thou hast taunted" (1 Samuel 17:45).

Adopting David as a Biblical forebearer of the colonists' rebellion was no simple matter, however. The Bible itself recounts young David's hesitancy to harm King Saul. Thus in 1759, with the popular King George II on the throne, preachers cited David's hesitancy to hurt the monarch as a means of discouraging rebellion.

Seeing in the subsequent pre-revolutionary stirrings against the later King George III a similarity to Absalom's perceiving his father, the elderly King David, as a weak and ineffective ruler, Faith Robinson Trumbull of Lebanon, Connecticut, embroidered her feelings on the current state of affairs. She and her husband, Governor Jonathan Trumbull, were deeply committed to the rebel cause. Faith's work, "The Hanging of Absalom," crafted in 1770, depicted David's son's thick hair ensnared in the branches of a tree, leaving him hanging and defenseless against attack, as recounted in 2 Samuel 18. Indicting George III through with her needle, Trumbull was arguing that England's irresponsible rule was subjecting the colonists to similar harm.

Once the war began, however, emphasis was placed on David as a positive figure of spiritual and strategic skill, and it was another offspring of the Davidic line who was seen as paralleling the tyrannical British monarch. A sermon by Peter Whitney on September 12, 1776, evoked the story of Rehoboam, the son of, and successor to, David's son Solomon. Just like Rehoboam in 1 Kings 12, Whitney railed, George III rejected "the counsel of the old men, and followed the impolitic advice of his young mates."[3] Alluding to the revolt that resulted from Rehoboam's oppressive policies, Whitney preached, "We need not wonder that the ten tribes of Israel fall off from the house of David" as a result of the abandonment of the "righteous governance for which God had long blessed them."[4]

Across the pond, English preachers understood their own Goliath-like role in the war. In 1776, the British Methodist John Fletcher warned that while the Americans might be wrongheaded Davids, they were Davids nonetheless. The Americans, Fletcher wrote, were "fasting and praying," as they hoped for Divinely granted victory, while the British were "ridiculing" the American as "fanatics, and scoffing at religion" while "running wild after pleasure." Prophetically predicting the unexpected colonial victory, Fletcher warned:

> If the Colonists throng the houses of God, while we throng playhouses, or houses of ill fame; if they crowd their communion tables, while we crowd the gaming table... if they pray, while we curse; if they fast, while we get drunk... If they shelter under the protection of heaven, while our chief attention is turned to our hired troops; we are in danger—in *great* danger... A youth that believes and prays as David, is a match for a giant that swaggers and curses as Goliath.[5]

Decades after the Revolution's success, the cause of a righteous fight for the spirit of America was claimed by both the North and South in the American Civil War. It is no surprise that each sought to bear the mantle of David. After all, as President Lincoln noted in his Second Inaugural Address, the two sides "read the same Bible and pray to the same God."

As Byrd documents in *A Holy Baptism of Fire and Blood*, following the defeat of the North at the Battle of Second Manassas during August 28 to 30, 1862, the North Carolinian Presbyterian minister Joseph Atkinson saw Stonewall Jackson as a modern-day slingshotter. "When we come to our own day," he preached, "may we not hope that Jackson, the Christian hero, the man of piety and prayer, with a fervency of spirit, like David's in the sanctuary, and a martial order like David's in the field, has been graciously given us as the interpreter and impersonation of the Christian element and the Christian consciousness of this grand conflict?"[6]

The North, in turn, saw in Jefferson Davis, the president of the Confederacy, as Absalom, whose rebellion, unlike in Trumbull's earlier rendering, was now deemed illegitimate. The Boston-based Baptist minister Daniel Eddy captured the tragic, but necessary, defeat of Absalom by his father's troops as a model for the North's motivations.

> There can be no glory in this war, however it may result, and whatever brilliant deeds may be done... Our great nation at its close will weep as David did over Absalom... it is our own blood that is flowing .... The last we see of Absalom, the traitor and the usurper, he is hanging on an oak... so perish all traitors, and for the good of the country, and the honor of humanity, and the glory of God, the sooner they perish the better![7]

The Northern Presbyterian George Duffield echoed the sentiment, decrying "the rebellion of the proud, luxurious, lascivious, unprincipled, murderous Absalom, against his noble, unsuspecting, too affectionate, and overindulgent father, David."[8]

A Vermont minister inspired by Lincoln's call for volunteers following the Confederate attack on Fort Sumter saw the coming battles as mirroring those fought by David's forces. Citing the words of Joab, David's commander, in 2 Samuel 10:12, he expressed his wish that the North would "be of good courage." "Let us play the men for our people," he thundered, "and for the cities of our God."

Joseph Gillespie, a friend of President Lincoln, recalled the president offering a hand of mercy and forgiveness to the South in a similar spirit. "Well," Gillespie recounts Lincoln musing, "some think their heads ought to come off; but there are too many of them for that, and for one, I would not know where to draw the line between those whose heads (it might be said) ought to come off or stay on."[9]

"My policy would be different," Gillespie said. "I would prefer to follow the example of King David. I have been recently reading the history of the Rebellion of Absalom, and would be inclined to adopt the views of David. When David was fleeing from Jerusalem, Shimei cursed him. After the rebellion was put down Shimei craved a pardon. Abishai, David's nephew, the son of Zeruiah, David's sister, said, 'this man ought not to be pardoned, because he cursed the Lords 'anointed.' David said, 'What have I to do with you, ye sons of Zeruiah, that you should this day be adversaries unto me? Know ye that not a man shall be put to death in Israel.'"

A slayer of giants whose faith stirred generals to battle, a prophet whose words powered patriots, a monarch who inspired mercy, David has long served as the shepherd of Americans' courage that, against all odds, God would grant us victory. And that is another reason to celebrate today.

CHAPTER EIGHT

Esther in America

Stuart Halpern

The Book of Esther, read during the Jewish holiday of Purim, has a special place in American history. Though some have argued that the unifying Biblical story for Americans is the account of the Israelites' exodus from Egypt, the courage of the eponymous heroine of the Book of Esther has also been a source of succor and moral inspiration in America since the days of the colonies.

In the tale, Esther, after being taken to the palace of King Xerxes to be his queen, heroically risks her life for her people. At the urging of her cousin Mordecai, she acts to save her fellow Jews from the plot of the king's wicked adviser, Haman.

During the decade preceding the American Revolution, as colonists began rebelling against the British, newspapers and preachers turned to Esther's story to articulate their own struggle for freedom. Upon the repeal of the Stamp Act in 1765, the *Boston Gazette* declared that whoever had suggested King George III enact such a law was "as great an Enemy... as was wicked Haman to the Jews."[1] The *New York Journal*, in 1774, noted that like George III, the Persian king "reigned over many distant provinces," and was, "by his prime minister, induced to oppress, and take measures to destroy many of his subjects."[2] Lord Bute—and later, Lord North—were British Hamans.

In a sermon titled *The Character of Haman*, Thomas Reese thundered, "No principles of religion, virtue or humanity can restrain the wretch, whose ruling passion is the lust for power."[3] King George III, like Xerxes, was "too ready to believe evil of his subjects, and to comply with the oppressive measures of his prime minister."[4] After the Revolution, president of the College of New Jersey (later Princeton) John Witherspoon compared the story of Esther to the story of America, preaching that "We have also an instance in Esther in which the most mischievous designs of Haman, the son of Hammedatha the Agagite against Mordecai the Jew, and the nation from which he sprung, turned out at last to his own destruction, the honor of Mordecai, and the salvation and peace of his people."[5]

Americans also turned to Esther in the fight against slavery. In an influential 1836 pamphlet, Angelina Grimké urged Southern white women to act like the Jewish queen. Arguing that the sin of slavery would lead to the moral destruction of all of American society, she encouraged them to risk their own lives, as Esther had done, to ensure the survival of their people. "Is there no Esther among you?" she asked rhetorically, "Read the history of this Persian queen, it is full of instruction."[6]

Later, Sojourner Truth also quoted Esther in a pivotal women's rights rally in New York City. "There was a king in the Scriptures," Truth said, "and then it was the kings of the earth would kill a woman if she come into their presence; but Queen Esther come forth, for she was oppressed, and felt there was a great wrong, and she said I will die or I will bring my complaint before the king."[7]

Nine days before Abraham Lincoln issued the Emancipation Proclamation, pastor William Weston Patton quoted to him Mordecai's request of Esther that she risk her standing to achieve the salvation of her people. Patton asked,

> "who knoweth whether thou art come to the kingdom for such a time as this?" And your memorialists believe that in Divine Providence you have been called to the Presidency to speak the word of justice and authority which shall free the bondman and save the nation.[8]

Americans today are not as biblically literate as their forebears. But Esther's teachings should continue to resonate. Esther chose covenant over comfort. When Mordecai asked her to risk her life on behalf of her people, Esther sat in the lap of nobility. And yet she chose loyalty—to her family, to her people, and to their traditions.

Since the nation's inception, Americans have found comfort, inspiration, and courage in Esther's pages. She continues to teach us that a polity can only truly flourish when ancient traditions and beliefs are not squashed in the name of unity, but celebrated.

CHAPTER NINE

American Samson

Stuart Halpern

Bible-readers who come across the birth of Samson as described in the Book of Judges might take the time to ponder the long-haired, muscular anti-hero's afterlife in the American political imagination. His story seems like one straight out of a comic book—one with a parental advisory warning.

Designated in his mother's womb as a savior of his people, Samson proceeded to demonstrate a passionate affinity for foreign women. His long hair, grown since childhood, was sheared by his lover, the treacherous Delilah, thereby sapping him of his miraculous strength. He met his end in a blind, suicidal final act of destroying a Philistine temple, to whose pillars he had been chained.

While comparisons between Biblical leaders like Moses and American Presidents Washington and Lincoln have been well documented, Samson, despite his rough living and tragic ending, has appeared in rather surprising American historical contexts.

In 1771, amid the Stamp Act crisis, Samuel Adams saw what were to become revolutionary efforts through the lens of the ancient Israelite judge: "The Sons of Liberty... animated with a zeal for their country then upon the brink of destruction, and resolved at once to save her, or, like Samson, to perish in the ruins, exerted themselves with such vigor as made the house of Dogon [the Philistine god] to shake from its very foundation."[1]

The episode in Judges 16 in which Samson crumbled the pillars of the temple of Dagon, sacrificing himself in defeating his Philistine enemies, was also invoked in the Massachusetts state assembly. In the debate over ratifying the Constitution, the Reverend Samuel Stillman sought to calm the fears of Anti-Federalists. Invoking Samson's final act, Stillman argued that:

> Should Congress ever attempt the destruction of the particular [state] legislatures, they would be in the same predicament with Samson, who overthrew the house in which Philistines were making sport at his expense; them he killed indeed, but he buried himself in the ruins.[2]

During the republic's fraught early years, Thomas Jefferson also turned to Samson, as he often had in his youthful writings. In a letter to the Florentine merchant Philip Mazzei, Jefferson decried the infiltration of the newly formed federal government by men Jefferson regarded as supportive of aristocracy and even monarchy. "It would give you a fever," he wrote, "were I to name to you the apostates who have gone over to these heresies, men who were Samsons in the field and Solomons in the council, but who have had their heads shorn by the harlot England."[3]

To Jefferson, England was playing the role of the deceitful temptress Delilah, seducing Federalist Samsons into the clutches of their previous overlords. The letter ended up being published without Jefferson's permission, sparking a scandal. Some, it seemed, presumed George Washington himself to be the "Samson in the field" to whom Jefferson referred.

This was far from the first time Jefferson invoked the Samson story. In Jefferson's childhood commonplace book (even in the before-Twitter times, teenagers were sharing their ad hoc observations in written form), scholars have noted the preponderance of quotations from John Milton's *Samson Agonistes*. Jefferson's difficult relationship with his mother, it is suggested, caused him to relate to the lonely, troubled Samson, who also suffered at the hands of a woman.

The African American community has also long held Samson in high regard. As Nyasha Junior and Jeremy Schipper comprehensively document in their *Black Samson: The Untold Story of an American Icon*, both enslaved and free blacks in America bore the name during colonial times. And leading abolitionists often saw inspiration in his tale.

In his 1842 anti-slavery poem "The Warning," Henry Wadsworth Longfellow depicts the "poor, blind Samson in this land, Shorn of his strength and bound in bonds of steel," whose enslavement threatens the integrity of America, "the vast Temple of our liberties."[4] In a letter a year before his infamous raid, the militant white abolitionist John Brown wrote, "I expect to effect a mighty conquest, even though it be like the last victory of Samson." After his arrest, Brown wrote in another letter, citing Judges 13:5:

> "He shall begin to deliver Israel out of the hand of the Philistines." This was said of a poor erring servant [Samson] many years ago; and for many years I have felt a strong impression that God had given me powers and faculties, unworthy as I was, that He intended to use for a similar purpose.[5]

In his lament over Brown's execution, Frederick Douglass noted: "Like Samson, he has laid his hands upon the pillars of this great national temple of cruelty and blood, and when he falls, that temple will speedily crumble to its final doom, burying its denizens in its ruin."[6]

At Douglass's funeral, in turn, the president of Howard University, the Reverend Dr. Jeremiah Rankin, spoke of how God had sent Douglass to fight against slavery, intending, "I will set this Samson of Freedom in your temple of Dagon, and his tawny arms shall yet tumble its columns about the ears of the worshipers."[7]

Booker T. Washington and Nat Turner also were compared to Samson, and later writers including Langston Hughes, Ralph Ellison, and James Baldwin weaved his exploits into their prose. Malcolm X and Martin Luther King Jr. each spoke often of Samson, with the latter advocating for a more peaceful resolution of the battle of civil rights than that of the Israelite temple-toppler.

In the Biblical text itself, Samson was a long-suffering loner. He was born after a unique angelic revelation and destined to live a solitary life tinged with tragedy. But in America, it turns out, he found company among Founding Fathers, presidents, abolitionists, and civil rights leaders. Though his story may have originated in ancient Israel's period of tribal warfare, his selfless acts of heroism have continued to resonate in the United States.

CHAPTER TEN

America's Favorite Prophet

Stuart Halpern

Everyone's favorite Passover guest is a ghost.

In one of the most mystical moments in the traditional festival dinners known as the Seder, Jews across the globe pour a glass for Elijah—that mysterious ancient prophet whose arrival will signify the messianic redemption. And they open the door for his anticipated entrance.

For those who might need a refresher on Elijah's Biblical backstory, the Book of Kings describes how this native of Gilead, circa 900 BCE, had the ability to declare famine, resuscitate dead children, outshine and then slaughter 450 prophets of Ba'al in a game of "who worships the real true God?" rebuke the wicked King Ahab, hear God's "still small voice" (per the King James Version rendering of 1 Kings 19:12) on a mountain after despairing of his ability to inspire his fellow Israelites to repent, and mentor his successor Elisha before ascending to Heaven in a chariot amid a whirlwind. His eventual return, the tradition goes, will come when the world is to be redeemed.

While Jews think about Elijah primarily at Passover, he's actually been a fixture of American political culture from the very beginning—not only at Passover, and not even only for Jews.

Upon George Washington's death on December 14, 1799, the Pennsylvanian Lutheran priest Samuel Magaw offered a sermon titled "An Oration Commemorative of the Virtues and Greatness of General Washington." In it, Magaw invoked Elijah both to praise the president's virtues as everlasting—and to signal the preacher's own political support for John Adams as the bearer of Washington's mantle in the election of 1800. He sermonized:

> The consolation is that your venerable Chief is not to be considered as mouldering in dust, and gone forever—but, *gone a little before*, assuredly invested with a life unperishable... as the sage Franklin expressed, on a valuable friend's decease... "His carriage was first ready, and he is gone before us. We could not all conveniently start together; and why should you and I be grieved at this, since we are soon to follow, and *we know where to find him*."—He hath gone before you! He hath ascended like Elijah, in his triumphal car, and bids us follow."[1]

Reassuring his flock that their leader had appointed a worthy successor as Elijah had appointed Elisha before ascending to Heaven, Magaw continued: "He hath left, meanwhile, an exalted portion of his spirit, and his mantle, to an ADAMS."[2]

A fellow Philadelphian preacher, William Rogers, offered a similar message on February 22, 1800, referring to Adams as being "Like Elisha of Old... may he possess a double portion of the Spirit and virtues of his once intimate—affectionate—but now entombed friend!"[3]

To these preachers, Washington, like Elijah, was a wonderworking figure beyond time. His legacy unperishable, he left behind a national moral compass to be followed by future generations.

Despite preachers' politics, Thomas Jefferson defeated Adams in the election of 1800. Yet Elijah would remain. In an 1817 letter from Adams to Jefferson regarding the recently defeated Napoleon, Adams evoked the prophet in a critique of the French emperor. "A Whirlwind raised him and a Whirlwind blowed him a Way to St Helena," Adams wrote. "He is very confident that the Age of Reason is not past; and So am I; but I hope that Reason will never again rashly and hastily create Such Creatures as him."[4] In 1865, the Italian artist Constantino Brumidi rendered a fresco that adorns the US Capitol building. In it, Washington is sitting amid the clouds of Heaven. Titled "The

Apotheosis of Washington," it depicts America's first president being carried by a whirlwind.

Every Elijah needs his King Ahab—his nemesis—and Washington's was England's King George III. Thus, Charleston's John Lewis delivered a sermon titled "Naboth's Vineyard" in 1777. Just as Ahab had unlawfully seized the vineyard of and killed an innocent man in 1 Kings 21 at the urging of his wife Jezebel, Lewis argued, the British crown was unjustly stealing colonists' property for personal gain. It was up to General Washington to offer King George III's army an Elijah-style rebuke in the manner of 21:19's "hast thou killed and also taken possession?"

In America's earliest decades then, it was Elijah to whom Americans turned in referencing a peerless figure of political ambition, fortitude, and lasting civic influence.

Antebellum America was also visited by Elijah. In 1854, Congress passed the Kansas-Nebraska Act, repealing the Missouri Compromise. As historian Mark Noll notes in *America's Book: The Rise and Decline of a Bible Civilization*, President Franklin Pierce, who supported the South on this issue, was criticized as a "latter day Ahab, deaf to the warnings of his Elijahs, the anti-Nebraska clergy."[5] Abraham Lincoln, too, encountered Elijah—in the form of a letter from the former mayor of New York, Fernando Wood. Urging him to make peace with the South, Wood referenced the words describing Elijah in 1 Kings 19:12 when he wrote: "your Inaugural address... pointed out with prophetic vision... that after a bloody and terrible struggle 'the still small voice of reason' would intervene and settle the controversy."[6] Frederick Douglass had earlier praised the British emancipation of West Indies as having come "not by the sword, but by the word; not by the brute force of numbers, but by the still small voice of truth."[7] The former slave Wallace Willis also saw in Elijah the hope for a more tranquil and unified polity, as Daniel Matt notes in his recent biography of the Biblical figure. Willis's spiritual "Swing Low, Sweet Chariot" is a lyrical interpretation of the prophet's ascension.

To these advocates for national unity, it wasn't Elijah's fiery wonder-working whirlwind riding that resonated. It was his having heard God's quietly rendered call. Perhaps, they hoped, this tranquil Divine uttering might usher in a more united United States.

> I'm sometimes up, and I'm sometimes down
> Comin' for to carry me home
> But I know my soul is heavenly bound
> Comin' for to carry me home...
> If you get there before I do
> Comin' for to carry me home
> Tell all my friends that I'm a-comin' too

During and after Reconstruction, Elijah kept coming, sipping from the cup of liberation. Francis James Grimké, one of the leading African American clergy until his death in 1937, in a sermon in 1900, compared Elijah's efforts to steer Israel back toward its God to America's need to morally repent. "For years he had labored hard for the reformation of his countrymen," Grimké preached. "He saw the people rushing headlong into idolatry and every form of wickedness and under the direction and inspiration of the Almighty, he threw himself with all the energy and impetuosity of his nature into the work of reforming them."[8]

In 1909, William Jennings Bryan, later to become secretary of state, also evoked Elijah as a symbol of American courage. Addressing the Northwestern Law School banquet, he told the assembled: "We need more Elijahs in the pulpit today—more men who will dare to upbraid an Ahab and defy a Jezebel."[9]

American politicians continue to evoke Elijah today. In 2019, Hillary Clinton eulogized Congressman and civil rights advocate Elijah Cummings as having, like his Biblical namesake, "weathered storms and earthquakes but never lost his faith" as he "raised the next generation of leaders" and "even worked a few miracles."[10] With the road toward social equality taking longer than hoped, it was the harshness of Elijah's moral rebuke that was hearkened to.

The twenty-first century's self-help ethos has also enlisted Elijah. In her 2013 commencement address at Harvard, Oprah Winfrey told the graduates "If you're willing to listen to, be guided by, that still small voice that is the GPS within yourself, to find out what makes you come alive—you will be more than okay. You will be happy."[11]

Jews aren't the only ones, American history has shown, who have been looking for Elijah with expectant eyes. A harbinger of hope, a rebuker of the unrighteous, a hearer of stillness amid fractured times, the Seder night's specter continues to visit, stirring Americans to perceive in his cup their own redemptive possibilities.

CHAPTER ELEVEN

Why Everyone Loves Daniel

Stuart Halpern

With the recent cinematic return of ageless wonders Harrison Ford as Indiana Jones and Tom Cruise as *Mission Impossible*'s Ethan Hunt, it's time for another canonical hero to hit the silver screen. You know, that handsome ancient Israelite, bedecked in a multi-colored coat who found himself thrown into a pit but was also second-in-command in the palace of a foreign land, interpreting the nighttime visions of a king?

No, I'm not talking about Joseph—although the announcement that *Wicked* director Jon M. Chu will be helming a new iteration of Andrew Lloyd Weber's *Joseph and the Amazing Technicolor Dreamcoat* for Amazon Studios is welcome, to be sure.

I'm talking about Daniel.

His tale, told in his eponymous Biblical book, is rarely read, even among Orthodox Jews (it being written largely in Aramaic probably has something to do with it). The quick recap is that Daniel was taken into exile by the Babylonian forces a few years before they destroyed Solomon's Temple in Jerusalem in 586 BCE. There he interpreted dreams for the Babylonian king Nebuchadnezzar, was rewarded by being given royal robes, saw his three fellow-Israelite friends survive being thrown into a fiery furnace because of their faith in God and refusal to bow down to an idol, deciphered the writing on the wall (yes, that's where it comes from) that appeared before King Belshazzar, and had his own series of dreams.

Oh, and he had a certain run-in with nature's apex predators. It's that particular tale, told in Chapter 6, that has found a surprisingly large fan base—throughout American political history.

Daniel was thrown in the lion's den because he prayed to God while facing Jerusalem in violation of a law mandating that only the king was to be worshiped. The law had been passed by a group of nefarious palace officials looking to conspire against their Hebrew colleague, who dared to be different. Daniel survived and it was his antagonists who got their just deserts. Or rather, became dessert.

Americans from the revolutionary era, through the fight against slavery, to both sides of the political aisle today, have found inspiration in Daniel's series of adventures and carnivore-facing courage.

In 1775, preacher David Jones of Philadelphia tried to stir his congregations toward the cause of rebellion against the oppressive British. He sermonized that when Paul in the New Testament said to be "subject to higher power," he cannot have meant that we must be loyal to monarchs if they be unjust. Jones argued:

> We cannot suppose, either that this text enjoins absolute submission to all laws, which may be made in a land; for some are so wicked, oppressive and unjust in their nature and tendency, that the best of men have thought it their indispensable duty to disobey them. You may well remember, that Nebuchadnezzar made it a certain law, that all nations in his empire should, on pain of death, worship his golden image. Was it the duty of his subject to obey or not? The conduct of Shadrach, Meshach and Abednego will determine the point, who, refusing to comply, were cast into a fiery furnace. Remember also, when Darius, king of Persia, made a statute, that no man should petition either God or man, save himself, for thirty days, Daniel refused obedience unto the decree, because it was unrighteous.[1]

To Jones, Daniel and his friends modeled steadfast resistance against a tyrannical regime.

John Adams, later to become America's second president, believed that Daniel modeled leadership qualities for the young country. Writing to James Warren in April 1776, he said: "the Management of so complicated and mighty a Machine, as the United Colonies, requires the Meekness of Moses, the Patience of Job, the Wisdom of Solomon, added to the Valor of Daniel."[2]

The struggle for the abolition of slavery, and later civil rights, also saw Daniel's courage as inspiring the cause. A well-known spiritual used the story of Daniel in the lion's den as a metaphor for deliverance from slavery and injustice. The spiritual begins "didn't my Lord deliver Daniel... and why not every man?" Frederick Douglass, in Chapter 11 of his autobiography, writes that he "felt like one who had escaped a den of hungry lions." And in October 1864, Sojourner Truth, the escaped slave turned abolitionist and women's rights activist, thought of the story while visiting President Lincoln. Truth, who never learned to read or write, was a devoted student of the Bible. She saw in the Great Emancipator shades of Babylon's great visionary:

> I said to him, Mr. President, when you first took your seat I feared you would be torn to pieces, for I likened you unto Daniel, who was thrown into the lion's den; and if the lions did not tear you into pieces, I knew that it would be God that had saved you; and I said if he spared me I would see you before the four years expired, and he has done so, and now I am here to see you for myself.[3]

Decades later, in his "Letter from a Birmingham Jail," Martin Luther King Jr. drew comfort from Daniel's friends' faith amid the fire, musing: "Of course, there is nothing new about this kind of civil disobedience. It was seen sublimely in the refusal of Shadrach, Meshach and Abednego to obey the laws of Nebuchadnezzar because a higher moral law was involved."[4]

King's citation has been one of the twentieth century's plethora of Daniel invocations, ranging from the courtroom to Congress.

Amid the 1925 *Scopes* trial, the highly politicized case over whether evolution should be taught in schools, William Jennings Bryan argued that throwing man in with the rest of "thirty-four hundred and ninety-nine other mammals... including elephants" was tantamount to "putting Daniel in the lion's den!"[5]

Democratic Congressman Jim Wright, who would later go on to be Speaker of the House under President Ronald Regan, wrote in his memoirs of seeing the Catholic President John F. Kennedy address a powerful Council of Methodist Bishops. "I made a statement afterward," he recounted, "that Kennedy reminded me of Daniel in the lion's den. A few of my constituents got angry at me, accusing me of comparing Protestant ministers to lions. They were just looking for something to get shook up about. I'm glad I lived during the presidency of John F. Kennedy. It was a time when a man could have heroes and be unapologetic."[6]

In 1992, a campaigning President George H. W. Bush tried to galvanize support from the religious right. The *Washington Post* recounted that Atlanta pastor Charles Stanley told the congregation, and hundreds of thousands of TV viewers watching the live stream, that upon welcoming Bush, he had shown the president his favorite painting, an image of Daniel in the lion's den. "Daniel didn't have his eyes on the lions," Stanley said, even though their den was filled with bones. No, the *Post* recounts Stanley arguing, "Daniel kept his eyes on a ray of sunlight, on the Lord."[7]

Disgraced Illinois Governor Rod Blagojevich tried to robe himself in Daniel's garb while facing criminal charges of corruption, stating to CNN's Larry King "I felt that—understanding I was walking into something much like Daniel in the lion's den—the chances were pretty slim that I'd be able to convince them to bring my witnesses and prove my innocence."[8]

Bipartisan immigration reform efforts in 2013 also saw in Daniel a symbol of strength—for politicians going on TV. Commenting on the small group of Republicans like Marco Rubio participating in the collaborative effort, Democrat Chuck Schumer told Politico, "They're getting a lot of flak and they're showing strength."[9] Schumer lauded Rubio for going on conservative talk shows, including Rush Limbaugh's on Fox News, and advocating for the framework. "He's been Daniel in the lion's den," Schumer said.[10]

In January 2023, when Politico covered efforts to unseat chairperson of the Republican National Committee Ronna McDaniel, it titled its report "McDaniel in the Lion's Den."[11]

Daniel even made an appearance in the Congressional hearings held in the wake of the January 6, 2021 disturbances at the US Capitol, that being the day in which the presidential vote totals from the 2020 election were being certified. During two-and-a-half hours of testimony, Vice President Mike Pence's lawyer Greg Jacob described fleeing to a secure location with Pence as the mob chanting "hang Mike Pence" stormed into the Capitol. While in the secure bunker, Jacob said, he pulled out his Bible and turned to the story of Daniel in the lion's den. "Daniel 6 was where I went," he said, "and in Daniel 6, Daniel has become the second in command of Babylon, a pagan nation that he completely faithfully serves. He refuses an order from the king that he cannot follow, and he does his duty—consistent with his oath to God.... And I felt that that's what had played out that day."[12]

So many diverse figures have drawn from Daniel the ability to retain faith amid fear and strength of conviction amid conflict. From freedom fighters to those who see themselves falsely accused, preachers to pundits to presidents, fans of his story would no doubt make it a blockbuster. While it might take a bit longer to see Daniel follow Joseph into theaters near you, here's hoping.

After all, as that *other* guy likes to say, any dream will do.

CHAPTER TWELVE

Nathaniel Hawthorne and the Hebraic Strain in American Thought

Wilfred M. McClay

> But meanwhile, by alternations of Hebraism and Hellenism ... the human spirit proceeds, and each of these two forces has its appointed hours of culmination and seasons of rule.
>
> —Matthew Arnold, *Culture and Anarchy*[1]

Like a great many other historians and social scientists writing in the middle of the twentieth century, the émigré psychologist Erik Erikson was fascinated by what he called "national identity": the enduring characteristics that give any particular national culture its coherence and distinctiveness, the things that make a German German, a Russian Russian, and so on.

But what made an American American? That was more difficult. The example of his adoptive country was a puzzle for Erikson, well before the turn to multiculturalism, because it seemed to him that "whatever one may come to consider a truly American trait can be shown to have its equally characteristic opposite." Americans are so changeable; they may well find themselves cycling, in a single lifetime, in and out of such polarities as "open roads of immigration and jealous islands of tradition; outgoing internationalism and defiant isolationism; boisterous competition and self-effacing cooperation, and many others." Perhaps, Erikson concluded, a nation's identity, rather than being a simple unitary thing, must be understood as "derived from the ways in which history has, as it were, counterpointed certain opposite potentialities, the ways in which it lifts this counterpoint to a unique style of civilization, or lets it disintegrate into mere contradiction."[2] Perhaps a national identity is better described then as the product of a field of competing forces, something that arises out of a web of tensions between opposing tendencies, a series of ongoing, evolving, and never-settled debates.

Such a formulation might help us grasp how it could be the case that a land, envisioned from its beginnings as the natural home of the Enlightenment—a "New" World free of bondage to customs, traditions, and the burden of history itself, "the land of the future . . . a land of desire for all those who are weary of the historical lumber-room of old Europe," in Hegel's famous words, of those who are eager to invent the world afresh—could also be the land where the New England Puritans settled, consciously modeling themselves upon the Israelites fleeing Egypt for the Promised Land, intent upon creating the millennial kingdom, the vision of a truly righteous nation that had been perverted first by the Catholic Church and then by the leaders of the English Reformation.[3] And a land that would subsequently become an asylum for religious believers of all stripes, and that to a far greater extent than any of its European counterparts has maintained its characteristic religious beliefs and practices, and incorporated them into a great many dimensions of public life and law.

In short, the same nation that Henry Steele Commager dubbed "the Empire of Reason" was also the land that religious believers saw as a fulfillment of Biblical prophecy, a New Zion and a New Jerusalem, a nation destined for a redemptive role in the history of the world.[4] The land of Benjamin Franklin and Thomas Jefferson was also the land of Cotton Mather and Jonathan Edwards. How to explain this?

In some respects, these polarities were not polar at all, since the optimism of the Enlightenment and the apocalypticism of the Puritans were both premised upon the belief that the world as given need no longer be taken as given, but could and should and would be made new. But in a deeper sense, these seeming opposites recall the great opposition articulated by the Church father Tertullian, between "Athens" and "Jerusalem," between Greek philosophy and Biblical religion, the twin poles that, as Leo Strauss argued, make Western civilization what it is.[5] Athens stands for the spirit of free rational inquiry undertaken in a fully intelligible world whose contours and dimensions are fully commensurable with our powers of understanding. Jerusalem stands for the spirit of piety, which concedes the weakness of human understanding and the inadequacy of unaided human nature, and insists that we are utterly reliant for guidance upon the few ways in which God has revealed Himself and His will to us, and that such reliance constitutes a wisdom superior to any ratiocination, since God's ways are not ours. It is by our faith that we are saved and not by our knowledge; and there is "nothing better than the fear of the Lord... nothing sweeter than to take heed unto the commandments of the Lord."[6]

The antagonism, Strauss argued, between these two "conflicting roots" is "the core, the nerve of Western intellectual history," and the secret of the West's vitality—a life lived "between two codes," in fundamental and unresolved tension.[7] We would no longer be ourselves, should we become all one or all the other.

A variant version of this antagonism was offered by Matthew Arnold in one of the essays collected in his famous 1869 book *Culture and Anarchy*, in which Arnold proposed a contrast between "Hellenism" and "Hebraism."[8] He considered the two to be competing "spiritual disciplines," each aiming at man's perfection or salvation. "The uppermost idea with Hellenism," wrote Arnold, "is to see things as they really are; the uppermost idea with Hebraism is conduct and obedience." These divergent conceptions were in turn rooted in divergent perceptions, divergent experiences. "As Hellenism speaks of thinking clearly, seeing things in their essence and beauty, as a grand and precious feat for man to achieve, so Hebraism speaks of becoming conscious of sin, of wakening to a sense of sin, as a feat of this kind."[9] Hellenism celebrates man's capacity for perfection and glory, in and through the exercise of his own power; Hebraism reminds him of his capacity for ignominy and shamefulness, in and through the same exercise. Neither impulse could ever succeed in driving the other away entirely; each enjoyed its season of dominance, and its season of recession; both had roles as successive elements in an unfolding economy of mind and spirit.

But what had Hebraism to do with the America of the mid-nineteenth century? There could be no doubt what impulse was dominant in the America of the 1830s and '40s. The official mood of Jacksonian America was one of swaggering optimism, in which the steady westward expansion of the country was matched by the booming expansion of its economy, and by an equally irrepressible expansion in the range of human possibility. It was a time of profound religious revivalism, with strong millenarian overtones, and of widespread interest in radical social reform, in which almost every dimension of American life, from the "relic" of slavery to the status of women to the patterning of family and community life, was held up to the light, with an eye toward its improvement and eventual perfection. The leading literary figures of the period, such as Ralph Waldo Emerson and Walt Whitman, envisioned the ideal American future as a life of radical, unconditioned form of freedom, a romantic restoration of our lost wholeness and vitality and individuality, available to any with the wit and boldness to seize it.

But then there was Nathaniel Hawthorne, who lived to stand athwart such hot enthusiasms and throw cold water on them. Hawthorne stalked the era's official optimism like a shadowy grey apparition, propelled by a spirit of Hebraic skepticism, and he did so all the way up to the cataclysm of the Civil War. Just as he wrote his *Blithedale Romance* (1852) as a wry put-down of the utopian delusions behind the Brook Farm experiment in communal living, so his entire *oeuvre* formed a stern and consistent rebuke to the giddy optimism of his age, and the false hopes and hidden terrors it failed to recognize. Yet he, too, was quintessentially American: as American as Emerson, as American as the Puritans. As American as the Salem Witch Trials.

At all events, Hawthorne became a distinguished representative of the Hebraic strain—submerged, recessive, but never entirely lost during these years of antebellum optimism—in American thought. His hard and challenging insights were, and are, all the more valuable for being wrung out of times that were so unfriendly to their expression. Such too would be the genius of Abraham Lincoln, who when it came time for his Second Inaugural Address in 1865, resisted the temptation to exult in the South's defeat, but instead invoked a startlingly Hebraic conception of the Civil War's carnage as an atonement for the nation's sins, a form of absolution imposed by a just but inscrutable Deity.

Hawthorne has more than merely historical interest to us now. He was not only remarkably insightful in his own day, but is also remarkably prescient about certain dilemmas in our own times, dilemmas that only the most far-sighted could have imagined in his day. Such, in any event, is the case I wish to make in this essay.

It might seem a large and implausible claim, and a steep mountain to climb. There are few, if any, of the classic American authors whose texts exude more of an air of dusty antiquity and desuetude and precious quirkiness than do those of Hawthorne. But that perception is deceptive—which is not surprising, given how deceptive and tricky and self-concealing an author Hawthorne was. For those dusty, quirky works turn out to be strangely clairvoyant, valuable in the surprising ways that the best old books are valuable—in presenting us with truths we could never otherwise have suspected or imagined, truths that we moderns have neglected or forgotten or disallowed or repressed.

In 1991 the art critic Robert Hughes published an influential interpretation of the explosive development of modern art; the book was called *The Shock of the New*.[10] But that title recycled a shopworn cliché, one that is not very shocking by now. The really interesting story is not the shock of the new, but the shock of the old, the message of the past—often a terrible and fearful wisdom—that bides its time in silence for many years in old texts and old artifacts, quietly awaiting its rediscovery. This is the kind of insight in which Hawthorne specializes.

That is not to say, though, that it is easy to bring readers, especially young ones, to recognize and experience the shock of the old. And

Hawthorne presents a particular challenge for many of us. Consider, for example, the exalted status accorded *The Scarlet Letter*, Hawthorne's 1850 masterpiece, the first indisputably great work of American literature. For much of the twentieth century, an acquaintance with *The Scarlet Letter* was considered an essential part of every American high-schooler's education. I doubt this is still true today. It is hard to imagine a more bizarre, and more futile, candidate for a literary rite of passage, one better calculated to establish a permanent aversion to classic literature in young people's minds.

I refer here not only to the baroque style of his writing, but to the story itself, which seems impossibly remote. What readers find in *The Scarlet Letter* is the story of a Puritan minister and a married woman who had a secret love affair, and feel remorseful about it afterward, especially the minister, a sensitive fellow who also turns out to be a hypocrite and a bit of a coward. The woman, a beautiful and impressively resilient spirit who bore a love-child out of that furtive encounter, is publicly humiliated by the close-knit Puritan community for her transgression. The minister chooses to conceal his part in the matter, although profound feelings of guilt gnaw away at him. Meanwhile the cuckold husband turns up in disguise, his identity known only to his wife. He is a coldhearted villain who is "on" to the guilt of the minister, schemes to get even with them both, while degenerating into an ever more loathsome monster in the process. In the end, most everyone lives, or dies, unhappily ever after. Pretty depressing stuff. Especially if your default assumption is that everyone would have been much better off, if they could just have, you know, Gotten Over It and Moved On.

Leaving aside the spidery indirection of *The Scarlet Letter*'s prose, and the notable lack of motion in its plot, what really dooms it for present-day readers is the alien intensity of its moral universe. How could such a hell-fired, guilt-ridden, sin-soaked tale possibly make headway with American young people? Part of Hawthorne's message makes sense to them, the part they've been trained to hear—that the Puritan religious and social code (as Hawthorne understood it) was excessive, cruel, sexist, and inhuman, that it wrung all the beauty and joy out of life, and that the actions of the avenging husband, Roger Chillingworth, though he was technically the wronged party, were ultimately far more sinister than those of the unconfessed adulterer, the Rev. Arthur Dimmesdale, and his near-blameless lover, Hester Prynne, who is the one forced to wear the scarlet A, as a public symbol of her sin. It makes sense to them only if it is read as a book with a liberatory theme.

Hawthorne allows a bit of room for this interpretation. But what present-day students can't comprehend is what all the fuss is about—why Dimmesdale felt so guilty, why he couldn't confess, why he couldn't "move on," why what he and Hester did together *was* in fact a grievous sin, why our sins and the sins of our forebears are inseparable from who and what we are, why those sins must be paid for, why it is almost impossible to pay for them fully, and yet why sins that remain unacknowledged and unconfessed and unpaid will surely destroy our souls. The central premise in Hawthorne's imaginative world—his insistence that the weight of the sinful human past, in one's own life, in the life of one's family, and in the life of one's city and country, can never be denied or wished away—is likely to be lost on a generation raised on cheerful and optimistic therapeutic affirmations. The only thing shocking is the thought that that an entire village of people could ever have thought this way, and believed this way.

This incomprehension may reflect our moral progress, as a more tolerant, more live-and-let-live society, more forgiving, less willing to train the heavy artillery of shaming and punishment on what are characteristic human foibles. Less optimistically, it may merely reflect a shift in the objects and actions toward which we aim that same artillery, so that intolerance and judgmentalism are now the intolerable sins upon which the firepower of our moral wrath is trained, with equivalent ferocity of non-judgmental judgment.

But surely the incomprehension reflects our tendency to vastly underestimate the claims that guilt makes upon our hearts and minds, whether we like it or not; and the fact that our secular age has lost the metaphysical and religious supports that once provided means by which sin could be addressed does not mean that sin and guilt have lost any of their power over us. On the contrary; it is a Hebraic insight, *par excellence*, to acknowledge that sin is never cost-free, but must be paid for, in blood or penitence, a statement that is as true psychologically as it is theologically. As the late novelist David Foster Wallace said, in his novel *Infinite Jest*, "The truth will set you free. But not until it is finished with you."[11] A Hebraic sentiment with which Hawthorne would agree heartily, and that his work consistently seeks to affirm. But how can that price be effectively paid, how can there ever be such a thing as absolution, in an era of unbelief? That, too, is a question that Hawthorne's work forces us to consider.

And so with those reflections in the background, we can return to Hawthorne and see what he might be telling us about ourselves. Perhaps it will help to first spend some time introducing this strange, nocturnal, and backward-looking author himself, who thought and lived in so many respects against the prevailing American grain.

Born in Salem, Massachusetts, on the Fourth of July in 1804, Hawthorne was a paradox from start to finish; the isolated and brooding scion of an old and rooted family who became the first great literary voice of a boisterous, restless new nation.[12] He found endless ways of embodying this tension, in a life that was both cautiously provincial and perpetually unsettled, tied as it was to a New England homeland in which he never really felt at home, but which he could never really leave for long, and never left mentally. He was both deeply proud of his Puritan family pedigree and deeply troubled by it, not least by the fact that his great-grandfather John Hathorne [sic] had been one of the judges in the infamous Salem witchcraft trials of the seventeenth century. There was a family tradition, one that formed the basis for his 1851 novel *The House of the Seven Gables*, that the family house retained a curse brought down upon it by that forebear's cruel deeds. Hawthorne may have changed the spelling of his own surname partly to put a little distance between himself and that heritage, and avail himself of the American promise of a fresh beginning. But at the same time he never ceased to acknowledge, reflect on, and even wallow in that very heritage, including its ugliest elements, in ways that profoundly affected his view not only of his own past, but that of the American nation.

His father was a sea captain who died in Dutch Surinam of yellow fever when Nathaniel was only four. So he grew up with his eccentric, reclusive mother and sisters in an entirely female-dominated house. His own tendencies toward introversion and bookishness were only accentuated by a youthful foot injury, which kept him out of school and indoors a great deal of the time. By the time he went off to college at Bowdoin in 1821, he was already fairly certain that he would not aspire to any of the conventional masculine careers—business, the clergy, the law, medicine—that might have been open to him from a college education. Instead, he was already setting his sights upon becoming "an Author, and relying for support upon my pen." But those ambitions also had a nationalistic tinge to them, for he hoped, as he told his mother, to produce works that would be regarded as equals to the "proudest productions of the scribbling sons of John Bull."[13]

The years at Bowdoin were important for a variety of reasons. He came out of his shell a bit, and initiated some of the most lasting relationships of his life, notably his lifelong friendship with Franklin Pierce, a future president of the United States. In the company of Pierce and other Bowdoin friends, he discovered a passion for partisan politics, settling easily into the political sympathies of a Jacksonian Democrat, an outlook that would stay with him for the rest of his life, and help immunize him against the appeal of the Whiggery and evangelical reformism that otherwise dominated his literary circles. Such a rough-and-tumble practical-mindedness in politics might seem out of character with his authorial ambitions, but the two were united by a strong sense of American cultural destiny. The student commencement address at Hawthorne's 1825 graduation, delivered by fellow graduate Henry Wadsworth Longfellow and entitled "Our Native Writers," offered a passionate plea for a new American literature, "springing up in the shadow of our free institutions." Such words spoke directly to Hawthorne. For the desire to have a hand in creating such a distinctive American literature was, as Brenda Wineapple says, "the secret ambition lodged like a thorn in his own heart."[14]

But that ambition would be a long time in the realization. After college, he returned to Salem, and spent a mysterious ten years living in his mother's home, what he would call his "long seclusion," a period of incubating his talent, publishing stories here and there (though usually in near-complete anonymity), and struggling with the fears and loathings that such a self-imposed withdrawal and miserable isolation must have imposed upon him. Others found it incomprehensible why Hawthorne, who was an extraordinarily handsome man, with captivating eyes that were, in the admiring words of Elizabeth Peabody, "like mountain lakes seeking to reflect the heavens," would have chosen to withdraw into the blue chamber of his soul. But out of this tortured state would finally come, slowly but surely, a body of short fiction that would eventually make up his *Twice-Told Tales* (1837), the work with which he finally emerged in the public eye.

What was Hawthorne doing, during those ten years of seclusion? Well, it appears that among other things he embarked upon an intensive plan of reading. His reading list sprawled in every direction. He read Montaigne, Racine, Voltaire, and Rousseau, he read Wordsworth, Keats, Shelley, and Byron, and he read exotic travel literature, such as Hakluyt's *Voyages*, Pinckard's *Notes on the West Indies*, and the travel writings of the botanist John Bartram. But above all else, he immersed himself in the reading of American history. Hawthorne pored for hours and hours over the annals of New England towns such as Boston, Scituate, Plymouth, and Salem, over the papers of Thomas Hutchinson, the unfortunate governor of Massachusetts Bay who was forced to flee to England on the eve of the Revolution, and sermons and religious tracts of Puritans, Quakers, and Shakers. Hawthorne later became well-known for his complaint (in the preface to *The Marble Faun*) that America was "a country where there is no shadow, no antiquity, no mystery, no picturesque and gloomy wrong, nor anything but a commonplace prosperity, in broad and simple daylight."[15] But there is every reason to believe he was being ironic in those words. For his immersion in the American past during those ten years of seclusion had led him to a keen awareness of his native land's shadows, mysteries, and wrongs. These would supply him with all the literary resources he needed.

But to do so, he would need to go against the then-dominant narrative of American history. There were, to speak rather broadly, two main versions of that narrative. One was the typological and religious, the other was secular and progressive one. They were not, in the end, entirely distinct; they had a tendency to bleed into one another, and both had a triumphalist character. In the typological view, the settlement of New England was an "errand into the wilderness," a Divinely ordained mission to establish a pure church and a godly society which would serve as an example to the world, and an instrument of purification and redemption. Taking a somewhat larger view, the Protestant Reformation of which Puritanism was an important element was understood in this narrative as a great step toward the liberation of the individual and of individual conscience from the tyranny of the Church—from what Thomas Jefferson liked to call "monkish superstition"—a freedom that would find its political expression in the American Revolution, and in the republican political institutions of post-revolutionary America. It would be the American mission to spread these freedoms and institutions to the rest of the world.

This broad optimism about the progressive destiny of America reached a kind of culmination in the figure of Emerson, Hawthorne's contemporary and friend, and arguably the leading American writer of that era, whose romantic individualism and nature-worship were light-years removed from the moral severity of his Puritan forebears, but whose linkage of American destiny with the project of individual liberation could not have been stronger.

Consider the opening words of his book *Nature*, published in 1836, in which he laments the derivative and hand-me-down quality of so much of what then passed for American culture, and is impatient for the next phase in America's progressive ascent:

> Our age is retrospective. It builds the sepulchres of the fathers. It writes biographies, histories, and criticism. The foregoing generations beheld God and nature face to face; we, through their eyes. Why should not we also enjoy an original relation to the universe? Why should not we have a poetry and philosophy of insight and not of tradition, and a religion by revelation to us, and not the history of theirs? Embosomed for a season in nature, whose floods of life stream around and through us, and invite us by the powers they supply, to action proportioned to nature, why should we grope among the dry bones of the past, or put the living generation into masquerade out of its faded wardrobe? The sun shines to-day also. There is more wool and flax in the fields. There are new lands, new men, new thoughts. Let us demand our own works and laws and worship.[16]

One might have thought that Hawthorne would be inspired by just such sentiments, which echoed the call for American literary originality expressed by Longfellow at Hawthorne's Bowdoin commencement in 1825. But his work expressed a very different, and darker frame of mind, one much more powerfully drawn to the shadowy places of the past, and one more attuned to questions of individual and collective guilt. Hawthorne was not immune to the drift of the triumphalist narrative; but he felt compelled to challenge it, and complicate it. Hence, with the aptly named *Twice-Told Tales*, he became our first revisionist historian—although he did his revising in the form of imaginative literature and not a refashioning of historical accounts.

This collection of tales, all of them previously published, included some of his best-known short stories, including "The Fountain of Youth (later published as "Dr. Heidegger's Experiment")," "The Minister's Black Veil," and "The May-Pole of Merry Mount." (He had already written such classic stories as "Roger Malvin's Burial," "My Kinsman, Major

Molineux," and "Young Goodman Brown," but chose, for his usual mysterious reasons, not to include them.)[17] One could plausibly argue that Hawthorne, like Hemingway, was at his most inspired and luminous in his early short fiction. Certainly, one sees the characteristic lines of his thought and vision coming into view, fully formed, in ways that would not be much altered or improved upon in the later work. The penchant for symbolism and allegory; for spooky echoes of past crimes and sins, still immanent and lurking; for the creepy defamiliarization of ordinary life, which is seen to hide strangeness and horror beneath its thin veneer; for static characters frozen compulsively in moral dilemmas, often self-chosen; and for a diction that conveys gauzy, dreamlike distance rather than novelistic clarity and specificity—all were fully present in these stories, which had been polished to a high gloss of formal perfection.

Let me make these assertions more concrete by examining some of the work a bit more closely. Let's begin with the story "Young Goodman Brown" (276). The title character is parting at sunset from his wife, Faith, on a mysterious journey. Hawthorne does intimate that he is undertaking some "evil purpose," and his journey takes him into the darkness of the woods, which are spooky and full of unseen terrors—very different from the woods of Emerson's experience. He soon encounters an older man, with whom he had a prearranged appointment, and the two walk on together. This older man is described as a worldly man, at ease with the high and mighty, and he carries a staff which bears the likeness of a great black snake. Is he, we begin to wonder, a figure of the Devil, or someone in his service?

After a time, Young Goodman Brown begins to weary, and feel trepidation about this journey. He wants to turn back. Maybe this is all a mistake.

> My father never went into the woods on such an errand, nor his father before him. We have been a race of honest men and good Christians since the days of the martyrs, and shall I be the first of the name Brown that ever took his path and kept . . . (278).

The older man interrupts, and insists upon his own revisionist history:

> Such company, thou wouldst say," observed the older person, interpreting his pause. "Well said, Goodman Brown! I have been as well acquainted with your family as with ever a one among the Puritans; and that's no trifle to say. I helped your grandfather, the constable, when he lashed the Quaker woman so smartly through the streets of Salem; and it was I that brought your father a pitch-pine knot, kindled at my own hearth, to set fire to an Indian village, in King Philip's War. They were my good friends, both; and many a pleasant walk have we had along this path, and returned merrily after midnight. I would fain be friends with you for their sake."

Goodman Brown is shocked. "If it be as thou sayest, I marvel they never spoke of these matters.... We are a people of prayer, and good works to boot, and abide no such wickedness."

The Devil is telling him some home truths about his ancestors, and is twice-telling the tales.

> "Wickedness or not," said the traveler with the twisted staff, "I have a very general acquaintance here in New England. The deacons of many a church have drunk the communion wine with me; the selectmen of divers towns make me their chairman; and a majority of the Great and General Court are firm supporters of my interest. The governor and I, too.... But these are state secrets."

Goodman Brown continues to be shocked at these revelations, as they unravel all of his known moral universe. They meet a seemingly pious old woman on the path, and she turns out to be a devotee of the devil. Eventually, he ends up at a kind of Black Mass-like ceremony, deep in the forest, where is gathered an assemblage of seemingly all the people of the village, from the most "grave, reputable, and pious people, elders of the church, chaste dames and dewy virgins, to men of dissolute lives and women of spotted fame, wretches given over to all mean and filthy vice, and suspected even of horrid crimes."

Finally, a voice rings out: "Bring forth the converts!" and Goodman Brown automatically steps forward. So, we see that this night's event was intended all along to be a kind of initiation. The Devil-like figure points out to the converts that all the people they had formerly admired for their righteous lives were present in his "worshipping assembly." And he continues:

> This night it shall be granted you to know their secret deed: how hoary-bearded elders of the church have whispered wanton words to the young maids of their households; how many a woman, eager for widows' weeds, has given her husband a drink at bedtime and let him sleep his last sleep in her bosom; how beardless youths have made haste to inherit their fathers' wealth; and how fair damsels—blush not, sweet ones—have dug little graves in the garden, and bidden me, the sole guest to an infant's funeral. By the sympathy of your human hearts for sin ye shall scent out all the places—whether in church, bedchamber, street, field, or forest—where crime has been committed, and shall exult to behold the whole earth one stain of guilt, one mighty blood spot. (286-87)

And then Goodman Brown sees, to his horror, that his wife Faith is also there, among the initiates. The Devil says, in a tone approaching sadness, "Depending upon one another's hearts, ye had still hoped that virtue were not all a dream. Now are ye undeceived. Evil is the nature of mankind. Evil must be your only happiness. Welcome again, my children, to the communion of your race." And then ensues a kind of infernal baptism ceremony.

Suddenly Brown finds himself alone, with all the apparitions having vanished.

The next morning, as he wanders the streets of Salem, he is bewildered. He sees the same figures he saw the previous night, acting as if nothing had happened, and he finds them repulsive, and on returning home, brushes past his adoring Faith without even greeting her. Was it all a dream? We the readers never know. But we do know that Brown never recovers from his glimpse into the heart of darkness, and the rest of his life is lived in a sad and gloomy restiveness, as if the spell of that experience, or dream, has seared his heart and imagination with an image he can never forget: the whole earth as one stain of guilt.

Two other stories reinforce the same or similar themes. "The Minister's Black Veil: A Parable," is a story of the eighteenth century, but also in a Puritan setting, the town of Milford (371). A Reverend Hooper, a pious and admired clergyman whose character is thought to have been based on the great Puritan theologian Jonathan Edwards, decides unaccountably to place a black veil over his face, and to leave it in place permanently. The story oddly foreshadows Franz Kafka's novella *The Metamorphosis*, in which there is a similar drastic change in appearance, although the change in this case is entirely voluntary. We are told nothing whatever of Reverend Hooper's reasons for doing this. The fact that he was engaged to be married is sometimes adduced as a source of sexual anxiety, and while that is of course suggestive, I'm afraid it is also typical of the ways in which a reductive reading of Hawthorne may blind us to the deeper meanings in him. The story traces the reaction of the townspeople who strain to make sense of this bizarre act. Ironically, thanks to the presence of the veil, Hooper's preaching reaches heights of power that it had never before achieved, whether because of "the sentiment of the discourse or the imagination of the auditors," Hawthorne does not say. But the veil never budges, and all appeals to him to discard it fall on deaf ears. When he tells his fiancée that he can never remove the veil for the rest of his mortal life, she, naturally, bids him farewell. In the end, he comes to be regarded as a pariah, and Reverend Hooper delivers an anguished, haunting final speech:

> Why do you tremble at me alone, cried he, turning his veiled face round the circle of pale spectators. Tremble also at each other. Have men

> avoided me, and women shown no pity, and children screamed and fled, only for my black veil? What, but the mystery which it obscurely typifies, has made this piece of crape so awful?... I look around me, and, lo! On every visage a Black Veil! (384)

In other words, his veil serves as a mirror to them. They all are wearing a veil, they all are engaged in serial dishonesty, self-deception, dissembling, concealment, secret sin. His own veiling has had the disturbing effect of provoking that realization. The veil typifies—meaning that it is a "type" of—the comprehensive sinfulness of all the village. That is the meaning of the parable, a meaning that echoes the conclusion of "Young Goodman Brown."

Finally, there is "My Kinsman, Major Molineux," a tale from the early stages of the American Revolution, and therefore even closer to Hawthorne's time (68). A young man named Robin who has come of age and is eager to make his way in the world, leaves his country home and goes to Boston in search of his uncle, Major Molineux, one of the British colonial governors, and reputedly a man of influence. He looks and looks, and asks everywhere after his kinsman, but no one can (or will) tell him anything. One has the sense, as one generally finds in Hawthorne, that there is a secret, something being withheld, at the bottom of this mystery. In the meantime, Robin finds Boston to be in a wild and mind-boggling state, a topsy-turvy carnival-like atmosphere in which it is hard to find his way, in which familiar things have taken on an unfamiliar aspect, and in which the scent of anarchy and license, even violence, is in the air. Finally, he discovers the secret: his kinsman is in the process of being expelled from the town, by a fiendish and pitiless mob employing one of the cruelest and most humiliating means possible: by tar and feather. As the crowd mocks his kinsman and laughs at him, Robin finds himself strangely excited, and being "seized upon" by the "contagion" of general laughter, ends up letting out the loudest laughter of all (86). The story ends with him being advised to stay in the city, where he can "rise in the world, without the help of [his] kinsman, Major Molineux."

It is an appalling ending, resembling the ending of "Young Goodman Brown," and the takeaway from the story is accordingly complex. But surely a part of its meaning is in its implicit revision of the American past. Hawthorne wants to remind us that the American Revolution, the central event in American history, the glorious touchstone of national identity, was also an event ringed about with terror and torture and blood-soaked brutality. Hawthorne almost certainly based the story of Major Molineux in part on the ordeal of Thomas Hutchinson, a colonial justice and lieutenant governor and Loyalist whose mansion was pitilessly destroyed by a revolutionary mob whose savagery was matched only by its destructive thoroughness.[18] In presenting revolutionary Boston as a den of violent and transgressive scoundrels, who would remorselessly victimize a man of dignity and standing, Hawthorne is again digging down into the American past, and finding materials that cast doubt upon the greater narrative, and the presumed virtuousness of the present.

So, these writings could hardly have been more opposed to the sunny, expansive, and forward-looking spirit of Emerson, or the spread-eagle national enthusiasm of an expanding Jacksonian America. Hawthorne was of the same milieu as Emerson, but took a very different view of matters. He is a diagnostician of guilt.

And yet, one might ask, does it follow that the kind of guilt he depicts is a guilt to which we can or should be able to relate easily? Aren't these gauzy fables tied inextricably to the peculiarities of an outmoded Puritan severity, a severity we are happy to have put behind us? Where is a Reverend Hooper to be found in the contemporary landscape?

True enough. But the point that bears bringing out for our present purposes is that the guilt being depicted in Hawthorne is relentless and unrelieved. It is a phenomenon with few remaining metaphysical supports, and in which all expiatory exits have been blocked. In Hawthorne's world, there is no possibility of absolution for sins committed, no sacrament of atonement, no way of offloading the weight or discharging the debt, no obviation, no oblation, no satisfaction, no way of putting it behind and moving on.

In fact, however, there are even deeper themes in Hawthorne that may never before have been as salient as they are in our own times. Consider a story such as "The Birth-mark," in which a scientist insists on removing from his beautiful wife's left cheek a crimson birthmark, her sole imperfection—and inadvertently kills her in the process (764). Or "Earth's Holocaust," in which a fire begun to rid the world of its "accumulation of worn-out trumpery" ends up consuming everything—and leaving the world no better (887). Or "The Celestial Rail-road," in which the hard path of Bunyan's *Pilgrim's Progress* is replaced by an easy and convenient railway—but one that leads its comfortable passengers not to the Celestial City but to hell (808). Or "Rappaccini's Daughter," a complex allegory in which a beautiful young woman, as an experiment in the control of nature by her scientist father, has been raised on a diet of poisonous plants to make her self-sufficient—and ends up being killed by her lover when he administers an antidote to the poison (975).

It is astonishing to read the critical examinations of these texts by Hawthorne scholars, and see how often they completely miss the point of them, and interpret them in terms of biographical, sexual, or current events. All of which observations may or may not be true. But such readings are essentially trivial in comparison to the profounder meanings that fairly leap off of these pages today, for all but the most distracted or insensate readers. Those meanings may be the most compelling reason why Hawthorne deserves a fresh reading, not only by academics and schoolchildren dragooned into reading him, but by everyone.

For these irony-drenched allegorical tales, with their constant reversals and inversions, are also warnings about the moral perils of human efforts to gain mastery over the terms of human existence. What a bitter sadness it would be, Hawthorne reflected at the end of "Earth's Holocaust," if "Man's age-long endeavor for perfection" served only to "render him the mockery of the Evil Principle, from the fatal circumstance of an error at the very root of the matter" (906). And what was that error? It was lodged in the heart, "the little, yet boundless sphere"; all the misery of world derives from that "original wrong." The human heart is where the problem is, and where the only solution can be found. "If we go no deeper than the Intellect," he warned, striving "with merely that feeble instrument, to discern and rectify what is wrong," then the result will be no more substantial than a dream. And, one is tempted to add, he knew whereof he spoke.

Interestingly, Hawthorne's appeal to the heart over the intellect aligns him Emerson, and with the very same romanticism that was sweeping through the salons of Boston and Concord in his day. So too did the dreamy and gothic elements in his fiction. But if Hawthorne was partly a romantic, he was even more of a Hebrew prophet, a throwback to the Isaiah who reviled the hardened and self-satisfied hearts of his contemporaries, and prophesied how it was that the hidden things would come to the light, and the pitiful wisdom of the wise would be destroyed. If he was not quite able to re-embrace the theology of his forebears in all its details, his invocation of an "original wrong" was a long and respectful bow to them, and to the explanatory power of their most fundamental assertion.

If the fear of God is the beginning of wisdom, however, it is so partly because such fear protects us against the fatal presumption of mastery—a fearlessness much more to be feared than fear itself.

Where then does that leave us? The progress of our scientific and technological knowledge in the West, and of the culture of mastery that have come along with them, has worked to displace the cultural centrality of Christianity and Judaism, the great historical religions of the West. But it has not been able to replace them. For all its achievements, modern science has left us with at least two overwhelmingly important, and insoluble, problems for the conduct of human life. First, modern science cannot instruct us in how to live, since it cannot provide us with the ordering ends according to which our human strivings should be oriented. In a word, it cannot tell us what we should live for, let alone what we should be willing to sacrifice for, or die for.

Secondly, science cannot do anything to relieve the weight of guilt on our souls, a weight to which it has added appreciably, precisely by its rendering us able to be in control of, and therefore accountable for, more and more elements in our lives—responsibility being the fertile seedbed of guilt. That growing weight seeks opportunities for release, seeks transactional outlets, but finds no obvious or straightforward ones in the secular dispensation. Instead, more often than not we are left to flail about, seeking some semblance of absolution in an incoherent post-religious moral economy that has not entirely abandoned the concept of sin, but lacks the transactional power of absolution or expiation without which no moral system can be bearable.

Hawthorne's stories do not offer a solution to any of these problems. But they do present the problems with an uncanny brilliance. The version of early New England that he conjures in his stories is a distant mirror of our own dilemmas, and as such, tell us something true about ourselves and our current condition. We may even hope that this truth will set us free—once it is finished with us.

CHAPTER THIRTEEN

The Story of Hagar and American Exile

Ariel Clark Silver

In American history as in the Book of Genesis, the figure of Hagar represents the themes of possession, dispossession, homelessness, exclusion, and exile.

Though an Egyptian female slave, Hagar bears Abraham his first son, Ishmael, when his wife Sarah is unable to conceive. After producing an heir, she is mistreated, causing her to flee, only to be remanded, then finally rejected outright. When Hagar appears in the record, she is a possessed figure, enslaved and at the mercy of her masters, Abraham and Sarah. She is delivered to Abram and commanded to produce posterity for him, which she does, a son named Ishmael, meaning "God hears." But Sarah is jealous and believes that Hagar views her with contempt because she is childless. She decides to deal harshly with Hagar, causing her to run away with her child. Hagar is then visited by an angel of the Lord and commanded to return and submit. She is also told to name the child Ishmael because the "Lord hath heard thy affliction" (Genesis 16:11).

At the same time, she is given a blessing that her seed will be multiplied greatly. Her response: "Thou God seest me" (Genesis 16:13). The intimate submission of Hagar to Abraham is now repaid with Divine closeness. Though possessed by others, and captive to their will, Hagar is still reminded that she has been seen and heard. Once Sarah delivers her own child, Isaac, Hagar's fortunes change again. Sarah detects Ishmael mocking Isaac and demands that he and his mother be cast out. Though it appears to pain Abraham to send his son Ishmael away, he is reminded by the Lord that his "seed" lies with Isaac. A nation will also come of Ishmael, but Abraham is to disown his first child (see Genesis 21:9-14).

This narrative of dispossession and exile displayed in the Book of Genesis is so evocative that American writers return to it in multiple ways in the mid-nineteenth century, when American literature marks its own artistic beginning, claiming independence from the cultural influences of Europe, to which it had previously given so much heed. In his monumental work, *Moby-Dick* (1851), perhaps the first great American novel, Herman Melville opens with the line, "Call me Ishmael," directly invoking the story of Hagar and her affliction. Ishmael, a crew member on *The Pequod*, a commercial whaling ship, functions as the narrator of this epic, which follows the pursuit of Captain Ahab for the white whale that maimed him. Echoing the Biblical king who acted imperially, supported idolatry, and presided over moral decline in Israel, Ahab in *Moby-Dick* is also mortally wounded. Ishmael alone survives the disastrous encounter with the white whale, floating on a wooden trunk when he is finally rescued by *The Rachel*, a pointed allusion to the words of the prophet Jeremiah, where he recounts Rachel weeping for her lost children (Jeremiah 31:15). In this uniquely American saga, the dispossession of Ishmael is transformed into the possibility of restitution, both personally and nationally.

When Hagar and Ishmael are cast out into the wilderness in the text of Genesis, they are essentially free but are homeless and without resources. They are no longer enslaved, but they are left alone in desperate straits. However, Hagar discovers that God not only hears her, but also hears her son when he cries out in thirst. Then speaking directly to Hagar, the Lord opens her eyes to see a well of water, causing them to survive in the wasteland (see Genesis 21:17-19). The ironic nature of these interactions with and reward from the Divine—sight amid invisibility, water in the desert, a nation without a homeland—establish Hagar and Ishmael as counter characters with counter commentaries, a structure at work in both the Genesis account and *Moby-Dick*. Once Hagar has brought the Abrahamic covenant to life through Ishmael, she is discarded and left to die.

The harshness of exile for this homeless mother and child is made even more evocative when the figure of Hagar, the ancient African woman who fulfills the covenant of Abraham, becomes a trope for the plight of African Americans held in bondage and often made to bear children against their will. In mid-nineteenth century American literature, Hagar and Ishmael are drawn upon to reimagine both the racial and gendered dynamics of dispossession, specifically female dispossession. From advertisements for runaway slaves as early as 1840, we learn that slave owners drew on this slave woman in Genesis in naming their own female slaves. As one example of many, John L. Durand offered a twenty-dollar reward for the return of Hagar in a runaway advertisement on June 13, 1840, in the *Newbern Spectator*. Did they know the story well enough to anticipate that she would, in fact, run away?

In an extension of this typological reimagination of Hagar, slave women were also cast strangely as Madonnas to the children of slave owners. But they are presented as counter-Madonnas, excluded rather than embraced, and made to suffer for their solicitude as mothers. One aspect of the apologist argument for slavery was that slave women were lovingly incorporated into the homes of those who held them in bondage, the very assumption which governed Hagar's initial inclusion in the household of Abraham and Sarah. In both instances, these "Hagars" bore the children of their masters. One genre of early daguerreotype in mid-nineteenth century America was the Chattel Madonna, which presented black enslaved women as nursemaids to the white children of their slave owners, manipulating photographic images to create a false visual record of human bondage as a benign institution of nurture and care.

Slavery was also justified based on a reading of Genesis 16 that has taken Hagar's return to Sarah in response to the angel's command as a Divine warning and caution. In this ancient narrative, some saw support for the Compromise of 1850, a legal code that included the Fugitive Slave

Act, which obliged ordinary citizens throughout the United States to return runaway slaves to their masters. The abolitionist response to the scriptural reading of slave owners was to present the problem in more real and humane terms through fiction, as Harriet Beecher Stowe does in Chapter 12 of *Uncle Tom's Cabin* (1852) when Aunt Hagar and her son Albert are separated, the son auctioned to one man for plantation work and the mother sold for a pittance to another man. Stowe's characterization of Hagar turns away from rebuke and forced repatriation to emphasize the pathos of their dilemma: Hagar and her son are divorced not only from the household to which they have contributed so much, they are divorced from each other.

Even as the story of Hagar is called upon to encourage the submission of female slaves, and to expose the harshness of their condition, there is yet another strain of this narrative that emphasizes the strength and perseverance of this Biblical mother and child. When unexpected, seemingly Divine rewards are realized, Hagar is transformed from a figure of desperation into one of restoration and reconstruction. Two years before *Moby-Dick,* E. D. E. N. Southworth published *Hagar, or the Deserted Wife* (1849), a story about a woman abandoned and left destitute. This narrative of Hagar in America demonstrates that dispossession is often born of industrial and economic shifts and mechanization, dislocations that brought both crises and opportunities. Southworth invokes the figure of Hagar to demonstrate the female quest for sovereignty in nineteenth century America, determined to find water even in the desert.

In this work of both spiritual biography and autobiography, the protagonist, Hagar Churchill, is married but abandoned with young children by her husband, much like the author herself. Southworth responds to the loss of her husband Frederick, who sets out in search of gold in Brazil, by writing stories such as this one to keep her family from starving. In *Hagar, or The Deserted Wife*, she inscribes loss and retrieval through another art form: music. Hagar Churchill becomes an international star as a singer, transforming her dispossession. The restoration that Southworth envisions for Hagar, complete with the return of her husband, eluded her in her own life, but it demonstrates her belief in the female protagonist as the heroine of her own quest. Southworth remained single the rest of her life (never divorced and never reunited) but she succeeded professionally, publishing in *The National Era* and eventually on an exclusive contract with *The New York Ledger*.

In *The Deserted Wife*, the regeneration of Hagar is also linked to the restoration of a home. When the male Churchill line runs out, Hagar Churchill inherits a ruined hall in decay. Her perseverance in a social and economic wilderness suggests a triumph over alienation and homelessness, a spiritual compensation in which her property, posterity, and power are all redeemed, and she is returned, literally and figuratively, to the promised land. In the hands of Southworth, Hagar comes to represent all aspects of the covenant made with Abraham, the father of her child, Ishmael. The alienation that she once suffered is turned to re-engagement and renewal.

In *Moby-Dick*, Melville also recognizes that communities are built in the face of great antagonism. Many of Melville's most memorable characters in *Moby-Dick* are solitary—what Ishmael refers to in the text as *isolato*. To be alone is the common plight of all. The loneliness endured by both the Biblical Hagar and Hagar Churchill is repeated in *Moby-Dick* in the women who sit in grief and isolation at the Whaleman's Chapel in New Bedford. They are the counterpoint to the lonely sailors at sea, separated both from loved ones and from one another. Whatever unity they may feel with one another is forged through bonds of loss, a sense of dispossession also felt in *The Deserted Wife*. The return home is long and arduous and filled with privation.

The American romantic protagonist is part solitary outcast and part conquering hero. In the Biblical story of Hagar, her son Ishmael is set in contrast to Isaac, one the outcast, the other the expansionist. The figure of Hagar plays such an important role in American self-conception because she resides at the juncture of these tensions, embodying the racial and gendered dimensions of these forces often at odds with one another. Melville extends the juxtaposition of this narrative and counternarrative in *Moby-Dick* through Ishmael, by placing on either side of this outcast narrator a man more wild than he is defined to be in Genesis. On the one side is the former cannibal, Queequeg. When he prays to his idol, Ishmael prays with him, building a friendship that heals psychic and social rifts. On the other side is the monomaniacal Captain Ahab. Ishmael responds by offering a sensitive account of the wounds that have driven Ahab to his antagonistic pursuit of the white whale. Ishmael's own racial hybridity places him in the middle of these extremes. Though Ishmael is not able to achieve an all hands-on-deck solidarity among the ship's crew, and he ultimately loses his clan at sea, he alone endures the calamity caused by one of those wild men, and is saved on the floating trunk of the other.

Is it possible that there are blessings for being exiled and unchosen, excluded altogether from the house of covenant? Like his ancient counterpart, Ishmael in *Moby-Dick* survives by getting out. Those rewards are neither obvious nor immediately clear. We know that Hagar and Ishmael together are promised posterity and nation-status, but they do suffer and spend much time in the wilderness. At the mythic level, they get out of the Hebraic narrative quite early, and are spared generational famine in Canaan, bondage in Egypt, and decades of wandering in the Sinai Peninsula. If *Moby-Dick* is a novel of domestic heroism, it is heroism on the divide between wildness and domestication. The glorious rebuilding which Southworth imagines and enacts for her abandoned Madonna and children is sustained here on the remnants of a shipwreck. Like the weaver in the Arsacidean bower, Melville is quick to make clear that life and death are deeply interwoven: "life folded Death; Death trellised Life" (460).

Where Southworth sees in the plight of Hagar and Ishmael a house rebuilt, Melville sees primarily a house destroyed. In the wake of the Fugitive Slave Act, Melville could see that the practice of turning on one another could lead the nation to the terrible collapse of its democratic aspirations. Nowhere is this clearer than in *Battle Pieces*, where Melville renders the Civil War in words as Matthew Brady does in images: stark, severe, unflinching. This conflict, also between brothers and their parents, led to disastrous consequences. The opening piece, a tribute to the abolitionist John Brown, indicates that "the cut is on the crown. . . . And the stabs shall heal no more." After the war, one severe outcome was homelessness, not only for maimed soldiers, and women left widowed often with children in need, but also for freed men and women. Like Hagar and Ishmael, they were released from their oppressors but left in a vast and inhospitable wilderness, some four million of them. Considered refugees rather than citizens, they were miserable, hopeless, near starvation, and crowded into cities and US Army camps, destitute and without a place to claim as their own. The failure of Reconstruction forced many to return to the labor they performed as slaves, on contracts that often did not include shelter. When the black American expatriate sculptor Edmonia Lewis composed her *Hagar* in Rome in 1875, she may well have had been alluding to the contemporary plight of African Americans who were deeply dispossessed in their own country, often kept from ownership of any land that could hold promise for them.

During Reconstruction, Harriet Beecher Stowe returns to the figure of Hagar in her work *Woman in Sacred History* (1874). When writing of Hagar's encounter with the angel in the desert, Stowe suggests that it is "so universally significant of our every-day human experience, that it has almost the force of an allegory" (38). She then asks her readers, "Who of us has not yielded to despairing grief, while flowing by us were unnoticed sources of consolation?" (38). Her analysis of Hagar is otherwise unremarkable, in part because she sympathized more with Sarah. Unlike Southworth, who saw herself in the plight of Hagar, the deserted wife, who had to support her children through writing, Stowe was already a powerful literary woman who expected her husband to follow her wishes. Her concerns in the story have more to do with tensions between Abraham and Sarah than between Abraham and Hagar. It is only in Stowe's liberal treatment of another Biblical figure, Miriam, that we have any sense how she might have articulated the needs of Hagar, if only she could have seen them more fully. Stowe heralded Miriam's influence on laws that protected an unloved wife from a husband's partiality, mandated the consideration of the rights of captive women, secured the marriage-rights of purchased slave women, and forbade making merchandise of women in bondage. Her discussion of Hagar, Sarah, and Miriam after the Civil War was aimed at efforts to restore both black and white women to positions of respect.

The symbolic renderings of Hagar in American literature in the nineteenth century have been defined by dispossession and homelessness. In *Clarel* (1876), Melville recasts the experience of exile as a prolonged futile search over centuries for a spiritual home. Beginning his epic poem in Jerusalem, the home of covenant Israel, and concluding in Bethlehem, birthplace of the Christian redeemer, he takes his characters, including Agar, on an inconclusive pilgrimage through the landscape of faith and doubt. On this journey through a patriarchal wasteland, they are given little in the way of solace or confirmation. They are left alone as Melville mounts his critique of mainstream religionists who seek an easy confirmation of their beliefs through an application to Biblical texts. He recognizes that any real search for Divine understanding is going to require the kind of excruciating journey that Hagar endured in the wilderness.

Melville returns to Hagar in *Clarel* at a moment when it is clear that the process of Reconstruction has been deeply compromised. The religious and political degradation of the American republic comes into view through a woman, Agar, whose name invokes the figure of Hagar but who lacks direction from a clear voice. In the Biblical story of Hagar and Ishmael, the saving grace is the presence of a voice that guides them through the wilderness of exclusion, loneliness, and rejection. Now that voice has itself become homeless. When the Compromise of 1877 was passed the year after the publication of *Clarel*, effectively ending the democratic advances secured through Union victory in the Civil War, Melville's concerns for his country were confirmed. The American republic refused the Divine direction that might have led them out of the desert. Between the publication of *Clarel* and Melville's death in

1891, there was one more significant surge of voiceless and homeless mothers and children in America. These wandering mothers and children filled New York, crowding into tenement houses and taking work in sweated industries. In one final visual rendering of nineteenth-century dispossession, the photographer Jacob Riis created another generation of counter-Madonnas and children to remind us of the long and determined search for home that Hagar and Ishmael have come to represent across American history.

PART THREE

American Presidents' Appreciation of Jewish Contributions

CHAPTER FOURTEEN

The Bible and the Presidents

Tevi Troy

The Bible has long been a key part of American life, dating back to the colonial era. The Puritan settlers of New England placed enormous importance on individual reading of the Bible, and the literacy rate in New England grew towards 90 percent during the Revolutionary period. Captain Levi Preston, a New Englander who fought at the 1775 Battle of Concord, recalled the universality of the Bible on colonial bookshelves, saying, "The only books we had were the Bible, the catechism, Watts'[s] psalms and hymns, and the almanacs."[1]

Given the American populace's close connection to the Bible, it is unsurprising that this was true of American presidents as well. This link dates back to America's first president, George Washington, who referenced Psalm 82 in his First Inaugural Address, saying, "it would be peculiarly improper to omit in this first official Act, my fervent supplications to that Almighty Being who rules over the Universe, who presides in the Councils of Nations...."[2] Washington also famously used a Biblical reference in his letter offering comfort to the Hebrew Congregation at Newport, Rhode Island. Washington wrote, "May the Children of the Stock of Abraham, who dwell in this land, continue to merit and enjoy the good will of the other Inhabitants; while every one shall sit in safety under his own vine and figtree, and there shall be none to make him afraid."[3] While this letter is well known, it is one of fifty times Washington is known to have used the "vine and figtree" reference which appears multiple times in the Bible, in Micah 4:4, 1 Kings 4:25, and Zechariah 3:10.

America's third president, Thomas Jefferson, also used a Biblical reference in his inaugural address, expressing his hope that America should have "room enough for our descendants to the thousandth and thousandth generation," a reference to Exodus 20:6: "maintaining loving devotion to a thousand generations."[4] What was somewhat surprising about Jefferson's use of a Biblical reference is that Jefferson was both a deist and someone with an uncomfortable relationship to divinity. He even painstakingly crafted a Bible with no references to Jesus's divinity, cutting out those passages to make it more conducive to his reading of the text.

Other presidents of the founding generation also had a close relationship to the Bible. James Madison (the fourth president) studied Hebrew at the College of New Jersey—later known as Princeton—so that he could have a better understanding of the characters of the Bible. Similarly, John Quincy Adams (the sixth president) studied the Bible closely, and wrote letters to his son providing Biblical teachings including his belief that the Hebrew prophets were "Messengers, specifically commissioned of [God], to warn the People of their duty, to foretell the punishments which awaited their transgressions."[5] He also considered writing a history of the Jewish people after his presidency, but unfortunately nothing ever came of it.

Abraham Lincoln, the sixteenth president, may have been the president most closely associated with the Bible. As an avid reader, Lincoln's association with it began at an early age. He only had access to a few books, the Bible among them, but he read those books over and over. As Lord Charnwood writes in his biography of Lincoln, "these books he did read, and read again, and pondered, not with any dreamy or purely intellectual interest, but like one who desires the weapon of learning for practical ends, and desires also to have patterns of what life should be."[6]

Lincoln's close reading of what he viewed as "the best gift God has given to man" had an enormous impact on him.[7] He regularly referred to the Bible throughout his life—citing the Old Testament approximately three times as often as the New Testament. The Bible, along with Shakespeare, taught him a useful way of speaking for his political aspirations: common yet elevated speech. The citizens of the time would recognize and not resent his references, but he could still present himself as thoughtful and educated. This common but elevated style helped him connect with regular people.

The Bible became a staple in Lincoln's political and personal life. He read the Book of Job for comfort in challenging times. His favorite Biblical verse—"let us judge not, lest ye be judged" (Matthew 7:1)—served him well as he sought to reconcile the divided nation towards the end of the Civil War. He referred to the difficulties Americans were facing as "troub'lous times," citing Daniel 9:25. When he heard via telegraph that only four hundred delegates appeared at the 1864 Republican Convention, he showed a remarkable Biblical literacy by asking for a Bible and reading this on-point passage from 1 Samuel 22:2: "And every one that was in distress, and every one that was in debt, and every one that was discontented, gathered themselves unto him; and he became a captain over them; and there were with him about four hundred men."

Lincoln regularly referenced the Bible in his political speeches. He mentioned it in both his First and Second Inaugural addresses. In the first, Lincoln referred to the "better angels of our nature" as an argument against secession, a nod to the "better angels" of Matthew 23:12. His second address was replete with Biblical references including Genesis 3:19 ("wringing their bread from the sweat of other men's faces"), Matthew 18:7 ("Woe unto the world because of offenses"), and Psalm 19:9 ("the judgments of the Lord are true and righteous altogether").

Lincoln's most famous Biblical allusion was not a quote, though, but a way of thinking. In the Gettysburg Address, perhaps the most effective and influential speech of all time, Lincoln opened with the words, "Four score and seven years ago." Those words never appear in the Bible, but they were suggestive of Psalm 90:10, which described a man's life span as "threescore years and ten; and if by reason of strength they be fourscore years." Lincoln not only knew the reference, but he knew that his audience would know it as well.

Unfortunately, Lincoln's replacement was not nearly as deft with his Biblical knowledge, nor as respectful of the holy book, as he had been. At the same Second Inauguration where Lincoln reverently cited the Bible multiple times, then-Vice President Andrew Johnson gave an intoxicated disaster of a speech, culminating in him taking a Bible and loudly kissing it in front of a mortified crowd. Johnson's horrifying performance led to jokes about Caligula's horse having more dignity than the new Vice President of the United States (Johnson had replaced Hannibal Hamlin, Lincoln's first-term vice president). The spectacle established a stark contrast with Lincoln, and did not bode well for Johnson's poorly-regarded presidency, which he assumed after Lincoln's assassination.

James A. Garfield, the twentieth president, was the next president to be assassinated. Garfield was the only minister to become president of the United States. Growing up, his mother took him and his siblings to church on Sundays, and taught the Bible in their home. The lessons apparently took hold. He once wrote in his diary, "It pains my heart to see the ignorance and bigotry that is abroad in the land. I wish that men would let all human traditions alone and take the Bible alone for their guide."[8] He also believed that there was a higher calling for him, writing that "the hand of the Lord has been with me, and he has preserved me for some purpose, I know not what."[9] He became a teacher, and would often teach the Bible to his students.

He only served as president briefly, getting shot on July 2, 1881, (about four months after his inauguration) and dying two months later, on September 19, 1881. During his time in office, he was religious about not working on Sundays. Once, when a cabinet member at a Saturday meeting suggested meeting the next day to finish their business, he replied, "If you men want to meet tomorrow, you may do so, but I will not meet with you. I have a more important engagement each first day of the week that I never miss." When asked what was more important, he responded, "Upon the first day of each week, I have an engagement with my Lord around the communion table. That is where I will be tomorrow."[10] Garfield liked to cite the Bible, but he also had a sense of humor about it. He once said, referencing John 8:32, "The truth will set you free, but first it will make you miserable."[11]

Theodore Roosevelt was not assassinated, but as vice president he did become president as a result of the assassination of the twenty-fifth president, William McKinley. Roosevelt was knowledgeable about the Bible and would make reference to it in political contexts. However, his references were less formal than reciting Biblical verses. He seemed to treat the Bible as literature and used its common language to make political points. For example, he referred to reporters who failed to keep confidences as members of the Ananias Club. It was a cheeky reference, as Ananias was a character who died after lying to Peter. When Roosevelt was police commissioner of New York, he praised the "excellent work needing nerve and hardihood" of certain Jewish officers of the New York police force with a Hebraic reference, calling them "the Maccabee type."[12]

In 1912, Roosevelt engaged in his own betrayal, running against his friend and hand-picked successor William Howard Taft as a third-party candidate. This move allowed Democratic candidate Woodrow Wilson to defeat the split Republican party and win the election. Wilson was a religious man, who, like Garfield, did not wish to conduct government business on Sundays. He also would say grace before he ate and read the Bible nightly. This habit continued ever after Wilson's debilitating stroke in the fall of 1919. When his friend Ray Stannard Baker came to see him, he found Wilson in bed with both a detective book and the Bible by his side.

Calvin Coolidge was another Bible-loving president. He took books with him wherever he went, and along with copies of Dante, Tennyson, and Milton, there would always be the Bible. It is therefore unsurprising that Coolidge had a Bible near him in Vermont on August 3, 1923, when he learned that Warren G. Harding had died, making Coolidge president. When he took the oath of office, some say that Coolidge did not place his hand on the holy book, explaining that "it is not the practice in Vermont or Massachusetts to use a Bible in connection with the administration of an oath."[13]

Another vice president who stepped into the presidency after a death was Harry Truman. Truman was an obsessive reader in his youth, including reading the Bible in its entirety thrice. As with Teddy Roosevelt, who was another big reader, Truman incorporated the Bible into his thinking and into his rhetoric. After his presidency, when dismissing the relevance of public opinion polls, he used Biblical characters to make his point: "I wonder how far Moses would have gone if he'd taken a poll in Egypt? What would Jesus Christ have preached if he'd taken a poll in Israel?"[14]

The Bible played an important role in one of Truman's key decisions as president. In 1948, his administration was badly divided on the question of whether to recognize the new State of Israel. Truman was under heavy pressure from multiple quarters on the question, but he eventually decided to recognize the fledgling state. Later, he would make clear that his familiarity with the Bible shaped his decision, particularly the story of Cyrus the Great, the Persian king who allowed the Jews to return to Jerusalem after the first exile. When Truman was introduced at the Jewish Theological Seminary as "the man who helped create the state of Israel," Truman interrupted the introduction, saying, "What do you mean, 'helped create'? I am Cyrus!"[15]

Like with Coolidge, the Bible was part of the equation in the story of two other vice presidents who ascended to the presidency. After John F. Kennedy's tragic assassination in Dallas in November 1963, Lyndon Johnson took the oath of office in Air Force One. Johnson wanted a Bible but Air Force One did not have one, so he instead used a missal, a Catholic prayer book, which someone had found on board. The next vice president to take over in mid-term, Gerald Ford, insisted that Air Force One have a Bible on it going forward, a tradition that continues to this day.

Ford had the Bible on his mind as he made the transition from vice president to president. The night before he was sworn in, Ford and his wife Betty lay in bed holding hands and reciting one of Ford's favorite verses, Proverbs 3:5–6: "Trust in the Lord with all thine heart; / and lean not unto thine own understanding. / In all thy ways acknowledge him, / and he shall direct thy paths." The next afternoon he took the oath of office, with Betty by his side, over a Bible open to Proverb 3:5-6.

The most Bible-literate president ever may have been Jimmy Carter. He began memorizing Biblical verses at the age of three. At eleven, he declared his faith publicly. He and his wife Rosalynn even read passages of the Bible to one another, including, at least once, in Spanish. Carter not only read the Bible itself, but theologians as well, including Paul Tillich, Dietrich Bonhoeffer, Karl Barth, Martin Buber, and his favorite, Reinhold Niebuhr. He once wrote that "One of my greatest regrets was not meeting Niebuhr before he died."

Despite all of his Bible reading, Carter could be cutting, and the Bible played into that trait as well. While running for president, Carter disliked *Boston Globe* reporter Curtis Wilkie, and did not mind letting him know. Once, when he saw Wilkie entering a church service without a Bible in hand, he handed Wilkie a Bible and said, "Here. You probably need this more than anyone else."[16] In retirement, he continued to stick close to the Bible, writing *NIV Lessons from Life Bible: Personal Reflections with Jimmy Carter* in 2012.

Carter's immediate successor, Ronald Reagan, was not as religious as Carter, but he did have a close relationship with the Bible. In 1965, he took a dig at Lyndon Johnson in a speech, saying, "Our president is fond of quoting Isaiah, 'Come let us reason together.' Doesn't that sound cozy? But our president does not drop down a line further to quote 'If ye refuse ye shall be devoured by the sword.'"[17] On a more serious note, while running for president in 1980, Reagan praised the Bible before an evangelical crowd, saying, "All the complex and horrendous questions confronting us at home and worldwide have their answer in that single book."[18]

One president who could have challenged and may have even surpassed Carter in Biblical literacy was Bill Clinton. The historian Jonathan Sarna believed that "Bill Clinton appreciated the Bible more than any American president since Abraham Lincoln."[19] As with Carter, Clinton's connection with the Bible stemmed from his upbringing in the South. He knew the text cold. In 1996, after the death of Commerce Secretary and Clinton friend Ron Brown, Clinton's speechwriters wrote remarks for him that included a verse from Isaiah. When Clinton saw the passage, he said, "Oh this is Isaiah 40:31. It sounds like the New English translation. I prefer the King James version myself. That's the one I'll use."[20] In the speech, he quoted his preferred version of the verse from memory. Similarly, when some Christian leaders told him that they were praying for Clinton and cited a verse from I Chronicles, Clinton corrected them, saying the passage in question was actually from II Chronicles.

Clinton would also impress Jewish visitors with his knowledge. In advance of his speech noting the first ever peace deal with Israel and the Palestinians, Clinton said he read the entire Book of Joshua in preparation, which inspired him "to wear a blue tie with golden horns, which reminded me of those Joshua had used to blow down the walls of Jericho. Now the horns would herald the coming of peace that would return Jericho to the Palestinians."[21] After the death of Yitzhak Rabin, Clinton also went Biblical, citing the Torah portion of that week and its story of Abraham's willingness to sacrifice his son, Yitzhak (Isaac), out of devotion to the Lord.

Clinton was followed by George W. Bush, who also liked to cite the Bible. Bush read the entire Bible annually and would cite it to make political points. In one instance, he dodged a question on gay marriage by saying, "I shouldn't be taking a speck out of someone else's eye when I have a log in my own," which is a reference to Matthew 7:3.[22] The presidents since Bush have not been as devoted to the Bible. Obama explained his biblical reading in his book *The Audacity of Hope*, writing, "When I read the Bible, I do so with the belief that it is not a static text but the Living Word and that I must continually be open to new revelations—whether they come from a lesbian friend or a doctor."[23] He did read a daily devotional given to him by his faith-based director Joshua DuBois, but the devotional included thoughts from non-religious figures such as Johnny Cash and Nina Simone.

To the extent that Donald Trump has interacted with the Bible, it has generally been in the context of missteps. He did wave his own copy the Bible, a gift from his mother, at the Values Voter Summit in 2015, saying. "I brought my Bible!"[24] When asked in an interview that year to name his favorite Biblical verse, he did not offer any. When asked whether he preferred the Old or the New Testament, he said, "Probablyyyyyy, equal," adding, "The whole Bible is incredible."[25] More memorably, he flubbed a Bible reference at Liberty University in January of 2016, citing "two Corinthians," instead of "second Corinthians," which someone literate in the Bible would be more apt to say.[26]

As president, he was actually sworn in on two Bibles, a rarity, both the copy that his mother had given to him as well as Abraham Lincoln's Bible. But his most prominent presidential Bible moment was during the post-George Floyd unrest in the summer of 2020. Trump walked from the White House with an entourage to St. John's Church, where nearly every president has worshipped. His daughter Ivanka handed him a Bible from her purse and Trump held it up without opening it. NBC's Kristen Welker asked him, "Is that your Bible?" Trump's response: "It's a Bible." He did not hold it upside down, as some outlets reported, but it was a bad moment nonetheless.[27]

As for Joe Biden, he did cite the Bible in his inaugural address, quoting Psalms 30:5, "Weeping may endure for a night, but joy cometh in the morning."[28] In this, Biden was in line with recent presidents, who surprisingly have been more apt to quote the Bible in inaugural addresses than nineteenth century presidents. In the twenty-nine inaugural addresses from George Washington through William McKinley's second in 1901, eleven cited the Bible. Out of the thirty speeches since then, twenty-three presidents have cited the Bible. This increase in frequency makes sense in an increasingly disaggregated society in which we have fewer and fewer common reference points. Over the course of two centuries, American presidents have relied on a variety of sources of information and inspiration. As Americans moved away from the printed word and towards broadcast and screen technology, we have seen the advent of radio, records, movies, TV, CDs, iPods, YouTube, Twitter, iPads, TikTok, and so much more. And yet, despite all of these changes, the best source for inspiration—for presidents and everyone else—remains the Bible.

CHAPTER FIFTEEN

Correspondence between Hebrew Congregations and George Washington

George Washington's election as the nation's first president was certified on April 6, 1789, and he was sworn into office on April 30 at Federal Hall in New York City. An initial effort made that year to coordinate the drafting of a congratulatory letter from the nation's Jewish communities to be sent to President Washington failed. The following spring, the Mickve Israel Congregation in Savannah, Georgia, took the initiative to congratulate Washington on their own terms. In June, the Shearith Israel Congregation in New York City sent a letter to Jewish congregations in Newport, Rhode Island; Philadelphia, Pennsylvania; Richmond, Virginia; and Charleston, South Carolina, asking for their input and willingness to be included in an address sent to President Washington. Moses Seixas of the Touro Synagogue of Congregation Yeshuat Israel in Newport responded by saying that the New York congregation should have congratulated Washington much earlier, and expressed reservations about joining the letter. Later that summer, he wrote to Washington on behalf of his own congregation. Leaders of the Charleston congregation initially responded favorably to the request from New York, but hearing little in response, wrote again to ask that their name be removed from the letter. This request was not sent quickly enough, and the address was presented to President Washington on December 13, 1790.

Levi Sheftall, President of the Mickve Israel Congregation in Savannah, Georgia, to George Washington, May 1790.[1]

Sir,

We have long been anxious of congratulating you on your appointment by unanimous approbation to the Presidential dignity of this country, and of testifying our unbounded confidence in your integrity and unblemished virtue: Yet, however exalted the station you now fill, it is still not equal to the merit of your heroic services through an arduous and dangerous conflict, which has embosomed you in the hearts of her citizens.

Our eccentric situation added to a diffidence founded on the most profound respect has thus long prevented our address, yet the delay has realised anticipation, given us an opportunity of presenting our grateful acknowledgements for the benedictions of Heaven through the energy of federal influence, and the equity of your administration.

Your unexampled liberality and extensive philanthropy have dispelled that cloud of bigotry and superstition which has long, as a veil, shaded religion—unrivetted the fetters of enthusiasm—enfranchised us with all the privileges and immunities of free citizens, and initiated us into the grand mass of legislative mechanism. By example you have taught us to endure the ravages of war with manly fortitude, and to enjoy the blessings of peace with reverence to the Deity, and benignity and love to our fellow-creatures.

May the great Author of worlds grant you all happiness—an uninterrupted series of health—addition of years to the number of your days and a continuance of guardianship to that freedom, which, under the auspices of Heaven, your magnanimity and wisdom have given these States.

George Washington to the Hebrew Congregation in Savannah, Georgia, June 14, 1790.[2]

Gentlemen,

I thank you with great sincerity for your congratulations on my appointment to the office, which I have the honor to hold by the unanimous choice of my fellow-citizens: and especially for the expressions which you are pleased to use in testifying the confidence that is reposed in me by your congregation.

As the delay which has naturally intervened between my election and your address has afforded an opportunity for appreciating the merits of the federal-government, and for communicating your sentiments of its administration—I have rather to express my satisfaction than regret at a circumstance, which demonstrates (upon experiment) your attachment to the former as well as approbation of the latter.

I rejoice that a spirit of liberality and philanthropy is much more prevalent than it formerly was among the enlightened nations of the earth; and that your brethren will benefit thereby in proportion as it shall become still more extensive. Happily the people of the United States of America have, in many instances, exhibited examples worthy of imitation—The salutary influence of which will doubtless extend much farther, if gratefully enjoying those blessings of peace which (under favor of Heaven) have been obtained by fortitude in war, they shall conduct themselves with reverence to the Deity, and charity towards their fellow-creatures.

May the same wonder-working Deity, who long since delivering the Hebrews from their Egyptian Oppressors planted them in the promised land—whose providential agency has lately been conspicuous in establishing these United States as an independent nation—still continue to water them with the dews of Heaven and to make the inhabitants of every denomination participate in the temporal and spiritual blessings of that people whose God is Jehovah.

Moses Seixas, Warden of the Touro Synagogue of Congregation Yeshuat Israel of Newport, Rhode Island, to George Washington, August 17, 1790.[3]

Permit the children of the Stock of Abraham to approach you with the most cordial affection and esteem for your person & merits—and to join with our fellow Citizens in welcoming you to New Port.

With pleasure we reflect on those days—those days of difficulty, & danger when the God of Israel, who delivered David from the peril of the sword, shielded your head in the day of battle: and we rejoice to think, that the same Spirit who rested in the Bosom of the greatly beloved Daniel enabling him to preside over the Provinces of the Babylonish Empire, rests and ever will rest upon you, enabling you to discharge the arduous duties of Chief Magistrate in these States.

Deprived as we heretofore have been of the invaluable rights of free Citizens, we now (with a deep sense of gratitude to the Almighty disposer of all events) behold a Government, erected by the Majesty of the People—a Government, which to bigotry gives no sanction, to persecution no assistance—but generously affording to All liberty of conscience, and immunities of Citizenship: deeming every one, of whatever Nation, tongue, or language, equal parts of the great governmental Machine: This so ample and extensive Federal Union whose basis is Philanthropy, Mutual Confidence and Publick Virtue, we cannot but acknowledge to be the work of the Great God, who ruleth in the Armies Of Heaven and among the Inhabitants of the Earth, doing whatever seemeth him good.

For all the Blessings of civil and religious liberty which we enjoy under an equal and benign administration, we desire to send up our thanks to the Antient of Days, the great preserver of Men—beseeching him, that the Angel who conducted our forefathers through the wilderness into the promised land, may graciously conduct you through all the difficulties and dangers of this mortal life: and, when like Joshua full of days and full of honour, you are gathered to your Fathers, may you be admitted into the Heavenly Paradise to partake of the water of life, and the tree of immortality.

George Washington to the Hebrew Congregation in Newport, Rhode Island, August 18, 1790.[4]

Gentlemen.

While I receive, with much satisfaction, your Address replete with expressions of affection and esteem; I rejoice in the opportunity of assuring you, that I shall always retain a grateful remembrance of the cordial welcome I experienced in my visit to Newport, from all classes of Citizens.

The reflection on the days of difficulty and danger which are past is rendered the more sweet, from a consciousness that they are succeeded by days of uncommon prosperity and security. If we have wisdom to make the best use of the advantages with which we are now favored, we cannot fail, under the just administration of a good Government, to become a great and a happy people.

The Citizens of the United States of America have a right to applaud themselves for having given to mankind examples of an enlarged and liberal policy: a policy worthy of imitation. All possess alike liberty of conscience and immunities of citizenship. It is now no more that toleration is spoken of, as if it was by the indulgence of one class of people, that another enjoyed the exercise of their inherent natural rights. For happily the Government of the United States, which gives to bigotry no sanction, to persecution no assistance requires only that they who live under its protection should demean themselves as good citizens, in giving it on all occasions their effectual support.

It would be inconsistent with the frankness of my character not to avow that I am pleased with your favorable opinion of my Administration, and fervent wishes for my felicity. May the Children of the Stock of Abraham, who dwell in this land, continue to merit and enjoy the good will of the other Inhabitants; while every one shall sit in safety under his own vine and figtree, and there shall be none to make him afraid. May the father of all mercies scatter light and not darkness in our paths, and make us all in our several vocations useful here, and in his own due time and way everlastingly happy.

Hebrew Congregations of Philadelphia, New York, Charleston, and Richmond to George Washington, December 13, 1790.[5]

It is reserved for you to unite in affection for your Character And Person, every political and religious denomination of Men; and in this will the Hebrew Congregations aforesaid, yield to no class of their fellow Citizens.

We have been hitherto prevented by various circumstances peculiar to our situation from adding our congratulations to those which the rest of America have offerd on your elevation to the Chair of the Fœderal governmt. Deign then illustrious Sir, to Accept this our homage.

The wonders which the Lord of Hosts hath worked in the days of our Forefathers, have taught us to observe the greatness of his wisdom and his might, throughout the events of the late glorious revolution; and while we humble ourselves at his footstool in thanksgiving and praise for the blessing of his deliverance; we acknowledge you the Leader of the American Armies as his chosen and beloved servant; But not to your Sword alone is our present happiness to be ascribed; That indeed opend the way to the reign of Freedom, but never was it perfectly secure, till your hand gave birth to the Fœderal Constitution, and you renounced the joys of retirement to Seal by your administration in Peace, what you had achieved in war.

To 'the eternal God who is thy refuge', we Commit in our prayer the care of thy precious Life, and when full of years Thou shall be gatherd unto the People 'thy righteousness shall go before thee', and we shall remember amidst our regret, that the Lord hath set apart the Godly for himself; whilst thy name and thy Virtues will remain an indelible memorial on our minds.

George Washington to the Hebrew Congregations of Philadelphia, New York, Charleston, and Richmond, December 13, 1790.[6]

Gentlemen,

The liberality of sentiment toward each other which marks every political and religious denomination of men in this Country, stands unparalleled in the history of Nations. The affection of such people is a treasure beyond the reach of calculation; and the repeated proofs which my fellow Citizens have given of their attachment to me, and approbation of my doings form the purest source of my temporal felicity. The affectionate expressions of your address again excite my gratitude, and receive my warmest acknowledgments.

The Power and Goodness of the Almighty were strongly Manifested in the events of our late glorious revolution; and his kind interposition in our behalf has been no less visible in the establishment of our present equal government. In war he directed the Sword; and in peace he has ruled in our Councils. My agency in both has been guided by the best intentions, and a sense of the duty which I owe my Country: and as my exertions have hitherto been amply rewarded by the Approbation of my fellow Citizens, I shall endeavour to deserve a continuance of it by my future conduct.

May the same temporal and eternal blessings which you implore for me, rest upon your Congregations.

CHAPTER SIXTEEN

Abraham Lincoln's Biblical Meditation in the Second Inaugural Address

Daniel L. Dreisbach

As the sun broke through the clouds shortly after noon on a drizzly March 4, 1865, Abraham Lincoln, with one hand raised and the other on an open Bible, took the presidential oath of office for the second time.[1] He then added "so help me God," bent forward, and kissed the Bible to conclude the solemn ceremony conducted on the East Portico of the US Capitol.[2] This had been preceded by a brief, six-minute address before an enthusiastic crowd.

Delivered in the waning days of a devastating national conflict that claimed the lives of an estimated 750,000 men, Lincoln's Second Inaugural Address is widely acclaimed as one of the most eloquent of all presidential addresses. Lincoln himself considered it one of his finest speeches, telling a political colleague it was "perhaps better than . . . any thing I have produced."[3] It is also among the shortest inaugural addresses, a little over seven hundred words in length. The artfully crafted speech is a model of brevity and profound simplicity.

Lincoln's Second Inaugural, like his speech at Gettysburg a year and a half earlier, resounds with Biblical themes, phrases, and rhythms.[4] It is a profoundly theological meditation on the ways and purposes of the Divine in a bitter conflict in which both sides prayed to the same God and solicited the same God's assistance. Biblical texts shaped Lincoln's understanding of God and His involvement in the affairs of men and nations. The God of Lincoln's rumination was the God of the Bible—both the Old and New Testaments—as evidenced by his multiple references to Scripture indicating his conceptions of God's nature, character, and conduct in history.

Lincoln was well acquainted with the English Bible, specifically the King James, or Authorized, Version of the Bible. Those who knew him best reported that he had an intimate and thorough knowledge of the Scriptures and was known to commit lengthy passages to memory. His biographer and friend of a quarter century, Isaac N. Arnold, recalled that Lincoln "knew the Bible by heart. There was not a clergyman to be found so familiar with it as he."[5]

American politicians have long deployed Biblical language in their public orations because, as an authoritative and sacred text, its mere invocation lends rhetorical weight to their words. The evocative use of Biblical language stirs an audience's religious imagination. Civic uses of Scripture, which sometimes mimic pulpit oratory, are calculated to capture an audience's attention (with, perhaps, the fear of God), arouse a righteous passion, solemnify a discourse, project an aura of transcendence and truth, emphasize the gravity of an idea or argument, and/or underscore an argument's moral implications.[6] In the Second Inaugural, Lincoln also drew on Scripture to gain insights into the character and purposes of God, especially as they pertain to His providential involvement in history.

America has produced no political figure more fluent in Biblical language or adept in appropriating the distinct vernacular and cadences of the King James Bible than Abraham Lincoln. In his study of Lincoln's religion, William J. Wolf observed that "[n]o President has ever had the detailed knowledge of the Bible that Lincoln had. No President has ever woven its thought and its rhythms into the warp and woof of his state papers as he did."[7] Biographer William E. Barton similarly remarked that Lincoln "read the Bible, honored it, quoted it freely, and it became so much a part of him as visibly and permanently to give shape to his literary style and to his habits of thought."[8]

In the Second Inaugural, Lincoln drew on the Bible and religious language in ways essential to the mission and message of the occasion. In its seven hundred words, he mentioned the Deity fourteen times, quoted the Bible four times (two of which he placed in quotation marks), referenced prayer three times, and explicitly mentioned the "Bible" one time.[9] Unlike the Gettysburg Address, which is replete with Biblical language and themes but contains no direct quotations from the Bible, at least forty-five words of the Second Inaugural are direct or approximate quotations from the King James Bible. In addition, several phrases, such as "bind up the nation's wounds" (Psalm 147:3) and care for the widow and orphan (James 1:27; Isaiah 1:17), were almost certainly inspired by the Jacobean Bible.

Although he was not the first president to quote Scripture in an inaugural address, no president before or since has used the Bible so substantively and extensively. Among the assembled throngs in Washington, DC, to witness Lincoln's inauguration in March 1865 was the former slave Frederick Douglass who famously quipped that the president's "address sounded more like a sermon than a state paper."[10] More recently, historian Ronald C. White Jr. called it Lincoln's "Sermon on the Mount."[11] And, indeed, the second half of the speech sounds more like a lay sermon than a political oration.

The speech opened a window into how Lincoln had come to view and understand God, the work of Divine will and providence in history, and the war that had torn the nation asunder. In *Lincoln's Greatest Speech: The Second Inaugural*, Ronald C. White Jr. argued that "God's providence is the prism through which [Lincoln] carefully refracted the meaning of the war. Lincoln points beyond himself and his generals to God as the primary actor in the war."[12] The speech is premised on a belief in a superintending providential agent who is firmly in control of the affairs of men and nations and dispenses judgment and facilitates reconciliation according to His Divine plan and will. The calamitous conflict that had engulfed the continent during the preceding four years could only be understood in the light of God's will.

How, then, does one understand God's will in the present conflict, given that, as Lincoln observed midway through the address, both sides "read the same Bible and pray to the same God, and each invokes His aid against the other"? Lincoln's contemplation of this conundrum marked a shift in his rhetoric, signaling an intent, perhaps, to speak about the nation's plight less as the commander-in-chief and more as theologian-in-chief. At this point, he turned to Scripture to inform his analysis and argument. Biblical themes of sin, judgment, atonement, redemption, and restoration figured prominently in the remainder of the address.

"It may seem strange," Lincoln said, that men would have the temerity "to ask a just God's assistance in wringing their bread from the sweat of other men's faces." This was a reference to mankind's fall and God's punishment for sin in Genesis 3:19. Lincoln rephrased the Biblical text to emphasize the moral offense of slavery. The sweat of one's brow is the source of one's property. In Lincoln's rendering, it is sinful to deny another (that is, the slave) the fruits of his labor. Herein lies the sin of slavery.

Lincoln did not linger long on this point before somewhat unexpectedly pivoting to Jesus's instruction from the "Sermon on the Mount" to "[j]udge not, that ye be not judged" (Matthew 7:1). In a slight revision, Lincoln inserted "let *us*" judge not and replaced the Biblical "ye" with "we," suggesting that blame for the sin of slavery extended beyond the Southern states. More important, this injunction was the hinge that turned the oration towards its climatic concluding expression of reconciliation: "With malice toward none, with charity for all."

Before reaching that resolution, though, he considered the consequences of this sin. He first acknowledged that "[t]he Almighty has His own purposes," which, once again, underscored God's place at the center of his analysis. He followed this with another one of Jesus's sayings: "Woe unto the world because of offenses; for it must needs be that offenses come, but woe to that man by whom the offense cometh" (Matthew 18:7; see also Luke 17:1). Dispensing judgment is among the purposes that believers ascribe to the Almighty, Lincoln observed. The offense (or sin) of "American Slavery" is surely followed by "woe," and the woe of this sin was the incalculable carnage and death of the "terrible war." The war, in short, was Divine judgment due to "both North and South" for the offense. Then, in words surely discomfiting to his audience, he warned that God's will may yet require more shed blood before "this mighty scourge of war... pass[es] away." Lest we complain about the horrible punishment God inflicted upon the nation for this offense, Lincoln recalled, in the words of Psalms 19:9, "the judgments of the Lord are true and righteous altogether."

Lincoln's use of phrase "American Slavery" indicates that the offense of which he spoke implicated both the North and South, sparing no American from blame. This contrasts with an earlier assertion that the "peculiar and powerful interest" of slavery localized in the Southern states was the "cause of the war." In the Gettysburg Address, and here, Lincoln implied that atonement for this besetting sin and regeneration for the nation were accomplished through the sacrificial shed blood and death of the "brave men" in the "great civil war."[13] In the atoning shed blood of this war, the old Union—corrupted by slavery—died, giving hope for a new birth and new life for the Union.

At its theological core, the Second Inaugural is a meditation on the inscrutable ways of Divine providence in human affairs. Lincoln was not the first president to ponder the place of providence in the life of the nation. A third of George Washington's First Inaugural Address, for example, was devoted to a reflection on the "providential agency" at work in the nation's founding. "These reflections, arising out of the present crisis," Washington declared, "have forced themselves too strongly on my mind to be suppressed."[14] John Quincy Adams was the first president to quote directly from the Scriptures in an inaugural address. He did so, quoting Psalms 127:1, in a closing prayer humbly supplicating for Divine favor and an "overruling providence."[15]

Lincoln's Second Inaugural Address offered a more nuanced and searching reflection on the role of providence in the affairs of nations. Historian Mark A. Noll wrote that Lincoln invoked Scripture "in order to make a profound public statement about the superiority of Divine providence over any partisan grasp of God's will."[16] As the war dragged on and the costs of the conflict mounted, the president turned with increasing frequency to this topic. He wrestled with why God had allowed a "terrible war" of such "magnitude" and "duration." In a private 1862 meditation on the "divine will" widely regarded by historians as anticipatory of the themes examined in the Second Inaugural, Lincoln wrote that each side in a great contest "claims to act in accordance with the will of God."[17]

But it is not possible that both represent God's will. "The prayers of both could not be answered," he opined in the Second Inaugural. Surely one party in this dispute (and perhaps both) was wrong. Indeed, he wrote in the 1862 meditation, "[i]n the present civil war it is quite possible that God's purpose is something different from the purpose of either party." The one thing that can be said with certainty is that "[t]he will of God prevails."[18] The perfect, yet inscrutable, will and ways of providence escape the ability of "erring mortals... to accurately perceive them," he wrote to Eliza P. Gurney in September 1864.[19] "The Almighty has His own purposes," the president affirmed as the central theme of his celebrated oration. And we can have confidence that the "will of God prevails" and the "judgments of the Lord are true and righteous altogether."

Shifting his focus to the future, Lincoln concluded the address with a humble, poetic plea to a people divided and devastated by war to eschew triumphalism and vindictiveness in victory and acrimony and recrimination in defeat. "With malice toward none, with charity for all, with firmness in the right as God gives us to see the right, let us strive on to finish the work we are in." He called on his countrymen to "bind up the nation's wounds" and to care for those left by the war widowed and fatherless. Only through the difficult work of reconciliation can there ever be a "just and lasting peace."

CHAPTER SEVENTEEN

President Roosevelt and Vice President Fairbanks to Attendees of the Exercises in Celebration of the Two Hundred and Fiftieth Anniversary of Jewish Settlement in America[1]

In April 1905, the Trustees of Congregation Shearith Israel in New York City established an executive committee to prepare for a celebration commemorating the 250th anniversary of the arrival of Jewish people to North America—specifically, the 1655 leave of settlement granted by the Dutch East India Company that allowed Jews to travel to, settle within, and trade in New Netherland. On November 30, 1905—Thanksgiving Day—crowds gathered in Carnegie Hall for a full program of addresses that began with and was punctuated by musical selections from Mendelssohn, Bruch, and Handel. The day ended with the chorus and audience singing "My Country 'Tis of Thee," a benediction given by the rabbi of New York's Congregation Rodeph Sholom, and the reading of a letter from President Theodore Roosevelt.

Theodore Roosevelt to Jacob H. Schiff, Chairman of the Executive Committee, November 16, 1905.

My Dear Sir:

I am forced to make a rule not to write letters on the occasion of any celebration, no matter how important, simply because I cannot write one without either committing myself to write hundreds of others or else running the risk of giving offense to worthy persons. I make an exception in this case because the lamentable and terrible suffering to which so many of the Jewish people in other lands have been subjected, makes me feel it my duty, as the head of the American people, not only to express my deep sympathy for them, as I now do, but at the same time to point out what fine qualities of citizenship have been displayed by the men of Jewish faith and race, who, having come to this country, enjoy the benefits of free institutions and equal treatment before the law. I feel very strongly that if any people are oppressed anywhere, the wrong inevitably reacts in the end on those who oppress them; for it is an immutable law in the spiritual world that no one can wrong others and yet in the end himself escape unhurt.

The celebration of the two hundred and fiftieth anniversary of the settlement of the Jews in the United States properly emphasizes a series of historical facts of more than merely national significance. Even in our colonial period the Jews participated in the upbuilding of this country, acquired citizenship, and took an active part in the development of foreign and domestic commerce. During the Revolutionary period they aided the cause of liberty by serving in the Continental army, and by substantial contributions to the empty treasury of the infant Republic. During the Civil War, thousands served in the armies and mingled their blood with the soil for which they fought. I am glad to be able to say, in addressing you on this occasion, that while the Jews of the United States, who now number more than a million, have remained loyal to their faith and their race traditions, they have become indissolubly incorporated in the great army of American citizenship, prepared to make all sacrifice for the country, either in war or peace, and striving for the perpetuation of good government and for the maintenance of the principles embodied in our Constitution. They are honorably distinguished by their industry, their obedience to law, and their devotion to the national welfare. They are engaged in generous rivalry with their fellow-citizens of other denominations in advancing the interests of our common country. This is true not only of the descendants of the early settlers and those of American birth, but of a great and constantly increasing proportion of those who have come to our shores within the last twenty-five years as refugees reduced to the direst straits of penury and misery. All Americans well may be proud of the extraordinary illustration of the wisdom and strength of our governmental system thus afforded. In a few years, men and women hitherto utterly unaccustomed to any of the privileges of citizenship have moved mightily upward toward the standard of loyal, self-respecting American citizenship; of that citizenship which not merely insists upon its rights, but also eagerly recognizes its duty to do its full share in the material, social, and moral advancement of the nation.

With all good wishes, believe me,

Sincerely yours,

Theodore Roosevelt

Charles Warren Fairbanks to Jacob H. Schiff, Chairman of the Executive Committee, November 30, 1905.

My dear Mr. Schiff:

I greatly regret my inability to participate with you to-day in celebrating the two hundred and fiftieth anniversary of the Jews in America. The event is one which we may all take pleasure in observing with appropriate ceremony, for the Jewish people have contributed and are contributing their full measure to our national growth and strength. They are enamored of our institutions and are a part of that loyal, intelligent, conservative citizenship which constitutes the stay and support of the Great Republic. Our hearts are filled with gratitude in this house of national thanksgiving that Jew and Gentile enjoy absolute political equality, and dwell together in amity and good fellowship throughout the limits of the United States. Here they entertain for each other a high degree of respect and good will, and rejoice in their common national inheritance. They are alike profoundly touched by the atrocities inflicted upon the Jews in Russia. They are moved by a common fraternal impulse to make their protest against this master crime of modern times, and send their aid and sympathy to those in sore distress. I entertain the confident hope that the Jews in America may continue to enjoy the fullest possible measure of prosperity and happiness, and that freedom in our common country may forever continue to bless both Jew and Gentile.

Very respectfully yours,

Charles W. Fairbanks

CHAPTER EIGHTEEN

Jewish Contributions to American Democracy

Speech delivered by President Calvin Coolidge at the laying of the cornerstone of the Jewish Community Center Building, Washington, DC, May 3, 1925.[1]

We have gathered this afternoon to lay with appropriate ceremony and solemnity the cornerstone of a temple. The splendid structure which is to rise here will be the home of the Jewish Community Center of Washington. It will be at once a monument to the achievements of the past, and a help in the expansion of these achievements into a wider field of usefulness in the future. About this institution will be organized, and from it will be radiated, the influences of the civic works in which the genius of the Jewish people has always found such eloquent expression. Such an establishment, so noble in its physical proportions, so generous in its social purposes, is truly a part of the civic endowment of the nation's capital. Beyond that, its existence here at the seat of the national government makes it in a peculiar way a testimony and an example before the entire country.

This year, 1925, is a year of national anniversaries. States, cities, and towns throughout all the older part of the country will be celebrating their varied parts in the historic events which a century and a half ago marked the beginning of the American Revolution. It will be a year of dedications and re-dedications. It will recall the heroic events from which emerged a great modern nation consecrated to liberty, equality, and human rights. It will remind us, as a nation, of how a common spiritual inspiration was potent to bring and mold and weld together into a national unity the many and scattered colonial communities that had been planted along the Atlantic seaboard. In a time when the need of that unification, understanding, and tolerance which are necessary to a national spirit is so great, it will recall the fact that the Fathers not only confronted these same problems in forms far more difficult than they are today, but also solved them.

Among the peoples of the 13 colonies there were few ties of acquaintance, of commercial or industrial interest. There were great differences in political sentiments, even within the local communities, while there were wide divergencies among the several colonies, in origin, in religion, in social outlook.

If we would seek a fairly accurate impression of conditions at the beginning of the Revolution, we must attempt a really continental view of North America as it was in 1775. The group of new-born commonwealths, which we commonly refer to as "the original 13 colonies," and which in our minds represent a considerable measure of nationality already achieved, did not in fact even know that they would be 13 in number. No man, on the day of Lexington, could be altogether sure that the Revolution was more than a New England affair. It might or it might not draw the middle and southern colonies into its armed array of resistance. On the other hand, the 13 might have been joined by Canada, which was British in sovereignty, but chiefly French in population; by Florida and Louisiana, which were both mainly Spanish. In short, there might have been 14, 15, or 16 original colonies participating in the North American revolution against Europe, or there might have been less than a half dozen of them.

At that time, France had no territory within continental North America. But this condition had existed for only a short time since the end of the Seven Years' War. France had by no means become reconciled to this exclusion from a part in the North American empire; and only a little later, in the year 1800, under a new treaty with Spain, resumed the sovereignty of the Mississippi Valley. Three years after this, benefiting by the fortunes of the Napoleonic wars, President Jefferson confronted and promptly seized the opportunity to buy Louisiana from Napoleon. Even then, many years were yet to pass before the last claims of Spain should be extinguished from this continent.

I have recounted these scraps of territorial history, because unless we keep them in mind we shall not at all comprehend the task of unification, of nation building, that the Revolutionary fathers undertook when they not only dared the power of Great Britain, but set themselves against the tradition of the subordination to Europe of America. As we look back, we realize that even among the colonies of England there were few and doubtful common concerns to bind them together. Their chief commercial interests were not among themselves, but with the mother country across the Atlantic. New England was predominantly Puritan, the southern colonies were basically cavalier. New York was in the main Dutch. Pennsylvania had been founded by the Quakers, while New Jersey needed to go back but a short distance to find its beginnings in a migration from Sweden.

There were well-nigh as many divergencies of religious faith as there were of origin, politics and geography. Yet, in the end, these religious differences proved rather unimportant. While the early dangers in some colonies made a unity in belief and all else a necessity to existence, at the bottom of the colonial character lay a stratum of religious liberalism which had animated most of the early comers. From its beginnings, the new continent had seemed destined to be the home of religious tolerance. Those who claimed the right of individual choice for themselves had to grant it to others. Beyond that—and this was one of the factors which I think weighed heaviest on the side of unity—the Bible was the one work of literature that was common to all of them. The Scriptures were read and studied everywhere. There are many testimonies that their teachings became the most important intellectual and spiritual force for unification. I remember to have read somewhere, I think in the writings of the historian Lecky, the observation that "Hebraic mortar cemented the foundations of American democracy." Lecky had in mind this very influence of the Bible in drawing together the feelings and sympathies of the widely scattered communities. All the way from New Hampshire to Georgia, they found a common ground of faith and reliance in the scriptural writings.

In those days books were few, and even those of a secular character were largely the product of a scholarship which used the Scriptures as the model and standard of social interpretation. It was to this, of course, that Lecky referred. He gauged correctly a force too often underestimated and his observation was profoundly wise. It suggests, in a way which none of us can fail to understand, the debt which the young American people owed to the sacred writing that the Hebrew people gave to the world.

This biblical influence was strikingly impressive in all the New England colonies, and only less so in the others. In the Connecticut code of 1650, the Mosaic model is adopted. The magistrates were authorized to administer justice "according to the laws here established, and, for want of them, according to the word of God." In the New Haven code of 1655, there were 79 topical statutes for the Government, half of which contained references to the Old Testament. The founders of the New Haven colony, John Davenport and Theophilus Eaton, were expert Hebrew scholars. The extent to which they leaned upon the moral and administrative system laid down by the Hebrew lawgivers was responsible for their conviction that the Hebrew language and literature ought to be made as familiar as possible to all the people. So it was that John Davenport arranged that the Hebrew language should be taught in the first public school in New Haven. The preachers of those days, saturated in the religion and literature of the Hebrew prophets, were leaders, teachers, moral mentors, and even political philosophers for their flocks. A people raised under such leadership, given to so much study and contemplation of the Scriptures, inevitably became more familiar with the great figures of Hebrew history—with Joshua, Samuel, Moses, Joseph, David, Solomon, Gideon, Elisha—than they were with the stories of their own ancestors as recorded in the pages of profane history.

The sturdy old divines of those days found the Bible a chief source of illumination for their arguments in support of the patriot cause. They knew the Book. They were profoundly familiar with it, and eminently capable in the exposition of all its justifications for rebellion. To them, the record of the exodus from Egypt was indeed an inspired precedent. They knew what arguments from holy writ would most powerfully influence their people. It requires no great stretch of logical processes to demonstrate that the Children of Israel, making bricks without straw in Egypt, had their modern counterpart in the people of the colonies, enduring the imposition of taxation without representation!

And the Jews themselves, of whom a considerable number were already scattered throughout the colonies, were true to the teachings of their own prophets. The Jewish faith is predominantly the faith of liberty. From the beginnings of the conflict between the colonies and the mother country, they were overwhelmingly on the side of the rising revolution. You will recognize them when I read the names of some among the merchants who unhesitatingly signed the non-importation resolution of 1765: Isaac Moses, Benjamin Levy, Samson Levy, David Franks, Joseph Jacobs, Hayman Levy Jr., Matthias Bush, Michael Gratz, Bernard Gratz, Isaac Franks, Moses Mordecai, Benjamin Jacobs, Samuel Lyon, and Manual Mordechai Noah[sic].

Not only did the colonial Jews join early and enthusiastically in the non-intercourse program, but when the time came for raising and sustaining an army, they were ready to serve wherever they could be most useful. There is a romance in the story of Haym Salomon, Polish Jew financier of the Revolution. Born in Poland, he was made prisoner by the British forces in New York, and when he escaped set up in business in Philadelphia. He negotiated for Robert Morris all the loans raised in France and Holland, pledged his personal faith and fortune for enormous amounts, and personally advanced large sums to such men as James Madison, Thomas Jefferson, Baron Steuben, General St. Clair, and many other patriot leaders who testified that without his aid they could not have carried on in the cause.

A considerable number of Jews became officers in the continental forces. The records show at least four Jews as lieutenant-colonels, three as majors and certainly six, probably more, as captains. Major Benjamin Nones has been referred to as the Jewish Lafayette. He came from France in 1777, enlisted in the Continentals as a volunteer private, served on the staffs of both Washington and Lafayette, and later was attached to the command of Baron de Kalb, in which were a number of Jews. When de Kalb was fatally wounded in the thickest of the fighting at the Battle of Camden, the three officers who were at hand to bear him from the field were Major Nones, Captain de la Motta, and Captain Jacob de Leon, all of them Jews. It is interesting to know that at the time of the Revolution there was a larger Jewish element in the southern colonies than would have been found there at most periods; and these Jews of the Carolinas and Georgia were ardent supporters of the Revolution. One corps of infantry raised in Charleston, South Carolina, was composed preponderantly of Jews, and they gave a splendid account of themselves in the fighting in that section.

It is easy to understand why a people with the historic background of the Jews should thus overwhelmingly and unhesitatingly have allied themselves with the cause of freedom. From earliest colonial times, America has been a new land of promise to this long-persecuted race.

The Jewish community of the United States is not only the second most numerous in the world, but in respect of its Old World origins it is probably the most cosmopolitan. But whatever their origin as a people, they have always come to us, eager to adapt themselves to our institutions, to thrive under the influence of liberty, to take their full part as citizens in building and sustaining the nation, and to bear their part in its defense, in order to make a contribution to the national life, fully worthy of the traditions they had inherited.

The institution for which we are today dedicating this splendid home, is not a charity to minister to the body, but rather to the soul. The 14,000 Jews who live in this capital city have passed, under the favoring auspices of American institutions, beyond the need for any other benevolence.

They are planting here a home for community service; fixing a center from which shall go forth the radiations of united effort for advancement in culture, in education, in social opportunity. Here will be the seat of organized influence for the preservation and dissemination of all that is best and most useful, of all that is leading and enlightening, in the culture and philosophy of this "peculiar people" who have so greatly given to the advancement of humanity.

Our country has done much for the Jews who have come here to accept its citizenship and assume their share of its responsibilities in the world. But I think the greatest thing it has done for them has been to receive them and treat them precisely as it has received and treated all others who have come to it. If our experiment in free institutions has proved anything, it is that the greatest privilege that can be conferred upon people in the mass is to free them from the demoralizing influence of privilege enjoyed by the few. This is proved by the experience here, not alone of the Jews, but of all the other racial and national elements that have entered into the making of this Nation. We have found that when men and women are left free to find the places for which they are best fitted, some few of them will indeed attain less exalted stations than under a regime of privilege; but that the vast multitude will rise to a higher level, to wider horizons, to worthier attainments.

To go forward on the same broadening lines that have marked the national development thus far must be our aim. It is an easy thing to say, but not so simple to do. There is no straight and smooth and posted highway into the vast, dim realm of the tomorrows. There are bogs and morasses, blind roads and bad detours. No philosophy of history has ever succeeded in charting accurately the day of the future. No science of social engineering has been able to build wide and easy roads by which to bring up the van of human progress in sure and easy marches. The race is always pioneering. It always has been and always must be. It dare not tire of unending effort and repeated disappointments. It must not in any moment of weariness or inertia cease from pressing on. Least of all can we indulge the satisfactions of complacency, imagining that the sum of useful progress has been attained. The community or the civilization that ceases to progress begins that hour to recede.

The work of spiritual unification is not completed. Factional, sectional, social and political lines of conflict yet persist. Despite all experience, society continues to engender the hatreds and jealousies whereof are born domestic strife and international conflicts. But education and enlightenment are breaking their force. Reason is emerging. Every inheritance of the Jewish people, every teaching of their secular history and religious experience, draws them powerfully to the side of charity, liberty and progress. They have always been arrayed on this side, and we may be sure they will not desert it. Made up of so many diverse elements, our country must cling to those fundamentals that have been tried and proved as buttresses of national solidarity.

It must be our untiring effort to maintain, to improve, and, so far as may be humanly possible, to perfect those institutions which have proved capable of guaranteeing our unity, and strengthening us in advancing the estate of the common man. This edifice which you are rearing here is a fine example for other communities. It speaks a purpose to uphold an ancient and noble philosophy of life and living, and yet to assure that such philosophy shall always be adapted to the requirements of changing times, increasing knowledge and developing institutions. It is a guarantee that you will keep step with liberty.

This capacity for adaptation in detail, without sacrifice of essentials, has been one of the special lessons which the marvelous history of the Jewish people has taught. It is a lesson which our country, and every country based on the principle of popular government, must learn and apply, generation by generation, year by year, yes, even day by day. You are raising here a testimonial to the capacity of the Jewish people to do this. In the advancing years, as those who come and go shall gaze upon this civic and social landmark, may it be a constant reminder of the inspiring service that has been rendered to civilization by men and women of the Jewish faith. May they recall the long array of those who have been eminent in statecraft, in science, in literature, in art, in the professions, in business, in finance, in philanthropy, and in the spiritual life of the world. May they pause long enough to contemplate that the patriots who laid the foundation of this Republic drew their faith from the Bible. May they give due credit to the people among whom the Holy Scriptures came into being. And as they ponder the assertion that "Hebraic mortar cemented the foundations of American democracy," they cannot escape the conclusion that if American democracy is to remain the greatest hope of humanity, it must continue abundantly in the faith of the Bible.

PART FOUR

The Meaning of Jewish History for Americans

CHAPTER NINETEEN

Why Study American Jewish History?

Jonathan D. Sarna

For many years, history held a central place in the curriculum of the Jewish school. Lady Katie Magnus's *Outlines of Jewish History*, the first book issued by the Jewish Publication Society (1890), was the textbook of choice, and it taught readers unabashedly heroic history, filled with sentiment, homily, and romance. Its aim was to turn students into "loyal and steadfast witnesses"—to keep them true to their faith.[1]

History still constituted "the chief subject of study in the Jewish Sunday school" in 1932. A study by Julius B. Maller entitled *Testing the Knowledge of Jewish History*, published that year by the Union of American Hebrew Congregations, called for the "reconstruction of the history curriculum in the Jewish school, with a shifting of emphasis from dates and names to interpretation." Where Lady Magnus was primarily concerned with maintaining Jewish loyalty, Maller stressed that the "ultimate aim" of Jewish history was "to enrich the inner life of the Jewish child."[2] He explained that Jewish history:

> deals with true stories of Jews who lived, struggled and exerted their influence, who were instrumental in making things better or worse. If the teacher succeeds in making the past living and real to his pupils, they will learn the good that has resulted from acts of loyalty and integrity. They will realize why there were martyrs, why these men

> deserve our recognition and gratitude. After the children will have long forgotten most of the dates and names connected with the various periods of Jewish history, their understanding of the significance of these periods will remain. This understanding, which will probably continue to influence their behavior in later life, is one of the ultimate aims of Jewish education.[3]

The object of Jewish history, according to this view, was to create role models for Jewish children; to provide them with heroes from the past with whom they might identify and seek to emulate.

American Jewish history, when it entered the school curriculum, fell heir to all of these various goals. It sought to instill pride, promote loyalty, and create effective Jewish role models for young people to follow. In addition, the first high-school textbook in American Jewish history, Lee Levinger's *A History of the Jews in the United States* (1930), aimed to create "intelligent American Jews" who understood their home environment. The Jewish school, Levinger insisted, needed to compensate for the fact that there was "seldom much mention of the Jews" in the American history curriculum that students studied in public school.[4]

Notwithstanding all of these high-minded aims, history over the ensuing decades lost out in the competition for space within the Jewish school curriculum. Today, Bible, Hebrew, and holidays form the central themes of Jewish education; Jewish history, and especially American Jewish history, are neglected. Some teachers, seeing how little attention is paid to history in the secular curriculum, wonder why they should be teaching Jewish history at all.

Scholars have recently proposed a variety of new answers to the question of why Jewish history, and especially American Jewish history, should be taught. Their arguments may be summarized as follows:

- American Jewish history contextualizes contemporary challenges facing American Jews. It helps American Jews understand where they are by showing them where they have been and allows them better to appreciate what sets them apart both as Americans and as Jews.

- American Jewish history deepens students' understanding of America and shows them how their ancestors fit into the larger picture of American society.
- American Jewish history broadens students' horizons, helping them to appreciate different ways of life, different points of view, and the impact of change over time.
- American Jewish history teaches students how to read, understand, and internalize primary source texts.
- American Jewish history helps to deepen attachments to Judaism and the Jewish people.
- American Jewish history communicates the enduring power of religion in America and shows how Jews have formulated religious identity in a distinctively pluralistic setting.
- American Jewish history bridges the gap between collective experiences and personal stories. It helps students find the links between their own histories and the history of the Jewish people as a whole.
- American Jewish history encourages students to integrate Jewish and secular studies by forging chronological and conceptual links between them.
- American Jewish history is a form of collective Jewish memory, and as such a vital part of Jewish identity.
- American Jewish history offers students tools to think historically about what constitutes the Jewish family, Jewish space, Jewish religion, and Jewish work, how they themselves relate to these concepts, and ultimately what it means to be an American Jew.
- American Jewish history helps Jews appreciate the common past shared with other American Jews.
- American Jewish history helps provide Jews with a master story that unites them both vertically with their ancestors in

previous eras and horizontally with Jews who live in other communities. It makes them appreciate that they are part of something much larger than themselves and creates a shared sense of community.

- American Jewish history forms the basis for the shared Jewish memories that are basic to both Jewish identity and Jewish community.

Several of these objectives apply to all forms of history instruction.[5] The study of the past, these scholars suggest, places present-day problems in perspective and teaches valuable textual and evidentiary skills that students can put to practical use later in life. Other objectives might be used to justify teaching American Jewish history in a non-Jewish setting, as part of the American experience as a whole. The overwhelming majority, however, justify the teaching of American Jewish history on the basis of Jewish identity formation. The aim of American Jewish history teaching, they claim, is to link Jews one to another, to create shared Jewish memories, and to promote community.

Deepening students' Jewish identity is, of course, a noble endeavor, but using American Jewish history as the vehicle to accomplish this aim raises significant problems. What do we do, for example, about unpleasant facts: criminality, slaveholding, intermarriage, or even (for those who teach in a non-Orthodox setting) the postwar resurgence of Orthodoxy? How, moreover, will students react later in life when they learn the more complex realities of the American Jewish experience; will they feel that their religious educators betrayed them? Even now, are we providing students with a portrait of American Jewish history that is as multi-faceted and self-critical as their curriculum in American history? And, if not, what message are we unintentionally conveying—not just about American Jewish history but about Jewish education in general?

One prominent educator argues that "history is only meaningful when it becomes memory" and that the task of Jewish educators is to "give life to Jewish history by translating it into memory for our students."[6]

This, again, sounds like a noble goal, but as readers of Yosef Hayim Yerushalmi's *Zakhor: Jewish History and Jewish Memory* (1982) know the relationship between Jewish history and Jewish memory is anything but simple. Memory, after all, plays tricks; it is fleeting, selective, and highly subjective. Students need to learn how to distinguish history from memory; the distinction is essential to critical thinking. Chanukah, for example, is part of Jewish history; the so-called Chanukah miracle, the cruse of oil that kindled for eight days, is part of Jewish memory. Rabbi Judah Loew b. Bezalel of Prague (1525-1609) is part of Jewish history; the *golem* attributed to him (in a book published in 1909) is part of Jewish memory. Haym Salomon (1740-85) is part of Jewish history; his reputed funding of the American Revolution is part of Jewish memory. It is unquestionably important for educated Jews to absorb both Jewish history and Jewish memory, but the two should never be confused.

Elsewhere, I have spelled out a somewhat different set of reasons for teaching American Jewish history, placing less emphasis on identity and more on tensions and continuities within the American Jewish experience as a whole.[7] In rethinking the issue now, I am inclined to believe that there is yet another theme that deserves emphasis, one that those of us engaged in the study and teaching of American Jewish history too often take for granted, not realizing how much of an impression it can make upon our students. The theme is human potential—in our case, the ability of American Jews, young and old, men and women alike, to change the course of history and transform a piece of the world. American Jewish history is, after all, not just a record of events; it is the story of how people shaped events, establishing and maintaining communities, responding to challenges, working for change. That, perhaps, is the greatest lesson of all that American Jewish history can offer our students: that they too can make a difference; that the future is theirs to create.

CHAPTER TWENTY

What Jews Mean to America

Meir Y. Soloveichik

"Some people like Jews, and some do not." With these words Winston Churchill once divided humanity into two categories. Of these groups, Churchill certainly belonged to the former, so much so that a friend of his once reflected, "Even Winston had a fault; he was too fond of Jews." Churchill's own fondness for Jews, and wonder at Jewish history, was linked to his admiration of his predecessor as prime minister. In the same essay, Churchill cited Benjamin Disraeli as having said that "the Lord deals with the nations as the nations deal with the Jews." Churchill concluded, "We must admit that nothing that has since happened in the history of the world has falsified the truth of Disraeli's confident assertion."

Should we seek to summarize our current state of affairs, we could do worse than employ Churchill's words. Some people, very clearly, do not like Jews. On October 7, 2023—that very day, weeks before Israel even entered Gaza—rallies celebrating Hamas's massacre of Israelis could be found on the streets of American cities. Today, in my own neighborhood on Manhattan's Upper West Side, as I walk home from synagogue on the Sabbath, I am confronted by poster after poster of a hostage of Hamas that some fellow New Yorker has chosen to tear at, shred, or deface. As anti-Israeli hate consumed campuses, the blasé way in which the presidents of America's leading universities commented before Congress about the well-being of their own Jewish students reflected, as John Podhoretz, the editor of *Commentary*, wrote, "how unimportant the feelings or concerns of Jews are within the sociological landscapes they tend."

Yet in the face of this terrible trend, other events remind us of a striking feature of American life: Some people do like Jews, and in fact some like them a great deal. If one had told a Jew from several centuries ago that, in the year 2023, an antisemitic pogrom would take place and the attack would be celebrated by mobs around the world, this Jew would not have been at all surprised. Yet this Jew would have been astounded to learn that, in response to the celebration of this pogrom, one prominent political party of the most powerful country on earth summoned the presidents of some of the most important universities in the land to publicly admonish them for their failings as academic leaders. Such stories of stalwart, public defenses of Jews against a country's elites are not abundant in the annals of Jewish history.

Thus, the past terrible months have reminded us not only of the endurance of antisemitism, but also of the remarkable way in which both the state of the Jews and the Jewish state are a prominent preoccupation in American public life. As the (non-Jewish) *Wall Street Journal* columnist Walter Russell Mead has commented, the Jewish past and future maintain "a distinctive place in American historical consciousness and political thought." Israel, Mead remarks, may be "a speck on the map of the world," but it "occupies a continent in the American mind." After two millennia of persecution experienced by Jews at the hands of others, it remains a wonder that a multitude of Americans—almost certainly many millions—ardently embrace their own version of Disraeli's dictum, that God will treat America as it treats the Jews.

What this means is that the debates suffusing the halls of academia and Congress regarding Israel, and the place of Jews in American society, tell us even more about Gentiles than about Jews. It bespeaks two different trends within the West, and two very different possibilities for its future. Understanding why this is so requires us to study the story of the Jews in the West, and to grasp why the current moment offers a clarion call for those who care about the Western future—and the place of America within it.

What is the West? The historian Niall Ferguson, in his brilliant book *Civilization: The West and the Rest*, notes that the term has a certain elasticity. By "the West," some refer to the intellectual achievements that began in ancient Athens, others to the civilization that rose from the ruins of Rome and its empire; others look later, to the technological and economic advancements in the second millennium, which ultimately made possible Europe's profound impact on the world. Still others look even later, to the emergence of liberal democracy in the eighteenth century.

What is clear is that Jews existed long before the impact of Athens or Rome was felt in the world. Unsurprisingly, it was Mark Twain who found a pithy way to express this:

> The Egyptian, the Babylonian, and the Persian rose, filled the planet with sound and splendor, then faded to dream-stuff and passed away; the Greek and the Roman followed, and made a vast noise, and they are gone; other peoples have sprung up and held their torch high for a time, but it burned out, and they sit in twilight now, or have vanished. The Jew saw them all, beat them all, and is now what he always was.

The West's relationship with the Jews has always begun, subconsciously or explicitly, with a query: Why are they still here? As the Roman Empire embraced a new faith and what we call Christendom began to emerge, the question of Jewish endurance became particularly perplexing. Much of the moral vision of the Hebrew Bible, embodied above all by the Ten Commandments, lay at the heart of post-pagan, Christian civilization. But the very same Hebraic Scripture spoke of a Jewish ingathering in a rebuilt Jerusalem, and this had certainly not occurred; Jerusalem had been sacked by Rome in 70 CE, and Jews were forbidden even to enter the city. The Church understood itself as the new Israel, with the Biblical promises to God's chosen made manifest in its own success; yet Jews undeniably remained. The phenomenon was squarely addressed by the greatest Christian mind to emerge out of the ruins of the Roman Empire. Augustine of Hippo put it plainly: "Jews are not admitted into their city, and yet Jews there are."

Why, then, were there still Jews? For Augustine, Jewish endurance was indeed a miracle, but one that bespoke the Jewish loss of chosenness. Providence, for Augustine, had preserved the Jews as an eternal testament to the truth of Christianity. As deniers of the gospel, they were to be denied access to Jerusalem and to political restoration; but, just as Cain in Genesis was exiled by the Almighty but also protected by Him, Christians were forbidden to harm Jews so that Jewish powerlessness would eternally testify to the gospel. To the Jews, Augustine applied a verse in the Psalms: "Slay them not, lest my people forget: scatter them by thy power, and bring them down."

While Augustine's interpretation was not, to put it mildly, a recipe for Jewish equality, it also expressly prohibited assaults on Jews. Given alternative explanations of Jewish endurance that were yet to come, it certainly could have been worse. There is some truth to the wry reflection of the Jewish philosopher Moses Mendelssohn that "but for Augustine's lovely brainwave we would have been exterminated long ago." Under Augustinian theology, Jews were allowed to live and, in certain constrained circumstances, even succeed. Augustine's approach became the dominant theology of the West when it was adopted by Pope Gregory in the sixth century, so that pagans were forced to accept Christianity but Jews were not.

This spiritual and social stasis did not last. In the high Middle Ages we find an explosion of vicious violence against Jews in Europe, setting a terrible trend for the next thousand years. At the same time, lies about Jews were born in Europe that festered and spread, lies that maintain a powerful purchase even today.

Why was it at this moment that such virulent Jew-hate emerged? The answers often focus on economic aspects of medieval Jewish life. Forbidden to engage in many trades, Jews often served as moneylenders and as financial middlemen between the members of the ruling class and their subjects; all this bred terrible resentment. But this explanation is insufficient. The hatred aimed at Jews in the Middle Ages targeted not only the Jews themselves but Judaism; the blood libel asserted that Jews used the blood of Christian children in their Passover celebrations, and in the courts of kings the Talmud was denounced as a threat to Christians. All this reflects a more theological element to antisemitism.

To truly understand this hatred, we must focus on a phenomenon that, for Ferguson, was the source of much conflict in Europe over centuries but that also set the stage for eventual Western dominance. In contrast to the empires of the East, medieval Europe featured a number of nation-states; this meant that diverse national identities developed in Europe and contested for supremacy. An inventive effervescence emerged from this rivalry, says Ferguson, leading to the development of weaponry and other technology as countries "all encouraged commerce, conquest and colonization as part of their competition with one another."

Ferguson notes how this fierce competition between national identities often resulted in war, presenting great dangers to "those who lived at the frontiers between the dozen or so bigger European states." This is true, but it was often even more dangerous for Jews within those states. Nations developing their own sense of identity and national pride looked to the Jewish people's mysterious endurance and were suddenly reminded of their own temporality and finitude. The great early-twentieth-century Jewish thinker Franz Rosenzweig described this phenomenon: "Just as every individual must reckon with his eventual death, the peoples of the world foresee their eventual extinction, be it however distant in time." A love of one's own nation, he reflected, is "pregnant with the presentiment of death." But in Jews, Rosenzweig writes, a nation is given a reminder that there is one people that is not like theirs: "The peoples of the world foresee a time when their land with its rivers and mountains still lies under heaven as it does today, but other people dwell there; when their language is entombed in books, and their laws and customs have lost their living power. We alone cannot imagine such a time."

Jew-hate is rooted in resentment of this undeniable fact of history. The West emerged in all its vitality in a plethora of nations and national rivalries, but as each nation sought to establish its strength, the Jew became a mirror reminding it of its finitude. The result was rage, what the Jewish columnist Jonathan Rosenblum has called "eternity envy."

This is why, in medieval antisemitism, the very symbols of Jewish faith, endurance, and vibrancy were turned by antisemites into symbols of purported perniciousness. The Christian writer Robert Nicholson has correctly conjectured that the disease of antisemitism "almost always grows from a resentment of 'chosenness': the idea that the Jewish god appointed one nation, the nation of Israel, to play a special role in history." This hatred, he argues, becomes a "grand anti-myth that turns Jewish chosenness on its head and assigns to the people of Israel responsibility for all the world's ills."

Throughout European history, in the midst of this great competition among nation-states, many turned on the Jews as each acquired its own sense of self. In 1144, less than a hundred years after the Norman Conquest, the blood libel was born in England when the death of a boy named William of Norwich was blamed on the local Jews and insanely linked to Jewish Passover preparations; in 1190, the Jews were massacred at York; in 1290, the Jews were expelled. As medieval France reached new heights of power under "Saint Louis," the Talmud was targeted for its imagined sinister content and burned in the streets of Paris. The Jews were expelled from France not long after, in 1306. Immediately after Aragon and Castile completed the conquest of Iberia, unifying Spain and restoring it to Christian rule in 1492, the Spanish monarchs expelled all Jews who refused to convert and assimilate; over the next several centuries "Judaizers" who had secretly stayed were hunted down. In the mid seventeenth century, Bogdan Chmelnitzki's Cossacks helped fashion Ukraine's sense of nationhood in rebelling against the Polish-Lithuanian commonwealth, but they murdered and mutilated thousands of Jews in the process.

Then, in Western Europe, one polity pointed the way to a different relationship with the Jewish people. The Dutch republic, having earned independence from the Habsburgs, allowed Jews to come to Amsterdam, to build synagogues openly, and to create communities. For the scholar

Steven Nadler, this was because the Dutch "saw their own recent history—their campaign for political sovereignty, liberated from Spain, and for religious freedom from Catholic oppression—reflected in the Biblical story of the Israelite struggle for emancipation from bondage in Egypt and the subsequent fight to claim the lands that God had promised them." The Jews of the Netherlands thrived and looked to new opportunities. From Amsterdam, a Jewish petition was sent to another ruler, who had overthrown a king and established a republic; this man, Oliver Cromwell, expressed openness to a Jewish return to England, which occurred in 1656. In Britain and the Netherlands, the Jews were welcomed, but they were in no way political equals. It was in the New World that another republic would rise and reflect a new way of seeing the Jews—and a new way of seeing itself.

On July 4, 1776, a committee comprising John Adams, Benjamin Franklin, and Thomas Jefferson was created by the Continental Congress and charged with developing a seal and symbol of the nascent United States. These Founders suggested an image of Moses and Pharaoh at the splitting of the sea, along with a motto: "Rebellion to tyrants, obedience to God." The suggestion, ultimately not adopted, reflected not these men's devout religiosity but their deep understanding of American culture and the place of the Hebrew Bible within it.

The scriptural connection lies at the heart of the American vision. The very word "democracy" derives from ancient Athens, but there is one essential American idea of which the ancient Greeks never conceived: equality. "You don't get out of Plato and Aristotle," the scholar and bioethicist Leon Kass has reflected, "an account that would sustain the view of the equal dignity of every human being." Rather, liberal democracy rests on the sense that, as first stated in Genesis, "both man and woman [are] equally made in God's image." Only a notion of rights derived from the Creator was believed to be sustainable—which is why John Adams, looking with horror across the ocean at the godless revolution fought in France, predicted the tyranny that would result.

But America felt bound to the Hebrew Bible also because of the way it saw itself. It compared itself to Israel of old not only because, like the Dutch, it had overthrown an empire, but because—as it ultimately announced on its seal—it believed itself to be chosen by providence to present to the world a *novus ordo seclorum*, a new order for the ages, as ancient Israel had been chosen to bring the monotheistic message to humanity. Sometimes it takes a foreigner to see how uniquely American this Biblical attitude was. The late British Chief Rabbi Jonathan Sacks saw this quite clearly:

> It is no accident that the Founders of America turned to the Hebrew Bible, or that successive presidents have done likewise, because there is no other text in Western literature that draws on these themes—history, providence, covenant, responsibility, the need to fight for freedom in every generation—together in a vision that is at once political and spiritual.

"Israel, ancient and modern, and the United States are the two supreme examples of societies constructed in conscious pursuit of an idea," Rabbi Sacks concluded. Of all the writings of the Founders, it is a letter from George Washington to the Jews of Savannah in 1790 that best expresses this:

> May the same wonder-working Deity, who long since delivering the Hebrews from their Egyptian Oppressors planted them in the promised land—whose providential agency has lately been conspicuous in establishing these United States as an independent nation—still continue to water them with the dews of Heaven and to make the inhabitants of every denomination participate in the temporal and spiritual blessings of that people whose God is Jehovah.

Here, Washington tells his fellow citizens that the tales of the Exodus and of America parallel each other: The Jews were not only to be welcomed as equals in America; their story inspired America. For the first president, God's blessings bestowed upon the Jews had never been removed—and he hoped that his nascent nation could be similarly blessed.

Such a letter from a Gentile head of state to the Jews is perhaps unique in history. The letter's import was not only political but theological; for, in a remarkable way, the American relationship with the Jewish people turned much of Western history on its head. Whereas Augustine and his heirs saw Jewish endurance as a sign of Divine punishment, and whereas medieval Europe saw in Jewish eternity a threat to its own identity, America looked to the Jewish story as an indication of Divine blessing, and therefore as a source of inspiration for the sort of country America was called to be. America came to see itself as a covenantal nation proclaiming to the world a concept of equality that was the gift of God; the American Revolution, Abraham Lincoln argued, was fought not only for independence but for "that something that held out a great promise to all the people of the world to all time to come."

Of course, America from the very beginning violated its covenant by failing to honor the truth that "all men are created equal." It was to the imagery of the Hebrew Bible that America's greatest president turned in urging America to embrace its covenantal calling. And in so doing, Lincoln used language that also reflected the uniqueness of America in the Jewish story:

> I am exceedingly anxious that this Union, the Constitution, and the liberties of the people shall be perpetuated in accordance with the original idea for which that struggle was made, and I shall be most happy indeed if I shall be a humble instrument in the hands of the Almighty, and of this, his almost chosen people, for perpetuating the object of that great struggle.

"Almost chosen people" is a perfect phrase. What it means is that America is not Biblical Israel's replacement; it does not seek to supersede or supplant the Jews. It does not envy Israel's eternity but seeks to learn from it and be blessed by it; it is Biblical Israel's imitator, learning the lessons of Israel's story. Whereas other nations saw in Jewish eternity a reminder of their own ultimate demise, America, as Lincoln argued, learned from the Biblical story that it could hope that it would not "perish from the earth" if it remained true to its covenantal calling. The phrase "almost chosen people" warns and inspires America, implicitly embracing the faith that, despite centuries of exile, God's covenant with the original "chosen people" remained.

Then, in 1948, that faith was vindicated.

The 1940s were the worst, and the greatest, decade in modern Jewish history. Hitler saw the eternal Jewish people as the ultimate threat to his thousand-year Reich. Driven by jealousy and hatred of a people that refused to be destroyed, he was convinced that he would succeed, for the first time in history, in achieving its destruction. He came closer than most. Three years after his death, the modern state of Israel was born. By 1967, Jerusalem was a united Jewish city. "Jews are not admitted into their city," Augustine had commented, "yet Jews there are." Suddenly, as the Hebrew prophets had promised, Jerusalem was a Jewish capital once again.

But as modern Israel prospered, much of the West lost faith in itself—and in the process lost faith in faith. Many Europeans saw in a strong Jewish state a reminder of the Biblical past that Europe suddenly chose to elide and eschew. In 2004, a constitution for the European Union was created whose preposterous preface described the history of Europe without a single mention of Christianity. What had once been the center of the Western world sought to forget much of what it had once believed.

Amid the collapse of confidence within much of the West, the story of Israel, and of the Jews, became even more important to many Americans. One striking embodiment of this aspect of American life is House Speaker Mike Johnson, who, having just emerged from relative obscurity, took the stage at the pro-Israel rally on the Mall in November and delivered the single sentence that received perhaps the greatest response from the crowd: "Calls for a cease-fire are outrageous." Johnson's Evangelical Christian faith is central to his political persona, and to his support for the Jewish state; but, as Walter Russell Mead has argued, those who simplistically link American pro-Israeli policies to Evangelical influence "have missed at least half the story." It is not merely that many Americans of faith support Israel but that Israel's story supports faith. Many religious Americans, Mead argues, find in Israel the vindication of traditional Western, and especially American, beliefs. Israel's story is seen as the ultimate indication that "God exists; he drives history; he performs miracles in real time; God's word in the Bible is true."

The Lord deals with the nations, Disraeli said, as the nations deal with the Jews; and it is this providential connection between history and the Jewish people that has sustained many Americans' sense of self. Americans of faith see a Europe that has forgotten its Biblical past, a place once called Christendom that has for all intents and purposes ceased to exist; and they see a progressive culture in America that is hostile to all they believe. In the face of this, they draw inspiration from the endurance of democratic Israel, believing that with God's help the American vision can endure as well. In a striking way, a Jewish capital in the Middle East has become a capital for those still clinging to the Judeo-Christian tradition in the West, to those holding fast to the way in which America saw itself. Eric Cohen, of the Tikvah Fund, has insightfully noted how inspiration from Israel's miraculous story now joins Jews and Christians together: "Jerusalem, forever the Jews' city of hope and once again the West's, is now the emblem of our shared purpose: to work with faith, political will, and moral resolve to rescue and defend our shared heritage from destruction and decay."[1]

It is only with this in mind that we can truly understand the intense hatred directed at Israel from the American Left. Many point to a progressive ideology that divides all individuals into oppressors and oppressed, with Jews considered the former. There is truth to this interpretation, but it does not explain why Israel is hated with a vociferousness that exceeds other progressive obsessions. Progressives elementally understand that Israel, ancient and modern, is a profound source of inspiration in the way America sees itself as a covenantal people. Many progressives, meanwhile, are driven by the fierce belief that America has never been a nation dedicated to a great idea; preposterous Pulitzer Prize–winning articles argue that 1619, rather than 1776, marks America's founding. In this telling, America was never biblically inspired to promote the idea of equality to the world, and its story is entirely a tale of evil and oppression. Woke progressives hate Israel because they hate America; they work, above all, to undermine the notion that America can consider itself a covenantal nation, and they therefore hate the embodiment of the original covenantal nation.

If America's unique relationship with the Jewish people continues—and if the Jewish state continues to be a source of sympathy and admiration—then the entire progressive project, in its current form, is endangered. This is why the more the righteousness of Israel's current cause is revealed, the antisemites become more agitated and angry. Thus, we have those who claw at posters of child hostages, destroying evidence of the evil of Israel's enemies. The phenomenon is an example of the now-popular internet meme, taken from a British comedy show, in which one SS officer turns to another in a brief revelatory moment and asks: "Are we the baddies?" The answer, for these individuals, is too horrible to contemplate, and so they are driven, in a rage, to remove the images that indict not only Hamas but themselves as well.

The confrontation in Congress between Republican representatives and the university presidents was therefore more than a mere hearing; it embodied a choice between two ways of seeing the American future. And that means that the explosion of antisemitism endangers more than the Jews. In his magisterial biography of Harry Truman, David McCullough describes how the vice president was dragged away from his card game on Capitol Hill and rushed to the White House, where he was greeted by a somber Eleanor Roosevelt. "Harry," she said, "the president is dead." Shocked, not initially comprehending what this meant for him, he responded by offering Eleanor and her family consolation and support: "Is there anything I can do for you?" To this, Eleanor candidly replied, "Is there anything we can do for you? For you are the one in trouble now."

Since October 7, I have received numerous emails and messages from American faith leaders and non-Jewish friends expressing their concern for, and solidarity with, the Jewish people. The substance of their communication is essentially: Is there anything I can do for you? The messages are heartwarming, inspiring, and deeply appreciated. But my own initial reaction has been a desire to respond, in friendship, that the danger is truly not only for Jews, but for all of us as Americans: You are the one who is in trouble now.

Come what may, the Jewish people will endure. I believe that this is guaranteed by God; and I also understand, with gratitude, that there exists today a Jewish state that will win its war and prove itself again capable of defending itself. But the targeting of Jews on America's campuses and in its cities is a sign of a deep threat to the future of America, of the growing strength of those who hate the Biblical way in which America has seen itself.

Not long ago, I interviewed Natan Sharansky in Jerusalem. I described to him how, on a recent episode of "Jeopardy!", when presented with the most famous verse of the 23rd Psalm, none of the three contestants could identify the book of the Bible it came from. Given that his own memoir of the Gulag is titled "Fear No Evil," and that in it he recounts how important Reagan's celebration of the Bible was to those who studied it in Soviet prisons, I asked him how this contemporary Biblical ignorance made him feel.

As part of his response, Sharansky told a remarkable story. After an antisemitic attack in Paris, he asked the French philosopher Alain Finkielkraut whether Jews had a future in France. The real question, Finkielkraut replied, was whether France had a future in France: whether the French would continue to defend Western values. Sharansky added to me that he had never thought America would face the same question about itself. But now, he reflected, he saw in college campuses self-loathing from Americans and an attempt to erase their country's identity. The explosion of Jew-hate, for Sharansky, was a reflection of this same phenomenon; it posed the question of whether there was a future for America in America. It is, in other words, America that is in trouble now.

The rallies against Israel on college campuses and in the streets, and the explosions of antisemitism that have been made manifest in the past months, are more than just another episode in the millennia-long story of the Jews. This is a moment that asks Americans whether they see themselves as the Founders once did. On their answer hangs nothing less than the future of the free world, which is led still by an "almost chosen people" that welcomed the chosen people into its midst and, inspired by the Jewish Biblical story, became a beacon to the world.

CHAPTER TWENTY-ONE

The Message from Jerusalem

Eric Cohen

In an extraordinary speech on October 17, 2019 at the University of Notre Dame, US Attorney General William Barr bluntly addressed the deep malaise affecting large swaths of contemporary American society. Describing a breakdown of epic proportions, he adduced such now-familiar indices as the high incidence of broken families, the soaring suicide rates, the record levels of depression, the army of "angry and alienated young males," and of course the ever more widespread addiction to opioids and other drugs. American culture, he declared, is descending into "chaos."

Speaking at a Catholic university, to an audience that included a large number of religious Christians, Barr characterized this grim reality as both a disaster for untold numbers of American citizens and a genuine crisis for American society at large. What was responsible for it? What had changed?

The founding proposition of the American experiment was that Biblical morality—our nation's bedrock Judeo-Christian inheritance—could form and sustain a citizenry suited for modern liberty and self-government. That proposition would be tested over the ensuing centuries by multiple vicissitudes and even by civil war, yet through it all the American experience would continue to validate the Founders' faith in the "moral and religious" people for whom alone, as John Adams insisted, "our Constitution was made."

But no longer. Today, the Judeo-Christian moral system has not so much dribbled away as it has been actively attacked and severely weakened through a deliberate campaign of delegitimization by myriad enemies of religious morality. "Secularists, and their allies among the 'progressives,'" as Barr put it,

> have marshaled all the forces of mass communications, popular culture, the entertainment industry, and academia in an unremitting assault on religion and traditional values. These instruments are used not only affirmatively to promote secular orthodoxy but also to drown out and silence opposing voices.... Those who defy the creed risk a figurative burning at the stake.

Under way for a half-century and now accelerating at social-media speed, this liberation project has yielded the opposite of an increase in human happiness. Indeed, as today's toll of victims attests, the new religion of irreligion has "brought with it immense suffering, wreckage, and misery."

In the face of this social crisis—this moral, cultural, and existential crisis—what is to be done? In the past, noted Barr,

> societies—like the human body—seem to have had a self-healing mechanism: a self-correcting mechanism that gets things back on course if things go too far.... This is the idea of the pendulum. We have all thought that after a while the "pendulum will swing back."

But today, he maintains, it is no longer possible to rely on the pendulum effect. The destruction has been too thorough—and it has been greatly abetted by the "unprecedented degree of distraction" afforded by all the instruments of "digital stimulation" that divert us from real love, friendship, and communal responsibility, and by the "almost limitless ways of indulging all of our physical appetites."

And when social life degenerates and decays—when the negative civic consequences of this moral breakdown assert themselves—we look to the nanny state as the new savior. Or, as Barr put it, "in the face of all the increasing pathologies—instead of addressing the underlying cause, we have the state in the role of alleviator of bad consequences." Instead of curbing the pornographic degradation of love, we protect sexual license and turn a blind eye to its brutalizing effects especially on the young; instead of curbing the use of drugs, we legalize them and then demand "safe injection sites" for a new generation of addicts. Yet despite all of this human wreckage, the new secularist faith itself—the idea that freedom from the traditional moral order is our new birthright—is never questioned, let alone reconsidered, by its adherents. Quite the opposite: progressivism's religious rivals—America's traditionalist synagogues and churches, traditional schools and communities of faith—are targeted as public threats to the new "woke" morality.

An expert in law, Barr catalogued the various ways in which the secularist campaign has, with notable success, exploited (and distorted) aspects of the American legal order to infiltrate its dogmas into public policy, into our major corporations, and most ominously into the curricula and governing ethos of American public schools. He also described how progressive courts and regulators have simultaneously worked to hobble religious institutions and religiously affiliated private education. And he concluded with a clarion call to "fight for the most cherished of our liberties: the freedom to live according to our faith." For only in a political order that preserves religious freedom will the great project of Judeo-Christian renewal—and thus American renewal—truly have a chance.

Still, the defense of religious liberty, by itself, is only a precondition for renewal, not yet the restoration of our broken culture. "What is it," Barr rightly asks, "that can fill the spiritual void in the hearts of the individual person? And what is a system of values that can sustain human social life?"

Some Christians have an answer to that question. To halt the dangerous decline into post-Christian chaos, they have concluded that they need to recover a certain pre-Christian understanding of human life and human nature. That is, they need to return—morally, spiritually, politically—to the Hebrew Bible, and through it, especially, to the message of the city of Jerusalem: the Jerusalem of old and, no less, the Jerusalem, and the Israel, that now miraculously live again.

Indeed, consider this: at any gathering of religious Christians in America today, the loudest applause is often reserved for causes and events related to Zion: for the moving of the American embassy to Jerusalem, for formal US recognition of Jewish sovereignty in the land of Israel, for popular American support of our friend and ally, the Jewish state.

Why does the city of Jerusalem, and why does the state of Israel, stir so many Christian souls with such spirited resolve? Answers abound, both theological and political.

Theologically, many (though not all) evangelical Christians believe the return of the Jewish people to Zion is a crucial step on the road to ultimate redemption. Politically, many Christians see modern Israelis as the "fighting front line" in defending the Western world—the Judeo-Christian world—against radical Islam. More recently, many Christians have been appalled to see how a maligned and grotesquely caricatured Israel has been pressed into service as a favored target of certain radical secularists, mainly in Europe and Latin America but also in the US, for whom the Jewish state can be held up as the world's most offensive example of ethno-religious nationalism. For these Christians, standing up for Israel is a way of standing up against the most aggressive wing of the modern progressive project.

Yet these reasons for the modern Christian's enthusiasm for Israel do not quite get to the heart of the matter. The Christian yearns for Jerusalem because the Christian world itself is in a moral—indeed a metaphysical—crisis. While the cathedrals of Europe lie largely empty, and while Christianity in the United States, under siege by energized secularists, has been weakened internally by crippling scandals and waves of disaffection, Jerusalem, the ancient holy city reborn, stands for many as the city of hope, the spiritual center of a Western renewal anchored in the Hebraic moral system. In dark times—and religious Christians, of whom William Barr is one, surely believe we are living in dark moral times—Jerusalem renews and rekindles the spirit.

I witnessed the Christian passion for Zion firsthand when recently asked to speak to a few hundred religious Christians at the YMCA in

Jerusalem, across the street from the King David Hotel. A century ago or more, only a novelist (like George Eliot), a visionary (like Moses Hess), or a prophet (like Theodor Herzl) could have pictured such a scene. Me: a religious Jew. The audience: conservative Catholics and evangelicals, on a spiritual pilgrimage, eager to hear from one of their "elder brothers in faith." The setting: a YMCA in an Israel restored, in a city governed again by the long-exiled Jewish people, in a nation brimming with Jewish life. As it says in Ezekiel: "This land that was desolate is become like the garden of Eden; and the waste and desolate and ruined cities are fortified and inhabited."

Today's Christians are hardly the first to look to Jerusalem, incubator and carrier of the message of the Hebrew Bible, for courage and inspiration. Many figures in history, both ancient and modern, have tried to grasp the deeper meaning of the human story during visits to "the city of righteousness, the faithful city," where the human drama reveals itself most vividly.

What exactly is it that they see there? In 1949—in the immediate aftermath of the Holocaust and in the midst of the austere but euphoric beginnings of modern Israel—the Canadian Jewish poet and journalist A. M. Klein visited the country and, two years later, published a strange short novel, now largely forgotten, called *The Second Scroll.* Klein was on a quest to understand the transcendent significance of that specific place and time, with the gas chambers of Auschwitz still fresh in men's minds and the resurrection of Israel happening before his eyes.

The novel takes Klein's protagonist—a Jewish Odysseus of the spirit—on a great metaphysical adventure from the ghettoes of the Old World to the Sistine Chapel, and from Communism to Nazism. Seeking truth, enduring evil, he finally lands in Israel restored. There, on the lookout for a new revelation of God's purpose in the world—a "second scroll"—he turns at first to the otherworldly visions of redemption penned by Jewish mystics and poets. But then he has the true revelation: the revelation of the miracle of everyday Jewish life, reborn in the now-living-again language of the Hebrew Bible:

> In the streets, in the shops, everywhere about me I had looked but had not seen. It was all there all the time—the fashioning folk, anonymous and unobserved, creating word by word, phrase by phrase, the total work that when completed would stand as the epic revealed.
>
> They were not members of literary societies, the men who were giving new life to the antique speech, but merchants, tradesmen, day laborers. In their daily activity, and without pose or flourish, they showed it to be alive again, the shaping Hebrew imagination.... There were dozens, there were hundreds of instances of such metamorphosis and rejuvenation. Nameless authorship flourished in the streets.
>
> It was as if I was spectator to the healing of torn flesh, or heard a broken bone come together, set, and grow again.... And this discovered poetry, scattered though it was, had its one obsessive theme. It was obsessed by the miraculous.

This, for Klein, was the miracle: everyday Jewish existence, saturated and sanctified in the holy Hebrew language. The holiness of regular people, not merely the poets and mystics but mortal men and women creatively meeting their needs and tending their gardens. The poetry of life as the only true answer to the politics of death. The resurrection of God's chosen people—the descendants of Abraham, Isaac, and Jacob—working and singing and raising their children, living normal lives in the land of their forefathers.

But Klein also pointed to a deeper truth, and one still true today. For the Jews of Jerusalem, the miracle of normalcy was and is not normal. In Jerusalem, normalcy is awe-inspiring, a resurrection that reminds one of God's hand in the world (for in no other way could one explain the inexplicable survival and return of the Jews); but it is also haunted, a normalcy secured and preserved at great human cost out of the ashes of the Shoah and then in war after war. And, in Jerusalem, normalcy is ever-threatened: there are still many who seek to grind Jewish bones into nothingness, and they are armed with missiles pointed right at the holy city.

Here, then, lies the doubly paradoxical message of Jerusalem and the Jewish people understood as a light unto a troubled humanity. Normal life is an everyday miracle, revealed in the warm embrace of mother and child, in the sweet songs of praise (Hallel) sung on festival days, at a family meal in the *sukkah*, in bride and groom under the wedding canopy. And yet, for Jews as ultimately for all human beings, normal life is a fragile miracle, one whose preservation requires a more-than-normal spirit, a more-than-normal courage, a more-than-normal faith.

At a Jewish wedding, in blessing "the King of the universe Who created joy and gladness, bridegroom and bride," Jews still today continue to pray for ultimate restoration, for the day when there might again be heard "in the cities of Judah and the streets of Jerusalem the sounds of joy and gladness, of bridegroom and bride, . . . of young people at their song-filled feasts." And then our everyday, normal bridegroom breaks a glass—to commemorate the destruction of the ancient Temple and as a reminder of the pain, evil, and uncertainty that have repeatedly befallen the Jewish people in the past and whose mortal reality the joyful couple must accept, endure, and overcome. This is the human condition, on display in vivid Jewish colors for all the world to see, in the ancient capital of the ancient Israelite nation reborn.

If this is indeed a true revelation of the human condition, that Hebraic vision did not come to an end with the destruction of the Temple and exile from the land in the late first century CE, only to be brought back from the grave in the second half of the twentieth century. To the contrary: what would come to be called the "rabbinic way of life," largely conceived and enacted in exile, persisted through time, often in harsh conditions, by being centered theologically in the holiness of everyday human existence, protected and preserved by a tough-minded code of law that structured every aspect of Jewish existence. The most animal functions—our natural needs and drives—were governed by commandments intended to restrain the commanded from the temptations of reckless pleasure-seeking, to remind them through innumerable formulas of blessing and gratitude of the unmerited gift of life that can so easily be taken for granted, and to elevate prosaic bodily existence to the plane of transcendent purpose.

In exile, these rules preserved the spirit of Jerusalem from extinction. The secular Zionist Hess, writing in the 1870s, described rabbinic Judaism as the hard shell that protected the Jewish body from assimilation and destruction. As many keen observers (like Mark Twain) have noted, the most powerful empires—with their animal gods and wild ecstasies, and with the Jewish remnant often under their dictatorial thumb—ultimately collapsed. Yet the Israelites remained, as both people and idea, their sacred purpose still miraculously intact.

In today's Jerusalem reborn, as so many Christians bear inspired witness, the Hebraic vision of the commanded life has now transformed the revivified holy land into the moral capital of the West. Which is also why the enemies of Judeo-Christian civilization—both secularist and Islamist—now target Israel as enemy number one.

Cheering for Jerusalem at church revivals and CPAC conferences, religious Christians seem to grasp almost instinctively that Jews are the clearest evidence and starkest reminder of the Western world's fighting Hebraic spirit. In an age threatened by radical secularism and radical Islam, by cultural decadence and a pagan view of human life as the unbridled pursuit of personal pleasure, they share with Jews a common origin in Abraham, a common scripture in the Hebrew Bible, a common moral challenge—and a common civilizational purpose.

The covenant of Abraham began, after all, as a response to the moral and political crisis of universal man, when God concluded that the way to instruct mankind in the good was to instruct a particular people—the Israelites; and that the way to remind mankind of the fragility yet indestructibility of the good was the miracle of Jewish survival from exile to redemption as the ever-dying people that never dies.

The Hebrew Bible revealed to human beings the guiding truths of existence: that the world was created by a Being more powerful than nature; that human beings were created in the image of God; that human life is sacred and child sacrifice abhorrent; that human kings are answerable to an ultimate Judge; that eating and sex are morally significant activities, governed by laws that separate the sacred from the profane; that death is real but not final; that rearing children is life's greatest blessing and most important commandment; and that despite the horrible realities of history, human life is not tragic but redemptive, not the eternal recurrence of the same but a providential story in which the Israelites have been chosen to play a special role as a "light unto the nations" whose improbable existence through time depends always and ultimately on God.

Pilgrims—and the Christian moral imagination in general—have now returned to Jerusalem, looking to the Hebraic way of life for guidance and inspiration.

The Christian version of this moral and theological vision sprang from Judaism; and while the Christian branches and leaves have sometimes tried to suck the life out of the Jewish root, the armies of Christian pilgrims—and the Christian moral imagination in general—have now returned to Jerusalem looking to the Jews for guidance and inspiration. The new Christians seem to recognize that our fates—and the fate of the Judeo-Christian moral system itself—are now bound together.

Grave threats to the Hebraic way of life have always been with us—as the Bible itself describes, our ancient forebears had their Canaanite, Egyptian, and Babylonian rivals. But the modern age, as Barr eloquently explains, seems different. Paganism and terrorism are now aided and facilitated by the uncontrollable fruits of human rationalism. The crooked spirit of man is now armed with mankind's novel technological powers—be they genetic engineering, transgender surgery, and Internet pornography on demand or chemical, biological, and nuclear weapons proliferated on a mass scale. Human lust, you might say, has teamed up with the lab scientists.

Admittedly, defending and embodying the Hebraic way of life, with its governing strictures on human conduct and human relations, has always been hard. It demands the moral training of both body and soul, and it requires endurance: all the harder when society constantly invites us to let go, to give in, to adopt the apparently easier but ultimately dehumanizing path.

But today, for all the reasons expounded by Barr, the current moral challenge seems particularly difficult and dramatic. Anti-Biblical civilization is now on the offensive, with its leaders well-entrenched in the commanding heights of modern culture: the universities, the media, the schools, and now even the corporations. And these progressive prophets, in their secular temples, are armed with some very seductive arguments: that modern science has embarrassed the truth-claims of Biblical religion, and that religious morality is oppressive, judgmental, and unnecessarily prohibitive. A new form of compassion has thus become the dominant ethos of our age, and a well-policed moral relativism is now our dominant ideology. In this vision, every way of life is seen as equally good, including a variety of lifestyles that were once taboo; to think otherwise would make other people suffer under the weight of moral standards (and scarlet letters) that supposedly dehumanize and imprison them.

But not quite every way of life is tolerated. From the rainbow menu of moral pluralism, only the Biblical vision, propped up by harsh and archaic laws that restrict human freedom, is excluded. In the new progressive mind, traditional religious morality is now treated as a form of bigotry to be utterly restricted, rejected, and suffocated. In this, as Barr argued at Notre Dame, today's relativists show themselves to be draconian absolutists, ready to consign any who dissent from their dogmas to "a figurative burning at the stake."

Of course, the arguments of the new secularists can be readily answered, both in theory and in practice. One need only point to the myriad abandoned and damaged children from marriages with no intergenerational commitment to the family; the relations between men and women living without any hard-won traditional guidance about their distinctive roles in human life; the collapsing birthrates in the most advanced civilizations; the fruits of secular radicalism in the last century's Stalinist and Hitlerite nightmares, checked only by the warrior courage of believing Christians and Jews in battlefields military, political, diplomatic, and cultural.

The history of Judeo-Christian civilization itself is surely stained by many errors and sins—including the Christian mistreatment and persecution of Jews. But past errors and excesses are not grounds for present surrender to the new tyranny of moral liberationism. The Judeo-Christian moral vision is not always "nice" (to use the term that the late Allan Bloom identified as the moral credo of generations of his students, blissfully ignorant that the miracle of freedom is an unmerited gift, a hard-won achievement, and a condition in need of defense). Rearing children, facing death, preserving justice in the face of criminality—niceness alone is not enough, and niceness wrongly understood will only lead us astray. Our age needs moral toughness, not amoral niceness. The Hebrew Bible understood this from the very beginning.

For Western civilization to flourish, Judeo-Christian moral disarmament, or moral surrender, must come to an end. Traditional Jews and Christians must forcefully reassert that the Hebraic way of life—with its vision of sanctified normalcy, governed by the Hebrew Bible's moral code, and courageously defended—is good and true. They—we—should never be embarrassed by traditional Judaism or Christianity, and should never give up on our sacred moral heritage.

While Jews and Christians now face the same moral challenge, the Jewish people and the Christian faithful are differently situated with respect to it.

To begin with the Jews: Jerusalem may be the moral capital of the West, but Jews remain the ever-threatened people, with only a few million of them in the world and myriad grave perils to their very existence.

In Europe, the Jews who remain are threatened by new waves of anti-Jewish terrorism. Parties of the left and the right blame Jews (yet again!) as the cause of Europe's woes, with the most unceasing attacks coming from those claiming that the Jewish mistreatment of Palestinians is what stands in the way of Europe's Kantian dream of perpetual peace. Many Jews in Europe—perhaps most Jews in Europe—are now thinking about whether, or when, or how to leave. An old nightmare may be returning.

In America, anti-Jewish prejudice is on the rise, with the most outwardly visible Jews being targeted for mayhem or slaughter in synagogues, kosher markets, and rabbis' homes. The progressive campaign targeting Israel and friends of Israel as racist occupiers is doing tremendous damage on university campuses across the country. At the same time, among a large percentage of non-Orthodox Jews, the warm embrace of American liberty has gradually dissolved any strong sense of Jewish identity and weakened the rituals, obligations, and institutions that preserve and protect that identity. The new progressive culture is now more antithetical to traditional Jewish morality than ever before, and the new progressive legal agenda increasingly threatens to restrict or ostracize traditional Jewish practice. The secular Jew is often only faintly Jewish in his or her core life commitments, and the traditional Jew is potentially becoming less free.

In Israel, by contrast, Jewish life shines brightest. Like any normal nation, Israel has its share of corruption, imperfection, fecklessness, and internal division. No one is claiming that modern Israel is—or ever will be—a moral utopia. But the eternal ethos of Jerusalem once again shapes Jewish communities throughout the holy land. In their calendar, language, holidays, and landscape, Israeli Jews live in direct continuity with their Biblical past. And alone among the advanced nations of the West, Israel has a high birthrate: a deep sign of cultural vitality connecting past, present, and future. This is exactly the reality of normal life resurrected that the poet Klein recognized as a Divine miracle. And yet, in Israel, the physical dangers to Jewish existence are grave—the venomous hatred persists, while the missiles remain pointed at Zion from north, south, east, and west.

This should remind us of another mark of distinction. The Hebraic vision is not only a spiritual or moral vision. In Jewish thought and in the Jewish liturgy, it is also a political vision, a vision of the ingathering of the Jews, of the literal rebuilding of Jerusalem, of the restoration of the kingdom of David. In this vision, an underlying unity marries spiritual steadfastness with political sovereignty and strength.

In the current age, Jews will regularly be assigned a twisted role in history, as they always have been—accused of everything from greedily engineering and living off of Western civilization's moral decline, to traducing American interests at the behest of a malign Zionist cabal, to either heedlessly pressing the case for a dangerously utopian universalism or, contrarily, refusing to take the lesson of their own near-extermination by Hitlerite nationalism and incorrigibly clinging to their clannish and exclusivist attachments. The Jews will always be blamed for whatever may be thought to ail the body politic or used as fuel to energize other people's ideologies. But the real Jew stands for something else and something other: for the sanctification of normal life, shaped and governed by the commandments, combined with the political realism necessary to preserve normal life in the face of abnormally obsessed enemies.

Even as there are ample grounds for worry about the precarious state of the Jews, there may be ampler grounds for worry about the precarious state of Christians.

Jerusalem is thus the sacred city with the political (and military) will to defend itself—the fortified desert capital of Jewish exceptionalism. That God may be with us, after all, does not mean that God can achieve His purposes without us. Political leaders like Moses, Joshua, and Esther—or Theodor Herzl, David Ben-Gurion, and Menachem Begin—would surely never qualify as cuddly universalists. Without them, Jewish brides and grooms would never have had a safe canopy in Jerusalem under which to raise their voices in songs of joy to the Creator of the universe, Who may reward them with children just as He rewarded the longings of Sarah, Rebecca, and Hannah.

If this is the light going forth from Jerusalem, from generation to generation, it is also a stark reminder that even as there are ample grounds for worrying about the precarious state of the Jews, there may be ampler grounds for worrying (as Barr does) about the precarious state of Christian civilization.

Unlike Christian Scripture, Hebrew Scripture grappled in realistic terms, from the beginning, with man's "political-theological" problem. The books of Exodus, Joshua, Samuel, Esther—these are, among much else, master works of political realism. The founding of ancient Israel was precisely a story about preserving and defending holiness in a world marshaled against it.

And yet, for thousands of years after the destruction of the Temple, Jews, unlike Christians, compiled no real record of actually governing cities, states, or empires. By contrast, Christians did compile such a record, and with it there inevitably has come the legacy of past errors, including the abuse of Christian power by Christian kings and the unjust persecution of accused heretics by Christian tribunals. The descent into post-Christian chaos and anomie is largely driven by a misguided effort to correct for those errors: that is, by rescinding (once and for all) any Biblical claims on the human soul and the human city in a kind of cleansing or atonement.

How many Western Christians, having learned the wrong lessons from their past, have become unwilling or unable to defend themselves and their civilization against the moral, cultural, and political forces that assault that civilization? How many Christians have falsely concluded that Christian imperfection somehow invalidates the truths of the Judeo-Christian moral vision? At its best, the Christian West has spread the Biblical vision of man to billions of God-seeking people around the globe; and so, if Christianity forever neuters itself in a misdirected form of penitence—or "liberation"—then Judeo-Christian civilization is doomed. Contemporary Europe, alas, is exhibit A in this tragic story-in-progress.

That is emphatically not the message of, or from, Jerusalem.

The ultimate theological differences between Jews and Christians will never be resolved, and their respective places in human history can never—and should never—be the same. But as Jews and Christians, we share a vision of the human person shaped by the moral passion of Abraham, the law of Moses, the spiritual yearnings of David, and Hannah's longing for a child.

For too long, the prophets of anti-Biblical civilization have tried to discredit the Judeo-Christian way of preserving and perpetuating a dignified way of life in the face of human frailty and human evil. Our frailty and vices they have instead fed and encouraged, while to human evil they have naively or perniciously given a free pass and opened the gates of the city. In the absence of religious faith and religious morality, just as the great Catholic writer Flannery O'Connor warned decades ago, "we govern by tenderness"; and when such tenderness is detached from its ultimate source in a just and almighty God, "its logical outcome is terror. It ends in forced labor camps and in the fumes of the gas chamber." Seduced and paralyzed by our supposedly more compassionate form of relativism, virtue retreats as evil advances. This is the nightmare that Barr described in his Notre Dame speech, and that social observers like Charles Murray, Leon Kass, and Yuval Levin have been diagnosing for decades.

The challenge for traditional Jews and Christians is to regain the moral high ground of Judeo-Christian civilization by repudiating and fighting back against its enemies, by rekindling our own moral self-confidence, and by proclaiming and demonstrating that the Hebraic commandments are humanity's truest guide to the best way of life. We need to restore religious liberty, promote religious schools, reclaim the Biblical foundation of America and of the West, and protect modern Israel as a fragile miracle that should inspire Jews, Christians, and God-seeking people around the world.

That emphatically is the message of, and from, Jerusalem.

In 2000, Pope John Paul II visited Jerusalem for the first time. He prayed at the Western Wall and delivered a speech at Yad Vashem—a memorial museum whose story ends not with the destruction of the Jews but with the rebirth of Israel. In his speech, he declared:

> My own personal memories are of all that happened when the Nazis occupied Poland during the war. I remember my Jewish friends and neighbors, some of whom perished, while others survived. I have come

> to Yad Vashem to pay homage to the millions of Jewish people who, stripped of everything, especially of human dignity, were murdered in the Holocaust.
>
> We wish to remember. But we wish to *remember for a purpose* [emphasis added], namely, to ensure that never again will evil prevail, as it did for the millions of innocent victims of Nazism. Out of the depths of pain and sorrow, the believer's heart cries out: "I trust in You, O Lord: I say, 'You are my God'" (Psalms 31:14).

The improbable Jewish story—the resurrection of Jerusalem, a "broken bone come together, set, and grow[ing] again"—provides perhaps the most compelling grounds for believing that good, in the end, will indeed ultimately triumph over evil. For without God's election of the Jews, the Biblical vision of human life as sanctified normalcy, under commandment, courageously defended, might never have come into being. The Jews are the Divine message in the bottle.

Like his fellow Christian pilgrims in their multitudes, the pope came to Jerusalem not to crusade or to conquer but to draw inspiration from the chosen people in the holy land. He came to pray with and for his "elder brothers in faith." Jerusalem, forever the Jews' city of hope and once again the West's, is now the emblem of our shared purpose: to work with faith, political will, and moral resolve to rescue and defend our shared heritage from destruction and decay.

CONTRIBUTORS

Eric Cohen is CEO of the Tikvah Fund and the publisher of *Mosaic*. He is also one of the founders of Tikvah's Lobel Center for Jewish Classical Education.

Dr. Daniel L. Dreisbach is a professor in the School of Public Affairs at American University in Washington, DC. His many works include *Reading the Bible with the Founding Fathers* and *Thomas Jefferson and the Wall of Separation between Church and State.*

Dr. Mark David Hall is a professor at Regent University's Robertson School of Government and a senior fellow at the Center for Religion, Culture, and Democracy, and director of Religious Liberty in the States. His many publications include *Did America Have a Christian Founding? Separating Myth from Historical Truth.*

Rabbi Dr. Stuart Halpern serves as the senior advisor to the provost and deputy director and chief strategy officer of the Zahava and Moshael J. Straus Center for Torah and Western Thought at Yeshiva University. He has edited nineteen books, including *Proclaim Liberty Throughout the Land: The Hebrew Bible in the United States, Esther in America* and *The Promise of Liberty: A Passover Haggada.* His writings on the Hebrew Bible's impact on the United States have appeared in *The Wall Street Journal, Newsweek, Tablet, Jewish Review of Books, First Things,* and *The Jerusalem Post.*

Rabbi Dr. Dov Lerner is a member of the faculty at the Zahava and Moshael J. Straus Center for Torah and Western Thought at Yeshiva University and serves as the rabbi of the Young Israel of Jamaica Estates.

His rabbinic ordination is from Yeshiva University's theological seminary, RIETS, and his doctorate is from the University of Chicago's Divinity School.

Dr. Wilfred M. McClay is professor of History at Hillsdale College, where he holds the Victor Davis Hanson Chair of Classical History and Western Civilization. His book *The Masterless: Self and Society in Modern America* received the 1995 Merle Curti Award of the Organization of American Historians. Among his other books is the award-winning bestseller, *Land of Hope: An Invitation to the Great American Story.*

Dr. Jonathan Sarna is university professor and Joseph H. & Belle R. Braun Professor of American Jewish History at Brandeis University. He is among the most eminent historians of American Judaism, and his award-winning 2004 book *American Judaism: A History* remains an indispensable landmark in the field.

Dr. Ariel Clark Silver is assistant professor of English at Southern Virginia University and currently serves as president of the Hawthorne Society. She is the author of *The Book of Esther and the Typology of Female Transfiguration in American Literature* and a contributor to *Esther in America.*

Rabbi Dr. Meir Y. Soloveichik is director of the Zahava and Moshael J. Straus Center for Torah and Western Thought at Yeshiva University, and rabbi at Congregation Shearith Israel in Manhattan. Rabbi Soloveichik has lectured throughout the United States, in Europe, and in Israel to both Jewish and non-Jewish audiences on topics relating to Jewish theology, bioethics, wartime ethics, and Jewish-Christian relations. He is the author of *Providence and Power: Ten Portraits in Jewish Statesmanship* and *Sacred Time*, and the co-editor of *Proclaim Liberty Throughout the Land: The Hebrew Bible in the United States.*

Dr. Shaina Trapedo is an assistant professor of English at Stern College and a resident scholar at the Zahava and Moshael J. Straus Center for

Torah and Western Thought at Yeshiva University. Her current book project, *From Scripture to Script: The Hebrew Bible on the Early English Stage,* considers Shakespeare and his contemporaries' indebtedness to Judaism and its exegetical traditions.

Dr. Tevi Troy is a senior fellow at the Ronald Reagan Institute, a senior scholar and director of the Impact Office at the Zahava and Moshael J. Straus Center for Torah and Western Thought at Yeshiva University, and a former Deputy Secretary of Health and Human Services and senior White House aide. He is the author of five books on the presidency, including *The Power and the Money: The Epic Clashes Between Commanders in Chief and Titans of Industry*, named one of 2024's best books by *The Economist*, *The Guardian* and *The Week*.

Dr. John R. Vile is a professor of Political Science and dean of the University Honors College at Middle Tennessee State University. A specialist on the US Constitution and its amendments, he is the author of volumes on national symbols such as the US flag, the national anthem, the bald eagle, and the Liberty Bell, as well as being the author of *The Bible in American Law and Politics*.

ACKNOWLEDGMENTS

We are grateful to those publications, listed herein, that have allowed us to reprint materials that originally appeared in their pages.

"American Samson," *Tablet Magazine*, Stuart Halpern, 20 May, 2021.

"America's Favorite Prophet," *Tablet Magazine*, Stuart Halpern, 30 March, 2023.

"Esther in America," *First Things*, Stuart Halpern, 26 February, 2021.

"The Message from Jerusalem," *Mosaic*, Eric Cohen, 6 January, 2020.

"The Shepherd of American Courage," *Tablet Magazine*, Stuart Halpern, 2 July, 2023.

"What Jews Mean to America," *National Review*, Meir Soloveichik, 22 February, 2024.

"Why Everyone Loves Daniel," *Tablet Magazine*, Stuart Halpern, 8 August, 2023.

"Why Study American Jewish History?" *Torah at the Center*, Jonathan D. Sarna, Fall 2003.

NOTES

CHAPTER 1: WHY WE TEACH AMERICAN HISTORY IN FAITH-BASED SCHOOLS

1 Alexis de Tocqueville, *Democracy in America*, trans. James T. Schleifer (Indianapolis: Liberty Fund Press, 2014), 2:475.

2 "From John Adams to François Adriaan Van der Kemp, 2 October, 1818," Founders Online, National Archives, https://founders.archives.gov/documents/Adams/99-02-02-7005.

3 George Washington, *The Papers of George Washington*, Series 2, Letterbooks -1799: Letterbook 24, April 3, 1793 - March 3, 1797. April 3, - March 3, 1797, 1793. Manuscript/Mixed Material. https://www.loc.gov/item/mgw2.024/.

4 "From George Washington to the United Baptist Churches of Virginia, May 1789," Founders Online, National Archives, https://founders.archives.gov/documents/Washington/05-02-02-0309. [Original source: *The Papers of George Washington, Presidential Series*, vol. 2, 1 April 1789–15 June 1789, ed. Dorothy Twohig (Charlottesville: University Press of Virginia, 1987), 423–425.]

5 "From George Washington to the Hebrew Congregation in Newport, Rhode Island, 18 August, 1790," Founders Online, National Archives, https://founders.archives.gov/documents/Washington/05-06-02-0135. [Original source: *The Papers of George Washington, Presidential Series*, vol. 6, 1 July 1790–30 November 1790, ed. Mark A. Mastromarino. (Charlottesville: University Press of Virginia, 1996), 284–86.]

6 Peter L. Berger and Richard John Neuhaus, "To Empower People: From State to Civil Society," in Don E. Eberly, ed, *The Essential Civil Society Reader: The Classic Essays* (Lanham, MD: Rowman & Littlefield Publishers, Inc., 2000), 153.

7 Philip S. Gorski, "Breaching the Wall of Separation Between Church and State," *The Chronicle of Higher Education*, 30 July, 2012, https://www.chronicle.com/article/breaching-the-wall-of-separation-between-church-and-state/?sra=true.

8 Jonah McKeown, "US Catholic School Growth Slows After Two Years of Notable Increases, Data Show," *Catholic News Agency,* 10 February, 2023, https://www.catholicnewsagency.com/news/253607/us-catholic-school-growth-slows-after-two-years-of-notable-increases-data-show; "Catholic Health Care in the United States," Catholic Health Association of the United States, April 2023, https://www.chausa.org/about/about/facts-statistics; Tess Solomon, Lois Uttley, Patty HasBrouck, and Yoolim Jung, "Bigger and Better: The Growth of Catholic Health Systems," Community Catalyst, November 2020, https://www.communitycatalyst.org/wp-content/uploads/2022/11/2020-Cath-Hosp-Report-2020-31.pdf.

9 "Profile: Catholic Charities USA," *Forbes*, https://www.forbes.com/companies/catholic-charities-usa; "The Salvation Army Among Nation's Top 5 Favorite Charities–Forbes and The Nonprofit Times," *The Nonprofit Times*, December 20, 2022, https://

easternusa.salvationarmy.org/usn/news/the-salvation-army-among-nations-top-5-favorite-charities/.

10 José Casanova, *Public Religions in the Modern World* (Chicago: University of Chicago Press, 2011), 234.

11 "Quotations," National Park Service, 1 March, 2023, https://www.nps.gov/thje/learn/photosmultimedia/quotations.htm.

CHAPTER 2: JOHN MILTON: BREAKER OF CHAINS

1 Margaret Fuller, *Papers on Literature and Art* (New York: Wiley and Putnam, 1846), 38.

2 *Pirkei Avot* [Ethics of the Fathers] 5:3.

3 Rabbi Jonathan Sacks, *A Letter in the Scroll: Understanding Our Jewish Identity and Exploring the Legacy of the World's Oldest Religion* (New York: Free Press, 2001), 52.

4 Book 9, Lines 28-33. See John Milton, *Paradise Lost.* Revised second edition. (New York: Routledge, 2013), 469.

5 Book 1, Lines 14–16. See Milton, *Paradise Lost*, 59.

6 William Poole, *Milton and the Making of Paradise Lost* (Cambridge: Harvard University Press, 2017), 191-2.

7 Arthur Lovejoy, *The Great Chain of Being: A Study of the History of an Idea* (Cambridge: Harvard University Press), 1964.

8 Leon Kass, *The Beginning of Wisdom: Reading Genesis* (London, UK: Free Press: 2003) 46.

9 Arthur Lovejoy, "The Origins of Ethical Inwardness in Jewish Thought." *The American Journal of Theology* 11, no. 2 (1907): 232–33.

10 Hans Kohn and Craig J. Calhoun, *The Idea of Nationalism: A Study in Its Origins and Background* (New Brunswick: Transaction Publishers, 2005), 30–31.

11 Rabbi Jonathan Sacks, *Covenant & Conversation: Deuteronomy: Renewal of the Sinai Covenant* (Jerusalem, Israel: Maggid Books, 2019), 65.

12 Book 9, Lines 1053-4. See Milton, *Paradise Lost*, 531.

13 Book 12, Lines 557–70. See Milton, *Paradise Lost*, 673.

14 John Milton, *The Complete Poetry and Essential Prose of John Milton* (United Kingdom: Random House, 2009), 1083.

15 See Rabbi Israel Jacob Algazi, *Shalmei Zibbur* [Laws of Prayer] (Jerusalem: Ahavat Shalom, 2003), 116–17.

16 See Stephen Dobranski, *Reading John Milton: How to Persist in Troubled Times* (Redwood City, CA: Stanford University Press, 2022), 193.

17 See Nelson, *The Hebrew Republic*, chapter 1; *Political Hebraism: Judaic Sources in Early Modern Political Thought* (Jerusalem, Israel: Shalem Press, 2008), 191-258; *Judaic Sources and Western Thought: Jerusalem's Enduring Presence* (Oxford, UK: Oxford University Press, 2011), 76; Fania Oz-Salzberger, "The Jewish Roots of Western Freedom," *Azure* 13 (2002), 88-132; Fania Oz-Salzberger, "The Political Thought of John Locke and the Significance of Political Hebraism," *Hebraic Political Studies* 1, no. 5 (Shalem, 2006), 568–592. For more on Milton's exposure to rabbinic literature see: Frank Mattern, *Milton and Christian Hebraism: Rabbinic Exegesis in Paradise Lost* (Heidelberg, Germany: Winter, 2009); Jeffrey Shoulson, *Milton and the Rabbis: Hebraism, Hellenism, and Christianity* (New York: Columbia University Press, 2001); Jason P. Rosenblatt, *Torah and Law in Paradise Lost* (Princeton: Princeton University Press, 2022); Jason P. Rosenblatt, *John Selden: Scholar, Statesman, Advocate for Milton's*

Muse (Oxford, UK: Oxford University Press, 2021); *Milton & Toleration* (Oxford, UK: Oxford University Press, 2007), chapter 7; *Milton and the Jews* (N.p.: Cambridge University Press, 2008), 13-82; Harold Fisch, *Jerusalem and Albion: The Hebraic Factor in Seventeenth-Century Literature* (London, UK: Schocken Books, 1964); Golda Werman, *Milton and Midrash* (Washington, DC: Catholic University of America Press, 1995).

18 John Milton, *The Complete Poetry and Essential Prose of John Milton* (London, UK: Random House, 2009), 1028.

19 John Milton and D. M. Wolfe, *Complete Prose Works of John Milton*, 3, (New Haven: Yale University Press, 1953), 542.

20 Book 12, Lines 24–29. See Milton, *Paradise Lost*, 647.

21 Book 12, Lines 69-74. See Milton, *Paradise Lost*, 650.

22 Rabbi Jonathan Sacks, *The Home We Build Together: Recreating Society* (London, UK: Bloomsbury Academic, 2007), 227.

23 Rufus Wilmot Griswold, cited in Margaret Fuller, *Papers on Literature and Art* (New York: Wiley and Putnam, 1846), 38-39.

24 Margaret Fuller, *Papers on Literature and Art* (New York: Wiley and Putnam, 1846), 38-39.

25 See John Greenleaf Whittier, *At Sundown* (London, UK: Houghton, Mifflin, 1892), 55.

26 Book 4, Lines 75. See Milton, *Paradise Lost*, 219.

27 Book 4, Lines 93-96. See Milton, *Paradise Lost*, 220.

28 Book 4, Lines 108–09. See Milton, *Paradise Lost*, 221.

29 Book 12, Line 587. See Milton, *Paradise Lost*, 674.

CHAPTER 3: THE JUDEO-CHRISTIAN TRADITION AND THE RISE OF AMERICAN RELIGIOUS LIBERTY

1 Frank Lambert, *Separation of Church and State: Founding Principle of Religious Liberty* (Macon: Mercer University Press, 2014), 142; David Holmes, *The Faith of the Founding Fathers* (New York: Oxford University Press, 2006), 22; Jon Butler, "Coercion, Miracle, Reason: Rethinking the American Religious Experience in the Revolutionary Age," in *Religion in a Revolutionary Age*, ed. Ronald Hoffman and Peter J. Albert (Charlottesville: University Press of Virginia, 1994), 29.

2 Daniel L. Dreisbach and Mark David Hall, ed. *The Sacred Rights of Conscience: Selected Readings on Religious Liberty and Church-State Relations in the American Founding* (Indianapolis: Liberty Fund Press, 2009).

3 David G. Dalin, "Jews, Judaism, and the American Founding," in Daniel L. Dreisbach and Mark David Hall, ed. *Faith and the Founders of the American Republic* (New York: Oxford University Press, 2014), 63.

4 Mark David Hall, *Proclaim Liberty Throughout All the Land: How Christianity Had Advanced Freedom and Equality for All Americans* (Nashville: Fidelis Publishing, 2023), 9-33; Eric Nelson, *The Hebrew Republic: Jewish Sources and the Transformation of Political Thought* (Cambridge: Harvard University Press, 2020). *Proclaim Liberty Throughout the Land: The Hebrew Bible in the United States: A Sourcebook*, ed. Meir Y. Soloveichik, Matthew Holbreich, Jonathan Silver, and Stuart W. Halpern (New York: The Toby Press, 2019) describes and gives numerous examples of how American civic leaders were influenced and inspired by the Hebrew Bible from early Puritans through the end of the Civil War.

5 Hall, *Proclaim Liberty*, 9-33.
6 Thomas J. Curry, *The First Freedoms: Church and State in America to the Passage of the First Amendment* (New York: Oxford University Press, 1987); Andrew R. Murphy, *Conscience and Community: Revisiting Toleration and Religious Dissent in Early Modern England and America* (University Park: Penn State University Press, 2001); Anthony Gill, *The Political Origins of Religious Liberty* (New York: Cambridge University Press, 2008); and Nicholas Miller, *The Religious Roots of the First Amendment: Dissenting Protestants and the Separation of Church and State* (New York: Oxford University Press, 2012).
7 Dreisbach and Hall, *The Sacred Rights of Conscience,* 152.
8 John M. Barry, *Roger Williams and the Creation of the American Soul: Church, State, and the Birth of Liberty* (New York: Viking, 2012).
9 William Penn, "England's Present Interest Considered," 1675, in *The Political Writings of William Penn,* ed. Andrew R. Murphy (Indianapolis: Liberty Fund Press, 2002), 57.
10 *Ibid.*, 340 (emphasis in original).
11 Dreisbach and Hall, *Sacred Rights,* 118. See also Roger Williams, "Charter of Rhode Island and Providence Plantation," (1663) in *ibid.*, 115.
12 Richard Bauman, *For the Reputation of Truth: Politics, Religion, and Conflict Among the Pennsylvania Quakers: 1750–1800* (Baltimore: Johns Hopkins University Press, 1971), 1-15.
13 "Jewish Neighborhoods: Philadelphia," https://www.yiddishbookcenter.org/language-literature-culture/wexler-oral-history-project-films-features-news/features/jewish-neighborhoods/philadelphia#:~:text=Philadelphia%20has%20one%20of%20the,of%20whom%20were%20Yiddish%20speakers; Edwin Wolfe and Maxwell Whiteman, *The History of the Jews in Philadelphia from Colonial Times to the Age of Jackson*, 2nd ed. (Philadelphia: The Jewish Publication Society of America, 1975), 14.
14 Isaac Backus, *An Appeal to the Public for Religious Liberty* (1773), in Ellis Sandoz, ed., *Political Sermons of the American Founding Era* (Indianapolis: Liberty Fund Press) 359 (emphasis in original).
15 Dreisbach and Hall, *Sacred Rights*, 274.
16 *Ibid.*, 275, 273-76.
17 *Ibid.*, 270.
18 *Ibid.,* 395.
19 *Ibid.*, 175 (emphasis in original).
20 Williams's references to Locke are used by scholars who claim that ministers in the era abandoned their commitment to Christian political ideas and substituted in their place largely secular political ones. See, for instance, Michael R. Zuckert, *The Natural Rights Republic* (Notre Dame: University of Notre Dame Press, 1996), 172, 183-93, and *passim.* I respond to this claim in Mark David Hall, *Roger Sherman and the Creation of the American Republic* (New York: Oxford University Press, 2013), esp. 1-40.
21 Dreisbach and Hall, *Sacred Rights,* 178.
22 *Ibid.*, 459, vii. To be sure, there was the obvious political motive of attempting to convince Catholic Quebec to enter the War for Independence on the Patriot side.
23 Dreisbach and Hall, *Sacred Rights*, 459, vii-viii.
24 *Ibid.*, 241.
25 *Ibid.* See generally Daniel L. Dreisbach, "George Mason's Pursuit of Religious Liberty in Revolutionary Virginia," *The Virginia Magazine of History and Biography* 108 (2000), 5-44.

26 Backus "An Appeal to the Public for Religious Liberty" (1773) in Sandoz, *Political Sermons*, 339.
27 *Ibid.*, 339 and, generally, 331–68.
28 Dreisbach and Hall, *Sacred Rights*, 276.
29 *Ibid.*, 337.
30 *Ibid.*, 246.
31 For a good overview, see Vincent Phillip Muñoz, "If Religious Liberty Does Not Mean Exemptions, What Might it Mean? The Founders' Constitutionalism of the Inalienable Rights of Religious Liberty," *Notre Dame Law Review* 91 (2016), 1387-1418. Various religious liberty provisions are conveniently collected by Neil H. Cogan, *The Complete Bill of Right: The Drafts, Debates, Sources, and Origins* (New York: Oxford University Press, 1997), 1-52.
32 Technically, Congress had the power to pass such laws for the federal territories, but instead of doing so it guaranteed in the Northwest Ordinance that: "No person demeaning himself in a peaceable and orderly manner, shall ever be molested on account of his mode of worship or religious sentiments . . . " (1787) in Dreisbach and Hall, *Sacred Rights*, 236, 473.
33 *Ibid.*, 433.
34 *Laws of the State of New York* (Albany, 1886), 2: 637; James S. Kabala, *Church-State Relations in the Early American Republic, 1787-1846* (London: Pickering & Chatto, 2013), 94-95.
35 Dreisbach and Hall, *Sacred Rights,* 242-64; John K. Wilson, "Religion Under the State Constitutions, 1776-1800," *The Journal of Church and State* 32 (Autumn 1990), 764; Davis, *Religion and the Continental Congress,* 34; and Gerard V. Bradley, "The No Religious Test Clause and the Constitution of Religious Liberty: A Machine That Has Gone of Itself," *Case Western Law Review* 37 (1987), 681-87.
36 Dreisbach and Hall, *Sacred Rights,* 242.
37 *Ibid.*, 294-95.
38 Morton Bordon, *Jews, Turks, and Infidels* (Chapel Hill: University of North Carolina Press, 1984), 5.
39 Dreisbach and Hall, *Sacred Rights*, 243.
40 *Ibid.*, 388, 394.
41 *Ibid.*, 464.
42 Peter A. Lillback and Jerry Newcombe, *George Washington's Sacred Fire* (Bryn Mawr: Providence Forum Press, 2006), 321-22.
43 Daniel L. Dreisbach, *Reading the Bible with the Founding Fathers* (New York: Oxford University Press, 2017), 81, 211–27.
44 Hall, *Proclaim Liberty,* 165–97.

CHAPTER 4: THE HEBREW BIBLE AND THE POLITICAL CULTURE OF THE AMERICAN FOUNDING

1 Portions of this chapter were adapted from Daniel L. Dreisbach, *Reading the Bible with the Founding Fathers* (New York: Oxford University Press, 2017). All Biblical quotations in the chapter are taken from the Authorized (King James) Version of the Bible because this is the English language translation most widely used in the American founding era.
2 See Kenneth L. Woodward and David Gates, "How the Bible Made America," *Newsweek*, 27 December, 1982, 44 ("Now historians are discovering that the Bible,

perhaps even more than the Constitution, is our founding document."); Martin Marty, "America's Iconic Book," in *Humanizing America's Iconic Book: Society of Biblical Literature Centennial Addresses 1980*, ed. Gene M. Tucker and Douglas A. Knight (Chico, CA: Scholars Press, 1982), 3 (America "has more than the Declaration of Independence and the United States Constitution enshrined in a vault in its archival heart. The Bible also is there."); Donald S. Lutz, *A Preface to American Political Theory* (Lawrence: University Press of Kansas, 1992), 115 ("the Bible provided [Americans] with a coherent basis for thinking about politics."); Solomon Schechter, *Seminary Addresses and Other Papers* (Cincinnati: Ark, 1915), 48-49 ("This country is, as everybody knows, a creation of the Bible, particularly the Old Testament."); Andrew C. Skinner, "The Influence of the Hebrew Bible on the Founders of the American Republic," in *Sacred Text, Secular Times: The Hebrew Bible in the Modern World*, ed. Leonard Jay Greenspoon and Bryan F. LeBeau (Omaha: Creighton University Press, 2000), 13 ("Both the Hebrew Scriptures and the Christian New Testament have exerted tremendous influence on American life from the earliest periods of the Republic's history to the present day.")

3 See, for example, Wilson Carey McWilliams, "The Bible in the American Political Tradition," in *Religion and Politics*, ed. Myron J. Aronoff (New Brunswick: Transaction Books, 1984), 21 ("the founding generation rejected or deemphasized the Bible and biblical rhetoric").

4 See, for example, Isaac Kramnick and R. Laurence Moore, *The Godless Constitution: The Case Against Religious Correctness* (New York: W. W. Norton, 1996).

5 See Eric Kaufman, "American Exceptionalism Reconsidered: Anglo-Saxon Ethnogenesis in the 'Universal' Nation, 1776-1850," *Journal of American Studies* 33 (1999): 440 ("the American free population on the eve of revolution was over 60 per cent English, nearly 80 per cent British, and 98 per cent Protestant").

6 Barry A. Kosmin and Seymour P. Lachman, *One Nation Under God: Religion in Contemporary American Society* (New York: Harmony Books, 1993), 28-29.

7 Sydney E. Ahlstrom, *A Religious History of the American People* (New Haven: Yale University Press, 1972), 350; see also 124 ("Puritanism provided the moral and religious background of fully 75 percent of the people who declared their independence in 1776").

8 William R. Hutchison, *Religious Pluralism in America: The Contentious History of a Founding Ideal* (New Haven: Yale University Press, 2003), 20-21.

9 For lists of the many influential Founders affiliated with the Reformed theological tradition, see Mark David Hall, *Roger Sherman and the Creation of the American Republic* (New York: Oxford University Press, 2013), x, 9, 22, 60, 111, 142, 151.

10 Donald S. Lutz, *A Preface to American Political Theory* (Lawrence: University Press of Kansas, 1992), 136. For a description of Lutz's method of analysis and sample, see Donald S. Lutz, "The Relative Influence of European Writers on Late Eighteenth-Century American Political Thought," *American Political Science Review* 78 (March 1984): 189–97.

11 For purposes of his study, Lutz defined a citation "as any footnote, direct quote, attributed paraphrasing, or use of a name in exemplifying a concept or position." Lutz, "The Relative Influence of European Writers on Late Eighteenth-Century American Political Thought," 191. Not all of the citations counted in his study are tied to direct

quotations. Moreover, the study does not capture unattributed direct quotations, paraphrases, or allusions to the Bible, which students of the era know are found frequently in this literature. The society was sufficiently Biblically literate that many would have known a quote, paraphrase, or allusion was Biblical in origin even without quotation marks or explicit attribution. Lutz's study counts citations. It does not reveal whether the Bible or any other source was cited approvingly or disapprovingly, accredited or discredited in an examined text. It simply identifies the sources and reports the frequency with which sources were consulted. Lutz, "The Relative Influence of European Writers on Late Eighteenth-Century American Political Thought," 191.

12 Lutz, *A Preface to American Political Theory*, 136.

13 Lutz reported that his study excluded "the majority of sermons that had no references to secular thinkers." Lutz, *A Preface to American Political Theory*, 136.

14 Donald S. Lutz, *The Origins of American Constitutionalism* (Baton Rouge: Louisiana State University Press, 1988), 140.

15 See Ezra Stiles, *The United States Elevated to Glory and Honor. A Sermon, Preached before His Excellency Jonathan Trumbull, Esq L. L. D., Governor and Commander in Chief, and the Honorable the General Assembly of the State of Connecticut, Convened at Hartford, at the Anniversary Election, May 8th, 1783* (New Haven: Thomas and Samuel Green, 1783), 6.

16 George Washington was described by his compatriots as an American Moses, the deliverer of the ancient Hebrews, even more frequently than he was compared to Cincinnatus, the legendary Roman dictator-turned-farmer. For useful discussions of Washington as an American Moses, see Robert P. Hay, "George Washington: American Moses," *American Quarterly* 21 (Winter 1969): 780–91; Garry Wills, *Cincinnatus: George Washington and the Enlightenment* (Garden City, NY: Doubleday, 1984), 27-37; Richard V. Pierard and Robert D. Linder, *Civil Religion and the Presidency* (Grand Rapids, MI: Academie Books, 1988), 81-85.

17 Israel Evans, *A Discourse Delivered Near York in Virginia, on the Memorable Occasion of the Surrender of the British Army to the Allied Forces of America and France, Before the Brigade of New-York Troops and the Division of American Light-Infantry, Under the Command of the Marquis de la Fayette* (Philadelphia: Francis Bailey, 1782), 46. Evans, who had studied under John Witherspoon at the Presbyterian College of New Jersey in Princeton, was a chaplain to the New-Hampshire troops.

18 Stiles, *The United States Elevated to Glory and Honor*, 7.

19 Samuel Langdon, *The Republic of the Israelites an Example to the American States, A Sermon, Preached at Concord, in the State of New-Hampshire; Before the Honorable General Court at the Annual Election. June 5, 1788* (Exeter, NH: Lamson and Ranlet, 1788), 30.

20 Abiel Abbot, *Traits of Resemblance in the People of the United States of America to Ancient Israel. In a Sermon, Delivered at Haverhill, on the Twenty-eighth of November, 1799, the Day of Anniversary Thanksgiving* (Haverhill, MA: Moore and Stebbins, 1799), 6.

21 Thomas Jefferson, Second Inaugural Address, 4 March, 1805, in *Thomas Jefferson: Writings* (New York: Library of America, 1984), 523.

22 See generally John Coffey, *Exodus and Liberation: Deliverance Politics from John Calvin to Martin Luther King Jr.* (New York: Oxford University Press, 2014).

23 *Journals of the Continental Congress, 1774-1789*, ed. Worthington C. Ford et al. (Washington, DC: Government Printing Office, 1904-37), 5:517–18 (4 July, 1776).

24 *Journals of the Continental Congress,* 5:689–91 (20 August, 1776); Proposal for the Great Seal of the United States, [Before 14 August, 1776], in *The Papers of Benjamin Franklin*, ed. William B. Willcox (New Haven: Yale University Press, 1982), 22:562–63; Report on a Seal for the United States, with Related Papers, [20 August, 1776], in *The Papers of Thomas Jefferson*, ed. Julian P. Boyd (Princeton: Princeton University Press, 1950), 1:494–95; John Adams to Abigail Adams, 14 August, 1776, in *The Adams Papers*, series II, *Adams Family Correspondence*, ed. L. H. Butterfield (New York: Atheneum, 1965), 2:96.

25 During their struggle for independence, Americans often compared their plight with that of the Children of Israel exiting Egypt. For example, reflecting on the extraordinary challenges and successes experienced by the former "Thirteen Colonies" in their conflict with Great Britain, John Jay, then serving as the Chief Justice of the New York Supreme Court of Judicature, opined: "we should always remember, that the many remarkable and unexpected means and events, by which our wants have been supplied, and our enemies repelled or restrained, are such strong and striking proofs of the interposition of Heaven, that our having been hitherto delivered from the threatened bondage of Britain, ought, like the emancipation of the Jews from Egyptian servitude, to be forever ascribed to its *true cause*, and instead of swelling our breasts with arrogant ideas of our prowess and importance, kindle in them a flame of gratitude and piety, which may consume all remains of vice and irreligion." John Jay, *The Charge Delivered by the Honourable John Jay, Esq.; Chief Justice of the State of New-York, to the Grand Jury, at the Supreme Court, held in Kingston, in Ulster County, September 9, 1777* (Kingston: John Holt, 1777), 7, 8.

26 "Negro Plot. An Account of the Late Intended Insurrection Among a Portion of the Blacks of the City of Charleston, South Carolina," Israel Thorndike Pamphlet Collection (Boston: J. W. Ingraham, 1822), 36. https://www.loc.gov/item/97110190.

27 William Lloyd Garrison, *Garrison's First Anti-Slavery Address in Boston. Address at Park Street Church, Boston, July 4, 1829* (Old South Leaflets, No. 180), 10.

28 See generally Daniel L. Dreisbach, "Introduction," to *Faith and Liberty Bible* (Good News Translation), ed. Alan R. Crippen II, Peter L. Edman, et al. (Philadelphia: American Bible Society, 2021), xv-xx.

29 This theme is developed in Oscar S. Straus, *The Origin of Republican Form of Government in the United States of America* (New York: G. P. Putnam's Sons, 1887). See also Lutz, *A Preface to American Political Theory*, 116 ("The more religious [Founders] saw the history of the Jewish people in the Bible as important for understanding republican institutions since it described what they considered to be a Hebraic republic and then showed God's displeasure when the Hebrews replaced their republic with a king.").

30 Straus, *The Origin of Republican Form of Government in the United States of America*, 131.

31 Samuel Langdon, *Government Corrupted by Vice, and Recovered by Righteousness. A Sermon Preached before the Honorable Congress of the Colony of the Massachusetts-Bay in New England, assembled at Watertown, on Wednesday the 31st Day of May, 1775. Being the Anniversary fixed by Charter for the Election of Counsellors* (Watertown, MA: Benjamin Edes, 1775), 11, 12.

32 Thomas Paine, *Common Sense*, 1st ed. (Philadelphia: R. Bell, 1776), 13-15; see generally ibid., 12-29 ("Of Monarchy and hereditary succession").
33 Algernon Sidney, *Discourses Concerning Government* (London, 1698), 97.
34 Connecticut Farmer [Roger Sherman], *Remarks on a Pamphlet, Entitled "A Dissertation on the Political Union and Constitution of the Thirteen United States of NORTH-AMERICA"* (New Haven, 1784), 25-26.
35 "Speech of John Smith (NY,) 20 June, 1788," in *The Debates in the Several State Conventions on the Adoption of the Federal Constitution*, 2, ed. Jonathan Elliot, 2nd ed. (Washington, DC: Government Printing Office, 1836), 225–26.
36 Straus, *The Origin of Republican Form of Government in the United States of America*, 131. See also ibid., 139 ("In short, again and again, in and out of our halls of legislation, was the history of the Hebrew Commonwealth referred to, narrated, rehearsed, and analogies drawn therefrom by the advocates of a republican form of government in answer to those who favored monarchy, so that the admonitions of Samuel were as familiar to the people of American as the words of the Lord's Prayer.").
37 Stiles, *The United States Elevated to Glory and Honor*, 7.
38 See Samuel Langdon, *The Republic of the Israelites an Example to the American States*, 10.
39 Deuteronomy 16:18 ("Judges and officers shalt thou make thee"); see also Deuteronomy 1:13 ("Take you wise men, and understanding, and known among your tribes"). Civil magistrates, the Puritans taught, are just as much God's ministers as the person called to fill the pulpit.
40 Exodus 18:21. See also Deuteronomy 1:13 ("Take you wise men, and understanding, and known among your tribes"); 2 Samuel 23:3 ("The God of Israel said, the Rock of Israel spake to me, He that ruleth over men must be just, ruling in the fear of God."). See generally Daniel L. Dreisbach, *Reading the Bible with the Founding Fathers* (New York: Oxford University Press, 2017), 166–85.
41 Deuteronomy 16:18 ("Judges and officers... shall judge the people with just judgment").
42 Deuteronomy 16:19 ("Thou shalt not wrest judgment; thou shalt not respect persons, neither take a gift [bribe]").
43 Deuteronomy 16:20 ("That which is altogether just shalt thou follow").
44 See also Exodus 18:21 ("to be rulers of thousands, and rulers of hundreds, rulers of fifties, and rulers of tens").
45 Deuteronomy 16:18 ("Judges and officers... in all thy gates [and] throughout thy tribes").
46 James H. Hutson, *Religion and the Founding of the American Republic* (Washington, DC: Library of Congress, 1998), 81.
47 By republican government, the founders meant, at least, popular government, committed to the rule of law, in which government authority is derived from the consent of the governed and exercised through representatives freely and fairly chosen by the people.
48 See, for example, John Adams's remark in 1776: "Statesmen, my dear Sir, may plan and speculate for liberty, but it is religion and morality alone, which can establish the principles upon which freedom can securely stand. The only foundation of a free constitution is pure virtue." John Adams to Zabdiel Adams, 21 June, 1776, in *The Works of John Adams, Second President of the United States*, ed. Charles Francis Adams,

10 vols. (Boston: Little, Brown and Company, 1850-56), 9:401. On 11 October, 1782, the Continental Congress issued a Thanksgiving Day Proclamation, authored by the Presbyterian clergyman and signer of the Declaration of Independence, John Witherspoon, declaring that "the practice of true and undefiled religion... is the great foundation of public prosperity and national happiness." Thanksgiving Proclamation of 11 October, 1782, in *Journals of the Continental Congress, 1774-1789*, ed. Worthington C. Ford et al. (Washington, DC: Government Printing Office, 1904-37), 23:647. Writing in the midst of the French Revolution in 1792, Gouverneur Morris, a signer of the US Constitution, remarked: "I believe that religion is the only solid basis of morals, and that morals are the only possible support of free governments." Gouverneur Morris to Lord George Gordon, 28 June, 1792, in Jared Sparks, *The Life of Gouverneur Morris, With Selections from His Papers and Miscellaneous Correspondence*, 3 vols. (Boston: Gray and Bowen, 1832), 3:32. Writing in 1799 with the anti-Christian impulses of the French Revolution in mind and employing imagery reminiscent of Washington's Farewell Address, the Virginian Patrick Henry stated: "the great pillars of all government and of social life . . . [are] virtue, morality, and religion. This is the armor, my friend, and this alone, that renders us invincible. These are the tactics we should study. If we lose these, we are conquered, fallen indeed." Patrick Henry to Archibald Blair, 8 January, 1799, in *Patrick Henry: Life, Correspondence and Speeches*, ed. William Wirt Henry, 3 vols. (New York: Charles Scribner's Sons, 1891), 2:592. In an often cited 1799 case, the Maryland General Court opined: "Religion is of general and public concern, and on its support depend, in great measure, the peace and good order of government, the safety and happiness of the people." *Runkel v. Winemiller*, 4 Harris & McHenry, 429, 450 (Gen. Ct. Oct. Term 1799). Charles Carroll of Maryland, a Roman Catholic and signer of the Declaration of Independence, remarked: "without morals a republic cannot subsist any length of time; they therefore who are decrying the Christian religion, whose morality is so sublime & pure . . . are undermining the solid foundation of morals, the best security for the duration of free governments." Charles Carroll of Carrollton to James McHenry, 4 November, 1800, in Bernard C. Steiner, *The Life and Correspondence of James McHenry* (Cleveland: Burrows Bros., 1907), 475. John Adams wrote in an 1811 letter to Benjamin Rush: "religion and virtue are the only foundations, not only of republicanism and of all free government, but of social felicity under all governments and in all the combinations of human society." John Adams to Benjamin Rush, 28 August, 1811, in *Works of John Adams*, 9:636.

49 George Washington, Farewell Address, 19 September, 1796, in *The Writings of George Washington*, ed. John C. Fitzpatrick, 37 vols. (Washington, DC: Government Printing Office, 1931-40), 35:229. "Of all the dispositions and habits which lead to political prosperity, Religion and morality are indispensable supports. In vain would that man claim the tribute of Patriotism, who should labour to subvert these great Pillars of human happiness, these firmest props of the duties of Men and citizens.... And let us with caution indulge the supposition, that morality can be maintained without religion. Whatever may be conceded to the influence of refined education on minds of peculiar structure, reason and experience both forbid us to expect that National morality can prevail in exclusion of religious principle. It is substantially true that virtue or morality is a necessary spring of popular government. The rule, indeed, extends with more or less force to every species of free government. Who that is a

sincere friend to it can look with indifference upon attempts to shake the foundation of the fabric?"

50 David Ramsay, *The History of the American Revolution*, 2 vols. (London, 1790), 2:356.

51 Benjamin Rush, *A Plan for the Establishment of Public Schools and the Diffusion of Knowledge in Pennsylvania* (Philadelphia: Thomas Dobson, 1786), 15.

52 John Adams to Benjamin Rush, 2 February, 1807, in *The Spur of Fame: Dialogues of John Adams and Benjamin Rush, 1805-1813*, ed. John A. Schutz and Douglass Adair (San Marino, CA: The Huntington Library, 1966), 75-76.

53 John Dickinson, notes [n.d.]. R. R. Logan Collection, Historical Society of Pennsylvania. Copy provided courtesy of The John Dickinson Writings Project, University of Kentucky.

54 Benjamin Franklin, Constitutional Convention, 10 August, 1787, as quoted in James Madison's *Notes of Debates in the Federal Convention of 1787*, in *The Records of the Federal Convention of 1787*, ed. Max Farrand (New Haven: Yale University Press, 1911), 2:249.

55 See generally Marci A. Hamilton, "The Calvinist Paradox of Distrust and Hope at the Constitutional Convention," in *Christian Perspectives on Legal Thought*, ed. Michael W. McConnell, Robert F. Cochran Jr., and Angela C. Carmella (New Haven: Yale University Press, 2001), 293-306.

56 James Madison, Constitutional Convention, 11 July, 1787, as quoted in James Madison's *Notes of Debates in the Federal Convention of 1787*, in *The Records of the Federal Convention of 1787*, ed. Max Farrand (New Haven: Yale University Press, 1911), 1:584.

Humankind's radical depravity was a familiar theme in James Madison's writings and, more generally, in the political literature of the founding era. Because men are not angels, Madison famously counseled in *The Federalist No. 51*, "[a]mbition must be made to counteract ambition." *The Federalist* (Gideon Ed.), ed. George W. Carey and James McClellan (Indianapolis: Liberty Fund Press, 2001), 268. Although this is the most famous passage, it is certainly not the only passage, in *The Federalist Papers* that addresses humankind's fallen nature. See the warning in *No. 6*: do not forget "that men are ambitio[u]s, vindictive, and rapacious." *The Federalist No. 6*, 21. See also *The Federalist No. 15*, 73, 74; *The Federalist No. 24*, 119; *The Federalist No. 37*, 185 ("the infirmities and depravities of the human character."). It should be acknowledged that various political traditions recognize the fallibility of human actors, but the tradition that most influenced Americans of the founding era on this point was Reformed Protestantism.

Humankind's radical depravity was a central tenet of the Reformed or Calvinist theological tradition, which was well represented in late eighteenth-century America.

57 Some scholars have claimed that the design of Presbyterian ecclesiastical governance, with its emphasis on representative government, divided and distributed powers, and checks and balances, influenced the US Constitution. The constitution of the Presbyterian Church, which was crafted in Philadelphia at the same time the delegates at the Constitutional Convention were framing the US Constitution in Independence Hall, "was built on the same architecture of distrust" of a fallible, sinful human nature as the US Constitution. The two constitutions shared philosophical and operational assumptions, design elements, and structures of governance. Marci A. Hamilton, "The Calvinist Paradox of Distrust and Hope at the Constitutional

Convention," in *Christian Perspectives on Legal Thought*, ed. Michael W. McConnell, Robert F. Cochran Jr., and Angela C. Carmella (New Haven: Yale University Press, 2001), 304. As one Presbyterian Church historian has written, "whatever may be said of the similarities and the differences between the two constitutions, both were the result of those ideas of representative popular government of which our [Presbyterian] Synod was the outstanding illustration and the most influential advocate throughout the colonial period." Marci A. Hamilton, "The Reverend John Witherspoon and the Constitutional Convention," in *Law & Religion: A Critical Anthology*, ed. Stephen M. Feldman (New York: New York University Press, 2000), 63 n. 5, quoting Frederick W. Loetscher, "Address on the 200th Anniversary of the Adopting Act" (1929), 10.

58 This standard definition of an oath was repeated in the debates on Article VI of the US Constitution in the state-ratifying conventions. See, for example, the 30 July, 1788, speech of Judge James Iredell (NC), in Jonathan Elliot, ed., *The Debates in the Several State Conventions on the Adoption of the Federal Constitution*, 4, 2nd ed. (Washington: printed for the editor, 1836), 196. See also "Kentucky Constitution of 1792," art. VIII, § 5; and "Kentucky Constitution of 1799," art. VI, § 7, *Text of Kentucky Constitutions of 1792, 1799 and 1850* (Frankfort, KY: Legislative Research Commission, 1965). Virtually every late-eighteenth-century moral philosopher defined oaths in similar terms. See, for example, John Witherspoon, "Of Oaths and Vows," in *Lectures on Moral Philosophy*, ed. Varnum Lansing Collins (Princeton: Princeton University Press, 1912), 130.

59 Edward Coke, *The Second Part of the Institutes of the Lawes of England,* 1st ed. (London, UK: 1642), 41.

60 Edward Coke, *The Third Part of the Institutes of the Laws of England*, 1st ed. (London, UK: 1644), 26.

61 See, for example, the Treason Act of 1547, 1 Edw. VI, c. 12 § XXII (1547), in *Statutes of the Realm: Volume the Fourth* (1819), 22; and Treason Act of 1695, 7 & 8 Gul. III, c. 3 § II (1695-6), in *Statutes of the Realm: Volume the Seventh* (1820), 6.

62 Massachusetts "Body of Liberties" (1641), article 47.

63 See George Lee Haskins, *Law and Authority in Early Massachusetts* (New York: Macmillan, 1960), 152–53 (discussion of the Biblical origins and application of rules governing the number of witnesses needed in Massachusetts colonial law and English common law). See also *New-Haven's Settling in New-England, and some Lawes for Government* (London, 1656), reprinted in Charles J. Hoadly, ed., *Records of the Colony or Jurisdiction of New Haven* (Hartford, CT: Case, Lockwood and Co., 1858), 572.

For more on the requirement of multiple witnesses in the Western legal tradition, see John H. Wigmore, "Required Numbers of Witnesses; A Brief History of the Numerical System in England," *Harvard Law Review* 15, no. 2 (June 1901): 83-108; L. M. Hill, "The Two-Witness Rule in English Treason Trials: Some Comments on the Emergence of Procedural Law," *American Journal of Legal History* 12, no. 2 (April 1968): 95-111; Cade S. Palmer, "The Biblical Origin of the Constitution's Two-Witness Standard," *Journal of Church and State* 64, no. 2 (Spring 2022): 259–79.

64 *Cramer v. United States*, 325 US 1, 24 and nn. 36 and 37 (1945).

65 Massachusetts "Body of Liberties" (1641), articles 46 and 43.

66 See Thorp L. Wolford, "The Laws and Liberties of 1648," in David H. Flaherty, ed., *Essays in the History of Early American Law* (Chapel Hill: University of North Carolina Press for the Institute of Early American History and Culture, 1969), 167

(limiting punishment to forty stripes was a rule "of Biblical origin, not present in the common law").

67 "Rules and Regulations," *Journal of Continental Congress, 1774-1789*, ed. Worthington C. Ford, et al. (Washington, DC, 1904-37), 2:119 (30 June, 1775).

68 "An Act for the Punishment of certain Crimes against the United States," 1st Cong., Sess. II, Ch. 9, 1 US Statutes at Large 115-116 §§ 15, 16 (30 April, 1790).

69 Most Americans likely learned of this Judaic practice from the Apostle Paul's testimony that five times he suffered under Judeans "forty stripes save one" (2 Corinthians 11:24). See generally Markus Oehler, "The Punishment of Thirty-Nine Lashes (2 Corinthians 11:24) and the Place of Paul in Judaism," *Journal of Biblical Literature* 140, no. 3 (2021): 623–40.

CHAPTER 5: THE HEBRAICALLY-INSPIRED LIBERTY BELL AND ITS ROLE IN THE AMERICAN STORY

1 George Lippard, "The Fourth of July, 1776" in *Legends of the American Revolution or, Washington and his Generals* (Philadelphia: T. B. Peterson and Brothers, 1847), 397.

2 John C. Paige, *The Liberty Bell of Independence National Historical Park: A Special History Study*, ed. David C. Kimball (Denver: Denver Service Center, National Park Service, Department of the Interior), 85.

3 John C. Paige, *The Liberty Bell of Independence National Historical Park: A Special History Study*, ed. David C. Kimball (Denver: Denver Service Center, National Park Service, Department of the Interior), 95.

CHAPTER 6: PSALMS AND THE AMERICAN FOUNDING

1 "Shakespeare, William: The First Folio: Fine Books and Manuscripts, Including Americana. Part 1." Auctioned at Sotheby's in New York, 21 July, 2021, www.sothebys.com/en/buy/auction/2022/fine-books-and-manuscripts-including-americana-part-1/shakespeare-william-the-first-folio-2.

2 "Bible in English: A Spectacular Association Copy of the First Edition of the Geneva Bible: Fine Books and Manuscripts, Including Americana. Part 1: 2022." Auctioned at Sotheby's in New York, 21 July, 2021, www.sothebys.com/en/buy/auction/2022/fine-books-and-manuscripts-including-americana-part-1/bible-in-english-a-spectacular-association-copy-of.

3 "A Previously Unrecorded Copy of the Official Massachusetts printing of the Declaration of Independence: Fine Books and Manuscripts, Including Americana. Part 1: 2022." Auctioned at Sotheby's in New York, 21 July, 2021, https://www.sothebys.com/en/buy/auction/2022/fine-books-and-manuscripts-including-americana-part-1/a-previously-unrecorded-copy-of-the-official.

4 "The United States Constitution and the Bill of Rights: Fine Books and Manuscripts, Including Americana. Part 1: 2022." Auctioned at Sotheby's in New York, 21 July, 2021, https://www.sothebys.com/en/buy/auction/2022/fine-books-and-manuscripts-including-americana-part-1/the-united-states-constitution-and-the-bill-of-2.

5 "The Bible Collection of Dr. Charles Caldwell Ryrie," auctioned at Sotheby's in New York, 5 December, 2016, https://www.sothebys.com/en/auctions/2016/bible-collection-of-charles-caldwell-ryrie-n09539.html?locale=en.

6 James Barron, "Book Published in 1640 Sets a Record at Auction." *The New York Times*, 27 November, 2013, www.nytimes.com/2013/11/27/nyregion/book-published-in-1640-makes-record-sale-at-auction.html.

7 King James Bible, Psalms (40:16).
8 Abraham Joshua Heschel, *God in Search of Man* (New York: Farrar, Straus and Giroux, 1976), 26.
9 Midrash Tehillim 18:1.
10 See Hannibal Hamlin's *Psalm Culture and Early Modern English Literature* (Cambridge: Cambridge University Press, 2004).
11 Charles Whitworth, "The Penitential Psalms and Ash Wednesday Services in the Book of Common Prayer, 1549-1662", *Revue Française de Civilisation Britannique* [Online], XXII-1, | 2017. https://journals.openedition.org/rfcb/1222#bodyftn10.
12 Heather Dubrow, *The Challenges of Orpheus: Lyric Poetry and Early Modern England* (Baltimore: Johns Hopkins University Press, 2011).
13 "The Bay Psalm Book: America's First Printed Book." auctioned at Sotheby's, 4 April, 2016, www.sothebys.com/en/videos/the-bay-psalm-book-americas-first-printed-book?ref=gentle-reformation.
14 Glover's death, his next of kin stand-in, and novice apprentice who originally trained as a locksmith help explain the Bay Psalm Book's many errors, including typographical and spelling mistakes and pages bound out of order. See James Barron's "Book Published in 1640 Sets a Record at Auction." *The New York Times*, 27 November, 2013, www.nytimes.com/2013/11/27/nyregion/book-published-in-1640-makes-record-sale-at-auction.html.
15 Cotton, John, et al. *The vvhole booke of Psalmes faithfully translated into English metre. Whereunto is prefixed a discourse declaring not only the lawfullnes, but also the necessity of the heavenly ordinance of singing Scripture Psalmes in the churches of God.* (Cambridge, MA: Imprinted by S. Daye, 1640), Pdf. Retrieved from the Library of Congress, www.loc.gov/item/71002405/.
16 Irving Lowens, "The Bay Psalm Book in 17th-Century New England." *Journal of the American Musicological Society*, 8, no. 1, (Berkeley: University of California Press, 1955), 22–29. JSTOR, https://doi.org/10.2307/829584.
17 Henry Wilder Foote, "The Bay Psalm Book and Harvard Hymnody." *The Harvard Theological Review*, 33, no. 3, (New York: Cambridge University Press, 1940), 225–37. *JSTOR*, http://www.jstor.org/stable/1508093.
18 "The Bay Psalm Book: America's First Printed Book." Auctioned at Sotheby's 4 April, 2016. www.sothebys.com/en/videos/the-bay-psalm-book-americas-first-printed-book?ref=gentle-reformation.
19 See John Fea's *Was America Founded as a Christian Nation?: A Historical Introduction* (Louisville: Westminster John Knox Press, 2011).
20 "Letter from John Adams to Abigail Adams, 16 September 1774" [electronic edition]. *Adams Family Papers: An Electronic Archive.* Massachusetts Historical Society. http://www.masshist.org/digitaladams/.
21 On the beginnings of the Jewish community in Pennsylvania, see Toni Pitock's "Commerce and Community: Philadelphia's Early Jewish Settlers, 1736–76." *The Pennsylvania Magazine of History and Biography*, 140, no. 3, (Philadelphia: Historical Society of Pennsylvania, 2016), 271–303. *JSTOR*, https://doi.org/10.5215/pennmaghistbio.140.3.0271.
22 "Letter from John Adams to Abigail Adams, 16 September 1774" [electronic edition]. *Adams Family Papers: An Electronic Archive.* Massachusetts Historical Society. http://www.masshist.org/digitaladams/.

23 Eds. Meir Y. Soloveichik, Matthew Holbreich, Jonathan Silver, and Stuart W. Halpern, *Proclaim Liberty Throughout the Land: The Hebrew Bible in the United States: A Sourcebook* (New York: The Toby Press, 2019), 90.
24 Ibid, 13.
25 Percy Bysshe Shelley. *A Defence of Poetry and Other Essays*, 18 July, 2022. www.gutenberg.org/files/5428/5428-h/5428-h.htm.
26 Henry Wadsworth Longfellow, "A Psalm for Life" (1838).
27 Matt Miller, *Collage of Myself: Walt Whitman and the Making of Leaves of Grass* (Lincoln, NE: University of Nebraska Press, 2010), 25.
28 Walt Whitman, "Death's Valley," *Harper's Monthly Magazine* 84 (April 1892): 707–09. Whitman wrote this poem upon request of editor Henry Mills Alden in 1889 to accompany "The Valley of the Shadow of Death" (1867) by the American landscape painter George Inness, itself inspired by Psalm 23. The magazine didn't end up publishing Whitman's poem until a month after his death in March 1892.
29 "In US, Decline of Christianity Continues at Rapid Pace," Pew Research Center, 17 October, 2019.
30 "First Look: Codex Sassoon." Auctioned at Sotheby's on 15 February, 2023. www.sothebys.com/en/videos/first-look-codex-sassoon.
31 William Shakespeare, *Much Ado About Nothing*, ii, 3.61.

CHAPTER 7: THE SHEPHERD OF AMERICAN COURAGE

1 The Declaration of Independence.
2 John Witherspoon, "The Dominion of Providence over the Passions of Men," (Princeton: 1776), https://oll.libertyfund.org/pages/1776-witherspoon-dominion-of-providence-over-the-passions-of-men-sermon.
3 Peter Whitney, American Independence Vindicated (Boston: E. Draper, 1777; Ann Arbor: Early English Books Online Text Creation Partnership). https://name.umdl.umich.edu/N12438.0001.001.
4 James P. Byrd, *Sacred Scripture, Sacred War: The Bible and the American Revolution* (Oxford: Oxford University Press, 2013), 114.
5 *The Works of the Rev. John Fletcher*, 3 (London: John Mason, 1859), 153.
6 Joseph Atkinson, "God, the Giver of Victory and Peace," (1862) quoted in James P. Byrd, *A Holy Baptism of Fire and Blood: The Bible and the American Civil War* (Oxford: Oxford University Press, 2021), 149.
7 Byrd, *A Holy Baptism of Fire and Blood*, 75.
8 George Duffield quoted in *Byrd, A Holy Baptism of Fire and Blood*, 74.
9 "Lincoln's Idea of Mercy," *The Daily Times* (Columbus, GA), 26 February, 1876, https://gahistoricnewspapers.galileo.usg.edu/lccn/sn90052397/1876-02-26/ed-1/seq-2/.

CHAPTER 8: ESTHER IN AMERICA

1 Eran Shalev, "The Bible and the Creation of the Nation," in *The Oxford Handbook of the Bible in America*, ed. Paul Gutjahr, (New York: Oxford University Press, 2017), 350.
2 Eran Shalev, "Evil Counselors, Corrupt Traitors, and Bad Kings: The Hebrew Bible and Political Critique in Revolutionary America and Beyond," in eds. Dustin Gish

and Daniel Klinghard, *Resistance to Tyrants, Obedience to God: Reason, Religion, and Republicanism at the American Founding* (Lanham, MD: Lexington Books, 2013), 108.

3 Eran Shalev, "Evil Counselors," 109.

4 Eran Shalev, "Evil Counselors," 110.

5 John Witherspoon, "The Dominion of Providence over the Passions of Men." (Princeton: 1776), https://oll.libertyfund.org/pages/1776-witherspoon-dominion-of-providence-over-the-passions-of-men-sermon.

6 A. E. Grimké, "Appeal to the Christian Women of the South," http://nationalhumanitiescenter.org/ows/seminarsflvs/religionabolition/grimkechristianwomen.pdf.

7 Sojourner Truth quoted in *History of Woman Suffrage*, 1, eds. Elizabeth Cady Stanton, Susan Brownell Anthony, Matilda Joslyn Gage (Rochester, NY: Susan B. Anthony, 1889), 568.

8 W. W. Patton, "President Lincoln and the Chicago Memorial on Emancipation," Maryland Historical Society Fund Publication No. 27 (Baltimore: Maryland Historical Society, 1888), 14.

CHAPTER 9: AMERICAN SAMSON

1 "Candidus," *Boston Gazette*, 19 August, 1771, in *The Writings of Samuel Adams*, 2, ed. Harry Alonzo Cushing, (New York: G. P. Putnam's Sons, 1906), 201.

2 "Speech of Rev. Mr. Stillman, Debates, Resolutions and Other Proceedings of the Convention of the Commonwealth of Massachusetts Convened at Boston on the 9th of January, 1788 [...] for the Purpose of Assenting to and Ratifying the Constitution Recommended by the Grand Federal Convention," (Boston: Oliver & Munroe, 1808), 215.

3 "I. Thomas Jefferson to Philip Mazzei, 24 April 1796," *Founders Online*, National Archives, https://founders.archives.gov/documents/Jefferson/01-29-02-0054-0002. [Original source: *The Papers of Thomas Jefferson*, 29, 1 March, 1796–31, December 1797, ed. Barbara B. Oberg. (Princeton: Princeton University Press, 2002), 81–83.]

4 Henry Wadsworth Longfellow, "The Warning," *Poems on Slavery* (Cambridge: John Owen, 1844), 31.

5 "Captain Brown to Rev. Dr. Humphrey, Nov. 25, 1859," in *Life and Letters of John Brown*, ed., F. B. Sanborn (Boston: Roberts Brothers, 1885), 604.

6 "Capt. John Brown Not Insane," *Douglass' Monthly*, November 1859, in *Frederick Douglass: Speeches & Writings* (New York: Penguin Random House, 2022).

7 "Tribute by the Rev. J. E. Ranking, D. D., President of Howard University," *In Memoriam: Frederick Douglass*, (Philadelphia: John C. Yorkston & Co., 1897), 33.

CHAPTER 10: AMERICA'S FAVORITE PROPHET

1 Samuel Magaw, D. D., "An Oration Commemorative of the Virtues and Greatness of General Washington," (Philadelphia: J. Ormrod, 1800; Ann Arbor: Early English Books Online Text Creation Partnership), 39, https://name.umdl.umich.edu/N28428.0001.001.

2 Magaw, "An Oration Commemorative," 39-40.

3 William Rogers, "The Prayer, Delivered on Saturday the 22d of February, 1800, in the German Reformed Church, Philadelphia" (Philadelphia: J. Ormrod, 1800), 6.

4 "John Adams to Thomas Jefferson, 26 May 1817," *Founders Online*, National Archives, https://founders.archives.gov/documents/Jefferson/03-11-02-0320. [Original source: *The Papers of Thomas Jefferson*, Retirement Series, 11, 19 January to 31 August 1817, ed. J. Jefferson Looney (Princeton: Princeton University Press, 2014), 382–85.]
5 Quoted in Mark Noll, *America's Book: The Rise and Decline of a Bible Civilization, 1794-1911* (New York: Oxford University Press, 2022), 127.
6 Abraham Lincoln. *Abraham Lincoln Papers*: Series 1. "General Correspondence. 1833 to 1916: Fernando Wood to Abraham Lincoln, Monday, Proposal to end war. December 8, 1862," Series 1, manuscript and mixed material, https://www.loc.gov/item/mal2001200/.
7 Frederick Douglass, *Life and Times of Frederick Douglass Written by Himself*, (Cleveland: Park Publishing Co., 1881), 604.
8 "Discouragements: Hostility of the Press, Silence and Cowardice of the Pulpit," in *The Works of Francis J. Grimké*, 1, ed. Carter G. Woodson, (Washington: The Associated Publishers, 1942), 234.
9 "The Price of a Soul," *Speeches of William Jennings Bryan*, 2 (New York: Funk & Wagnalls Company, 1913), 364.
10 Kathryn Krawczyk, "Hillary Clinton Eulogizes Elijah Cummings with Biblical Analogy to 'Prophet' who 'Stood Against Corrupt Leadership,'" *The Week*, 25 October, 2019, https://theweek.com/speedreads/874388/hillary-clinton-eulogizes-elijah-cummings-biblical-analogy-prophet-who-stood-against-corrupt-leadership.
11 "Winfrey's Commencement Address," *Harvard Gazette*, 31 May, 2013, https://news.harvard.edu/gazette/story/2013/05/winfreys-commencement-address/.

CHAPTER 11: WHY EVERYONE LOVES DANIEL

1 David Jones, "Defensive war in a just cause sinless. A sermon, preached on the day of the continental fast, at Tredyffryn, in Chester County" (Philadelphia: Henry Miller, 1775).
2 "From John Adams to James Warren, 22 April 1776," Founders Online, National Archives, https://founders.archives.gov/documents/Adams/06-04-02-0052. [Original source: *The Adams Papers*, Papers of John Adams, 4, February–August 1776, ed. Robert J. Taylor (Cambridge: Harvard University Press, 1979), 135–37.]
3 Frederick Douglass, *Narrative of the Life of Frederick Douglass, an American Slave* (Boston: Anti-Slavery Office, 1845), 107.
4 Martin Luther King Jr., "Letter from a Birmingham Jail."
5 *The World's Most Famous Court Trial: Tennessee Evolution Case* (Cincinnati: National Book Company, 1925), 175.
6 Jim Wright, *Balance of Power: President and Congress from the Era of McCarthy to the Age of Gingrich* (Nashville: Turner Publishing, 1996), 71.
7 William Booth and John E. Yang, "Bush Courts Religious Right as Democrats Assail Record," *The Washington Post*, 2 March, 1992.
8 "Blagojevich: 'I'm Going to Clear My Name'" *CNN Politics*, 4 February, 2009, http://edition.cnn.com/2009/POLITICS/02/04/lkl.blagojevich/.
9 Politico Playbook Breakfast with Senators McCain and Schumer, *C-SPAN*, 30 January, 2013, https://www.c-span.org/video/?310686-1/politico-playbook-breakfast-senators-mccain-schumer.

10 Ledyard King, "Immigration Plan a Gamble for Marco Rubio," *USA Today*, 3 February, 2013, https://www.usatoday.com/story/news/politics/2013/02/02/rubio-pushes-immigration-overhaul/1884911/.

11 Rachel Bade, Eugene Daniels, and Ryan Lizza, "McDaniel in the Lion's Den," Politico, 23 January, 2023, https://www.politico.com/newsletters/playbook/2023/01/23/mcdaniel-in-the-lions-den-00078958.

12 "Who Are the Witnesses Testifying at the Jan. 6 Hearings?" *PBS News Hour*, 9 June, 2022, https://www.pbs.org/newshour/politics/who-are-the-key-players-in-the-jan-6-committee-hearings-so-far.

CHAPTER 12: NATHANIEL HAWTHORNE AND THE HEBRAIC STRAIN IN AMERICAN THOUGHT

1 Matthew Arnold, *Culture and Anarchy*, ed. Samuel Lipman (New Haven: Yale University Press, 1994), 93.

2 Erik H. Erikson, *Childhood and Society* (New York: Norton, 1950), 285-86.

3 Georg Wilhelm Friedrich Hegel, *The Philosophy of History*, trans. J. Sibree (New York: Dover Publications, 1956), 87.

4 Henry Steele Commager, *The Empire of Reason: How Europe Imagined and America Realized the Enlightenment* (New York: Doubleday, 1977); Ernest Lee Tuveson, *Redeemer Nation: The Idea of America's Millennial Role* (Chicago: University of Chicago Press, 1968).

5 Leo Strauss, "Progress or Return? The Contemporary Crisis in Western Civilization," *Modern Judaism*, Vol 1, No. 1 (May 1981), 17-45.

6 Ecclesiasticus 23:27 (KJV).

7 Strauss, op. cit., 43-45.

8 Arnold, op. cit., 86-95.

9 Ibid., 153.

10 Robert Hughes, *The Shock of the New: The Hundred-Year History of Modern Art—Its Rise, Its Dazzling Achievements, Its Fall* (New York: McGraw-Hill, 1991).

11 David Foster Wallace, *Infinite Jest* (Boston: Little, Brown, 1996), 973.

12 For biographical details I have relied chiefly on Brenda Wineapple, *Hawthorne: A Life* (New York: Knopf, 2003); and James R. Mellow, *Nathaniel Hawthorne in His Times* (Boston: Houghton Mifflin, 1980).

13 Wineapple, op. cit., 42-44.

14 Ibid., 57.

15 Nathaniel Hawthorne, *The Marble Faun: Or, The Romance of Monte Beni* (New York: Penguin, 1990), 3.

16 Ralph Waldo Emerson, *Nature and Selected Essays* (New York: Penguin, 2003), 35-36.

17 For Hawthorne's stories I have referred to the Library of America edition, which contains all the stories and much else besides. Nathaniel Hawthorne, *Tales and Sketches* (New York: Library of America, 1982). Page numbers hereinafter refer to this edition, and will be placed in the text.

18 A splendid account of these events is provided in Bernard Bailyn, *The Ordeal of Thomas Hutchinson* (Cambridge: Harvard University Press, 1974).

CHAPTER 13: THE STORY OF HAGAR AND AMERICAN EXILE

1 Douglas Anderson, *A House Undivided: Domesticity and Community in American Literature*. (Cambridge: Cambridge University Press, 1990).
2 Matthew Fox-Amato, *Exposing Slavery: Photography, Human Bondage, and the Birth of Modern Visual Politics in America* (Oxford: Oxford University Press, 2019).
3 Judith Fryer, *The Faces of Eve: Women in the Nineteenth Century American Novel* (New York: Oxford University Press, 1976).
4 Janet Gabler-Hover, *Dreaming Black, Writing White: The Hagar Myth in American Cultural History*. (Lexington: University Press of Kentucky, 2000).
5 Susan K. Harris, "Extending and Subverting: The Iconography of Houses in *The Deserted Wife*." In *Nineteenth-Century American Women's Novels: Interpretive Strategies*. (Cambridge: Cambridge University Press, 1990).
6 Roberta Ann Johnson, "African Americans and Homelessness: Moving Through History." *Journal of Black Studies*, 40, no. 4, 2010, 583–605.
7 Andrew Judd, "Hagar, Uncle Tom's Cabin, and Why We Cannot Agree on What the Bible Says about Slavery." *Bulletin for Biblical Research* 31.1 (2021): 1–15.
8 Jane M. Rudd, ed. *Literature & Photography: Interactions 1840–1990*. (Albuquerque: University of New Mexico Press, 1995).
9 David Reynolds, *Faith in Fiction: The Emergence of Religious Literature in America* (Cambridge: Harvard University Press, 1981).
10 Marion Ann Taylor, "Harriet Beecher Stowe and the Mingling of Two Worlds: The Kitchen and the Study" in Christiana de Groot, and Marion Ann Taylor eds., *Recovering Nineteenth-Century Women Interpreters of the Bible*, Society of Biblical Literature, 2007.

CHAPTER 14: THE BIBLE AND THE PRESIDENTS

1 "Why Capt. Levi Preston Fought," *The Historical Collections of the Danvers Historical Society*, 8 (Danvers, MA: Published by the Society, 1917), 70.
2 "Washington's Inaugural Address of 1789: A Transcription," National Archives and Records Administration, https://www.archives.gov/exhibits/american_originals/inaugtxt.html.
3 "From George Washington to the Hebrew Congregation in Newport, Rhode Island, 18 August 1790," Founders Online, National Archives, https://founders.archives.gov/documents/Washington/05-06-02-0135. [Original source: *The Papers of George Washington*, Presidential Series, 6, 1 July 1790–30 November 1790, ed. Mark A. Mastromarino. (Charlottesville: University Press of Virginia, 1996), pp. 284–86.]
4 Thomas Jefferson, First Inaugural Address, 4 March, 1801, https://avalon.law.yale.edu/19th_century/jefinau1.asp.
5 "From John Quincy Adams to George Washington Adams, 21 March 1813," Founders Online, National Archives, https://founders.archives.gov/documents/Adams/99-03-02-2264.
6 Lord Charnwood, *Abraham Lincoln* (Lanham, MD: Madison Books, 1996), 15.
7 Abraham Lincoln, "To the Coloured Men of Baltimore Upon Presentation of a Bible," 7 September, 1864, *Abraham Lincoln's Speeches*, ed. L. E. Chittenden, (New York: Dodd, Mead and Company, 1896), 346.

8 Theodore Clarke Smith, *The Life and Letters of James Abram Garfield*, 1 (New Haven: Yale University Press, 1925), 38.

9 Smith, *The Life and Letters of James Abram Garfield*, 59.

10 Howard E. Short, "President Garfield's Religious Heritage and What He Did with It," *Hayes Historical Journal*, 4, no. 2 (Fall 1983), https://www.rbhayes.org/research/hayes-historical-journal-president-garfield-s-religious-heritage/.

11 *Quote Junkie: Presidents Edition* (Hagopian Institute, 2008), 39.

12 Theodore Roosevelt, "On the Submission of the Memorandum Concerning the Kishineff Massacre," 15 June, 1903, in ed. Alfred Henry Lewis, *A Compilation of the Messages and Speeches of Theodore Roosevelt, 1901–1905* (Bureau of National Literature and Art, 1906), 484.

13 Ed., Stanley Coben, *Reform, War, and Reaction: 1912–1932* (Columbia: University of South Carolina Press, 1973), 382.

14 Nelson W. Polsby and Aaron Wildavsky, *Presidential Elections: Strategies and Structures of American Politics* (Lanham, MD: Rowman & Littlefield Publishers, 2008), 172.

15 Michael R. Beschloss, *Presidential Courage: Brave Leaders and How They Changed America 1789-1989* (New York: Simon & Schuster, 2007), 234.

16 Curtis Wilkie, *Dixie: A Personal Odyssey Through Events that Shaped the Modern South* (New York: A Lisa Drew Book/Scribner, 2001), 230.

17 Jonathan Darman, *Landslide: LBJ and Ronald Reagan at the Dawn of a New America* (New York: Random House, 2014), 288.

18 Martin E. Marty, *Religion and Republic: The American Circumstance* (Boston: Beacon Press, 1989), 149.

19 Quoted in Yair Rosenberg, "A Conversation with Bill Clinton's Rabbi," *Tablet*, 18 October, 2013, https://www.tabletmag.com/sections/news/articles/a-conversation-with-bill-clintons-rabbi.

20 Amy Sullivan, "Attn: White House Speechwriting Office," *TIME*, 6 February, 2009, https://swampland.time.com/2009/02/06/attn-white-house-speechwriting-office/.

21 Dennis Ross, *Doomed to Succeed: The US-Israel Relationship from Truman to Obama* (New York: Farrar, Straus and Giroux, 2016), 268.

22 Chris Good, "George W. Bush on Gay Marriage, Immigration, and Why Obama Kept His Terrorism Policies," *ABC News*, 7 July, 2013, https://abcnews.go.com/blogs/politics/2013/07/bush-on-gay-marriage-why-obama-kept-his-terrorism-policies.

23 Becky Bowers, "President Barack Obama's Shifting Stance on Gay Marriage," *Politifact*, 11 May, 2012, https://www.politifact.com/factchecks/2012/may/11/barack-obama/president-barack-obamas-shift-gay-marriage/.

24 Tom LoBianco, "Bible in Hand, Trump Makes Pitch to Religious Voters," *CNN*, 26 December, 2015.

25 Eric Zorn, "Trump Offers Revealingly Bad Answers About the Good Book," *Chicago Tribune*, 26 October, 2016.

26 Jessica Taylor, "Citing 'Two Corinthians,' Trump Struggles To Make The Sale To Evangelicals," *NPR*, 18 January, 2016.

27 "Meet the Press," *NBC News*, 7 June, 2020.

28 Joseph Biden, "Inaugural Address," 20 January, 2021, https://www.whitehouse.gov/briefing-room/speeches-remarks/2021/01/20/inaugural-address-by-president-joseph-r-biden-jr/.

CHAPTER 15: CORRESPONDENCE BETWEEN HEBREW CONGREGATIONS AND GEORGE WASHINGTON

1 "From George Washington to the Savannah, Ga., Hebrew Congregation, 14 June 1790," Founders Online, National Archives, https://founders.archives.gov/documents/Washington/05-05-02-0279. [Original source: *The Papers of George Washington, Presidential Series*, 5, 16 January 1790–30 June 1790, ed. Dorothy Twohig, Mark A. Mastromarino, and Jack D. Warren (Charlottesville: University Press of Virginia, 1996), 448–50.]

2 "From George Washington to the Savannah, Ga., Hebrew Congregation, 14 June 1790," Founders Online.

3 "From George Washington to the Hebrew Congregation in Newport, Rhode Island, 18 August 1790," Founders Online, National Archives, https://founders.archives.gov/documents/Washington/05-06-02-0135. [Original source: *The Papers of George Washington, Presidential Series*, 6, 1 July 1790–30 November 1790, ed. Mark A. Mastromarino (Charlottesville: University Press of Virginia, 1996), 284–86.]

4 "From George Washington to the Hebrew Congregation in Newport, Rhode Island, 18 August 1790," Founders Online.

5 "From George Washington to the Hebrew Congregations of Philadelphia, New York, Charleston, and Richmond, 13 December 1790," Founders Online, National Archives, https://founders.archives.gov/documents/Washington/05-07-02-0036. [Original source: *The Papers of George Washington, Presidential Series*, 7, 1 December 1790–21 March 1791, ed. Jack D. Warren Jr. (Charlottesville: University Press of Virginia, 1998), 61–64.]

6 "From George Washington to the Hebrew Congregations of Philadelphia, New York, Charleston, and Richmond, 13 December 1790," Founders Online.

CHAPTER 16: ABRAHAM LINCOLN'S BIBLICAL MEDITATION IN THE SECOND INAUGURAL ADDRESS

1 An earlier version of this chapter was published as "Lincoln's 700 Words of Biblical Meditation," *Law & Liberty*, www.lawliberty.org, (4 March, 2015).

2 Noah Brook's report to the *Sacramento Daily Union*, 12 March, 1865 (published April 10), reprinted in Michael Burlingame, ed., *Lincoln Observed: Civil War Dispatches of Noah Brooks* (Baltimore: Johns Hopkins University Press, 1998), 167–69.

3 Lincoln to Thurlow Weed, 15 March, 1865, in *The Collected Works of Abraham Lincoln*, ed. Roy P. Basler et al., 8 vols. (New Brunswick: Rutgers University Press, 1953), 8:356.

4 See Daniel L. Dreisbach, "Biblical Language and Themes in Lincoln's Gettysburg Address," *Perspectives on Political Science* 44, no. 1 (2015): 34-39.

5 Isaac N. Arnold, *The Life of Abraham Lincoln* (Chicago: Jansen, McClurg and Co., 1885), 45.

6 See generally Daniel L. Dreisbach, *Reading the Bible with the Founding Fathers* (New York: Oxford University Press, 2017), 71-94.

7 William J. Wolf, *Lincoln's Religion* (Philadelphia and Boston: Pilgrim Press, 1970), 131.

8 William E. Barton, *The Soul of Abraham Lincoln* (New York: George H. Doran Co., 1920), 275.

9 Abraham Lincoln, "Second Inaugural Address," 4 March, 1865, in Arthur M. Schlesinger Jr., and Fred L. Israel, eds., *My Fellow Citizens: The Inaugural Addresses*

of the Presidents of the United States, 1789-2009 (New York: Facts on File, 2010), 148–50. All quotations from Lincoln's Second Inaugural Address are taken from this source.

10 Frederick Douglass, *Life and Times of Frederick Douglass* (Hartford, CT: Park Publishing Co., 1882), 441.

11 Ronald C. White Jr., "Lincoln's Sermon on the Mount: The Second Inaugural," in *Religion and the American Civil War*, ed. Randall M. Miller, Harry S. Stout, and Charles Reagan Wilson (New York: Oxford University Press, 1998), 208–25.

12 Ronald C. White Jr., *Lincoln's Greatest Speech: The Second Inaugural* (New York: Simon & Schuster, 2002), 167.

13 Abraham Lincoln, "The Gettysburg Address" ("Bliss" copy), 19 November, 1863, in *Collected Works of Abraham Lincoln*, 7:23.

14 "Final Version [of Washington's First Inaugural Address]," [30 April, 1789], in *The Papers of George Washington, Presidential Series*, ed. W. W. Abbot et al. (Charlottesville: University Press of Virginia, 1987), 2:174.

15 John Quincy Adams, "Inaugural Address," 4 March, 1825, in Schlesinger and Israel, eds., *My Fellow Citizens*, 63.

16 Mark A. Noll, "William Jennings Bryan, Theodore Roosevelt, Woodrow Wilson, and the King James Version of the Bible," *Theology* 114, no. 4, (2011). 252.

17 Abraham Lincoln, "Meditation on the Divine Will," [2 September, 1862 (?)], in *Collected Works of Abraham Lincoln*, 5:403.

18 Lincoln, "Meditation on the Divine Will," 5:404, 403.

19 Abraham Lincoln to Eliza P. Gurney, 4 September, 1864, in *Collected Works of Abraham Lincoln*, 7:535.

CHAPTER 17: PRESIDENT ROOSEVELT AND VICE PRESIDENT FAIRBANKS TO ATTENDEES OF THE EXERCISES IN CELEBRATION OF THE TWO HUNDRED AND FIFTIETH ANNIVERSARY OF JEWISH SETTLEMENT IN AMERICA

1 These letters were first published in *Publications of the Jewish Historical Society* in 1906.

CHAPTER 18: JEWISH CONTRIBUTION TO AMERICAN DEMOCRACY

1 This speech was originally published by the Jewish Center in March 1940. This text is taken from an undated reprinting of that speech by the Jewish Welfare Board in New York City.

CHAPTER 19: WHY STUDY AMERICAN JEWISH HISTORY?

1 Katie Magnus, *Outlines of Jewish History* (Philadelphia: Jewish Publication Society, 1890), 333–34; Jonathan D. Sarna, *JPS: The Americanization of Jewish Culture* (Philadelphia: Jewish Publication Society, 1989), 29–33.

2 Julius B. Maller, *Testing the Knowledge of Jewish History* (Cincinnati: Department of Synagogue and School Extension of the Union of American Hebrew Congregations, 1932), v, vii, 138.

3 Ibid, vii-viii.

4 Lee J. Levinger, *A History of the Jews in the United States* (New York: Union of American Hebrew Congregations, 1949), vii–x, 3. On this and other textbooks in the field, see Jonathan B. Krasner, *Representations of Self and Other in American*

Jewish History and Social Studies Schoolbooks: An Exploration of the Changing Shape of American Jewish Identity (Ph.D. thesis, Brandeis University, 2002).

5 See Sam Wineburg, *Historical Thinking and Other Unnatural Acts* (Philadelphia: Temple University Press, 2001); Peter N. Stearns, Peter Seixas, and Sam Wineburg (eds.) *Knowing, Teaching and Learning History* (New York: New York University Press, 2000).

6 Regina Stein, "Teaching American Jewish History As A Story," *Moving Beyond Haym Salomon: The Teaching of American Jewish History to 20th Century Jews* (Philadelphia: Temple University / American Jewish Committee, 1996), 26–29.

7 Jonathan D. Sarna, "Toward A New Approach to the Teaching of American Jewish History," *The Principal* 31 (May/June 1986); idem, *The American Jewish Experience* (New York: Holmes & Meier, 2nd ed., 1997), xiii-xix; idem, "What's The Use of Local Jewish History," *Rhode Island Jewish Historical Notes* 12 (November 1995), 77-83.

CHAPTER 20: WHAT JEWS MEAN TO AMERICA

1 Eric Cohen, "The Message from Jerusalem," *Mosaic*, 6 January, 2020, https://mosaicmagazine.com/essay/history-ideas/2020/01/the-message-from-jerusalem/.

INDEX